ROSE BOWL DREAMS

THOMAS DUNNE BOOKS
ST. MARTIN'S PRESS ✠ NEW YORK

ROSE BOWL DREAMS

A Memoir of Faith,
Family, and Football

ADAM JONES

THOMAS DUNNE BOOKS.
An imprint of St. Martin's Press.

ROSE BOWL DREAMS. Copyright © 2008 by Adam Jones. All rights reserved. Printed in the United States of America. For information, address St. Martin's Press, 175 Fifth Avenue, New York, N.Y. 10010.

www.thomasdunnebooks.com
www.stmartins.com

Design by Jamie Kerner-Scott

Library of Congress Cataloging in-Publication Data

Jones, Adam.
    Rose Bowl dreams : a memoir of faith, family, and football / Adam Jones.—1st ed.
        p.   cm.
    Includes bibliographical references and index.
    ISBN-13: 978-0-312-37369-6 (alk. paper)
    ISBN-10: 0-312-37369-4 (alk. paper)
    1. Jones, Adam.   2. Sportswriters—United States—Biography.   3. Football—United States—Anecdotes.   4. College sports—United States—Anecdotes.   5. Faith—Anecdotes.   6. Mothers and sons—Anecdotes.   I. Title.
    GV742.42.A32 A3
    796.04'30973—dc22

                                                                                    2008018433

First Edition: August 2008

10 9 8 7 6 5 4 3 2 1

In Memory

Reba Killian Jones,
1931–2002,
who taught me to live in the moment

W. Mitchell "Bulldog" Jones,
1901–1994,
who taught me that the good life moves ever forward

CONTENTS

Contents

ACKNOWLEDGMENTS

Acknowledgments present an intimidating challenge to a first-time author. Not only am I amazed at exactly how many people stepped forward to help this effort, I am also not guaranteed of being a second-time author and thus being able to thank anyone whom I leave out this time around. This book started with Jim Hornfischer, who was my friend before he became my agent. Jim always had a vision for this project and never accepted anything less than my best work, for which I am both thankful and indebted. Sharon Hornfischer was equally supportive of me, far beyond the call of duty.

Peter Wolverton at Thomas Dunne Books has been a pleasure to work with and I couldn't have asked for a better editor, despite his obvious bias for the Alabama Crimson Tide and the SEC in general. Even on the difficult days, I reminded Pete that his publishing house was actually paying me to write about college football—every day is a good day under that circumstance. I would also like to thank assistant editor Elizabeth Byrne, who has been nothing but kind and responsive. In addition, production editor Kenneth J. Silver and copy editor Donald J. Davidson both do terrific work, although I know them only through their notations and memos.

Family is central to this book. My family begins with an old psychiatrist in the Texas Panhandle. Thanks, Dad, I hope I made Mom proud. My siblings, David and his wife Ellen, Molly, and Sam, could not have been more supportive or helpful, not only through their editorial assistance, but also in collecting photos and family history. Additionally, Sam gets high marks for his research on West Texas football and David for his work with the Panhandle Sports Hall of Fame. I love you all.

My mother-in-law, Patricia Florence, would have been one of the world's great copy editors, had she not instead decided to be one of the world's great transactional lawyers. Craig and Kristi Florence, Kirk and Elizabeth Florence, and all of their great kids have always welcomed me with open arms and have been both tolerant and amused that the Jones family history has bled into the Florence family history. I am very proud to be a Florence.

On the football side, Suzanne Halliburton of the *Austin-American Statesman* has covered the Longhorns almost exactly concurrent with my own fascination, dating back to her days at the *Daily Texan*. She has been generous with her time and patient with my attempts at rookie sports journalism. Thank you, Suzanne, for being a willing ear and helping me keep my facts straight. Thanks also to the Texas Tailgaters community, especially Vic Wang and Jeff Fowler.

There are several media professionals who have helped me greatly, including Adam Quisenberry with West Texas A&M University athletics, Patrick Smyth with the Denver Broncos, Cora Bullock and Avrel Seale with the University of Texas Alumni Association, and Joy Lawrence, Jim Sigmon, and Susan Sigmon with the University of Texas Athletics photography.

Acknowledgments

I appreciate the ongoing support and advice of Matthew Zemek of CollegeFootballNews.com, Peter Bean of Burnt Orange Nation, Tom Higley, one of the great Panhandle newspaper and radiomen, and the legendary Robert Heard, who has forgotten more Texas history than I will ever know and is a master of grammar and usage.

Chris Carson has not only taken some spectacular photographs of the Texas Longhorns in his career, he even managed to make me look good in the book jacket photo. Ryan Gravatt of Quicksilver Internet Solutions is the brains behind my college football site, www.jonestopten .com.

Many folks have read versions of the manuscript and everyone had something valuable to share. A special thanks to David D. Anderson, the student manager for the 1970 Texas Longhorn National Champions, for his insights on Darrell Royal and his knowledge of Texas high school and college football. Others who contributed include Brandon Aghamalian, Mike Turner, Lawrence and Jodi Leach, Jerry Valdez, and the Duke crew: Kevin Warmath, Dave Hepenstal, Garrick Francis, and David Feingold.

I would like to thank Jay Farrar because the music of Son Volt provided the soundtrack for many of the nights I stayed up working on this book.

Alisa Peppers served as my tour guide through both the geography and the culture of south Houston. She is one of the great Texas women and she and her husband, Reggie, are dear friends. Many others aided in my understanding of Houston, including Jimmy Wynn (whose hospitality I greatly appreciate), Cory Rountree, Patti Foster, Shirley Neeley, Ed Warken, athletic director of the Galena Park Independent School District, Kelly Raglin, executive director of the West Orem YMCA, and Dr. John Burruss, chief of psychiatry at Ben Taub Hospital and a lifelong friend.

The Reverend Samuel Smith took me in, called me brother and was a gracious host during an inspiring day at Mount Horeb Missionary Baptist Church. He is a remarkable man. Thanks, Papa. While at Mount Horeb, Bessie Latson and Shonda Washington fed me an unforgettable meal. I

Acknowledgments

greatly valued my lunchtime conversation with Reverend Willie Smith of Mount Horeb and Reverend H. J. Johnson of Cathedral of Faith, Dallas. These gentlemen aided in my understanding of the African-American church and the Missionary Baptist movement. The message that day was brought by the Bishop Gary Scott of Trinity Fellowship.

My own faith life has been guided by some wonderful pastors, but no one more so than the Reverend Howard F. M. Childers. I would also like to thank Reverend Jim Mayfield, Reverend Ann Beaty, and Reverend Robert Hall and the staff and members of Tarrytown United Methodist Church in Austin. It is my home.

Thanks also to the Friday morning men's Emmaus group: Mike, Rob, Jay, Bob, Jack, James, and Jim. We're not quite the Apostles, but a reasonably good group of guys nonetheless.

College football is not for the faint of heart and I would like to acknowledge every player who has had the guts to suit up for the Texas Longhorns. The magic doesn't happen without you. My thanks to John Haines, a member of the great 1983 Texas defense, who has always been willing to stop and talk football, and to Selvin Young, who confirmed for me a story about the power of faith.

My gratitude also goes out to all of the old WT Buffaloes, especially the late Hatcher Brown, Weldon "Bird Dog" Trice, Tod Mayfield, Maurice Cheeks, and the great number 7 himself: Reggie Spencer.

Thanks also to some Panhandle football fans who have contributed to the language and feel of the book: Owen Bybee, Birke Marsh (who coined the phrase: "couldn't throw feed to starving birds"), Benson Latham (who introduced me to the phrase: "to weave a tapestry of obscenities"), Todd and Susan Clark, Greg Stafford, whose family introduced me to live Southwest Conference football, Mike and Paige McKay, Mark and Marcy McKay, and David Milton. Also thanks to my fellow author Christopher J. Oglesby, redneck lawyer, storyteller, philosopher, and keeper of all things great about West Texas.

The book describes a very special group of friends, henceforth known as the Lone Star Drinking Club: Holly Jacques Turner, Juan Shepperd,

Acknowledgments

Ann Erickson, Courtney Johnson, Terry Lynch, and my favorite football fan and partner-in-crime: Zachary Peace Jones. I never want to watch the Horns without you, son.

To my sons, Ben and Charlie, thanks for making your father just a little bit happier every day. We have a lot of Longhorn football ahead of us.

Erin, I couldn't have done this without you. And I certainly wouldn't have wanted to, which describes everything about my life, come to think of it. I think chapter 16 sums it up best:

Of all the blessings that God had given me, of all the things in my life that I had taken for granted, one superseded all others. I was married to exactly the right woman.

So what chapter shall we write next?

Adam Jones
Austin, Texas
January 13, 2008

ROSE BOWL DREAMS

FAITH IN GOD AND FOOTBALL

God created college football as a grand gift to an imperfect world. I learned this as a very small boy living in the middle of the Texas Panhandle. There the horizon runs unbroken, separating the sky from the vast plains that sit at the top of the Caprock Escarpment, 3,500 feet above the Gulf of Mexico. There is nothing but barbed wire to resist the chill winter winds sweeping south from the Rocky Mountains. My grandfather often said the reason so many kids from the area served in the navy was because the Panhandle, which is sheet-metal flat with barely a tree to interrupt the sunsets, has the same horizon as the open sea.

Into this landscape, the good people of the Panhandle carved out a stadium to accommodate the West Texas State University Buffalo football team. West Texas State, WT for short, consecrated the Buffalo Bowl on September 26, 1959, just outside the small college town of Canyon. The bowl was built into one of the only natural valleys in the Panhandle, which obviated the need to build grandstand supports since the concrete could be poured downhill into the perfect concave mold. The stadium was equipped with electrical outlets under every other seat in the east-side chairback section, enabling any fan with an extension cord to make coffee and toast, listen to the call on the Buffalo radio network, huddle under an electric blanket, and watch television and the game at the same time. Such futuristic thinking made our stadium state of the art long before the luxury suite was invented. Senator Lyndon B. Johnson himself came to the grand opening. The stadium cozily accommodated 20,000 and on a fall Saturday night, despite the amenities, was usually half full, at best. The Buffalo Bowl's official name was later changed to Kimbrough Memorial Stadium, but nobody ever called it that, which

Frank Kimbrough Memorial Stadium. *(West Texas A&M Athletics)*

was a shame, seeing as Frank Kimbrough was a fine football coach and athletic director, with the good sense to pass on at a point when his reputation was fresh and the administration needed someone to name a stadium after.

In 1973, when I was six, I saw my first football game there. The Buffs defeated Drake, 13–10, in the season opener. The victory was one of only two for the Buffaloes in the entire season—the Buffs had a lot of seasons like that—but it nevertheless marked the beginning of a lifelong devotion to an ever-changing roster of college kids achieving sometimes remarkable, breathtaking victory and other times hugely disappointing and depressing loss on the gridiron.

In time I would come to believe that college football contained all of the joy, faith, pageantry, feeling, failure, and renewal that any person could hope for out of life. Even my faith in God would become intertwined with my faith in football. Though God was not likely amused by this, I believed that there was no greater test of faith than to tie oneself to the fortunes of a college football team. It's no accident that the fans of any particular squad are called "the faithful." I was faithful to the West Texas Buffaloes as a child and, later, after I put away childish things, to the great Texas Longhorns. My faith in college football carried me through life, death, and divorce. And to redemption. College football showed me that the divine will could be realized on 120 yards of freshly manicured turf. I find that most of my important memories project through the Technicolor prism of stadium Saturdays. Passions evoked by college football flowed through generations of my family, tying us all together. It bound me to my grandparents, parents, wife, sons, and a group of remarkable friends collectively known as the Lone Star Drinking Club. I believed in college football. My belief that a game could be a tonic to overcome all of life's troubles originated with my grandfather, who the old Buffaloes referred to as "Bulldog," and with my mom, who was the greatest college football fan I ever knew.

W. Mitchell "Bulldog" Jones was a star on the football field who would return to WT after his playing days to coach and teach. After

World War II, the university president appointed my grandfather dean of men, which made him responsible for every male undergraduate's well-being and comportment, especially those who played intercollegiate athletics and whose eligibility hung in the balance. When the Jones family arrived at Kimbrough Stadium on a fall afternoon, we were traveling with serious celebrity. We couldn't get to our seats without being told what a great man my grandfather was—even men who didn't stop to talk to us would give a quick nod and a respectful "Dean Jones" by way of greeting, as if they were walking across campus and afraid that the old man knew where they had been the night before.

My grandfather's love for the Buffs ran deep, but he knew entirely too much about the game to be a great college football fan. At games, he barely spoke; undisciplined or reckless play by the Buffaloes brought no worse than a disapproving shake of his flattopped head. He carried himself with the reserve of a federal bank. My father, W. Mitchell Jones Jr., whom the Buffalo faithful called "Dubya Mitch," could be counted on, maybe once or twice every Saturday, to jump out of his seat with enthusiasm. He was always Mr. Positive; booing or berating an official was completely out of his character. Among our traveling party, it was up to two great women to really bring the game to life with passions that reflected the unpredictable surges of the human spirit. My grandmother, the country-tough matriarch Audrey Jones, and my mother, Reba, knew how to bring the staid alumni side of the Buffalo Bowl to roaring life. They hollered. They yelled. They booed. The chorus of racket was often to their husbands' disapproval, which, of course, amounted to exactly diddly as an impetus to change their behavior. My grandmother just embraced the spirit of it all—the band taking the field, the ringing of the homecoming bell, the pageantry, the religion. My mother appreciated all that, but she also had a sharp strategic eye for the game before her. My mother's intellectual curiosity wouldn't allow her to be a casual fan, or a casual anything. She always wanted to know the details, the context, and the history. Nothing escaped her interest. This was the only way she ever experienced life and she expected the same of her children. She was always in the moment, believing life composed a grand adventure and that the world was privileged to have her play a part. Her dedication to the Buffaloes—her Buffaloes—was unceasing, even when they finished 2–9 and looked bad doing it.

My mother's voice echoing in the Kimbrough Memorial Stadium night was unadulterated bliss. Once the fight song started (with its shouted, pulsating bridge: "*W-T-S-U, Dubya-TEE-ess-YOO, Fight! Fight! Fight!*") and the homecoming bell started ringing, my mother cranked up the voltage. She didn't care one whit that our seats were with the venerable Dean Jones. She cheered every great play, booed the refs after a blown call, offered the Buffalo offensive coaching staff an unending stream of advice. The only time she was quiet was at the snap when the Buffs had possession—she was as knowledgeable as she was passionate. The passion shone through regardless of the score, the time remaining, or the down and distance.

For several years I learned, right between my two parents, proud members of the Class of '51, what it meant to care about a team's success more than rational thought should allow. My childhood football catechism might have held me in fine stead had my parents confined me to the Buffalo Bowl, but in the fall of 1975 they made the mistake of driving me to Austin. My sister, Molly, was a freshman at the University of Texas and it was parents' weekend. Everything about the University of Texas is bigger than everything about West Texas State; but as an eight-year-old I had no concept of the physical and emotional magnitude. The thirty-story administration building towering over campus—infamous as the site of one of the most awful mass murders in history, when Charles Whitman shot dead fourteen people from its observation deck in 1966—was bigger than the only skyscraper in Amarillo. That such a great structure belonged to a college and not a city was staggering to understand. There it loomed, right among enormous old-growth oaks and perfectly manicured quads between huge classroom buildings and dorms with their own zip codes.

As we walked to the stadium from the motel that Saturday, I remember how the throng expanded, tributary side streets spilling fans into the main university pathways until there was barely any room to move. It was like an endless stream of pilgrims moving toward the center of their college football universe. Eventually all paths converged on the tunnels leading into Texas Memorial Stadium. I clutched the back of my father's shirt as the usher tore our tickets and funneled us into a set of escalators ferrying folks up to the top of the west-side upper deck. Fourteen floors later we emerged on a huge mezzanine that overlooked the campus to the west and the State Capitol to the south. From there we entered the stadium, so high up it was dizzying. I watched birds fly underneath us. The deck sat at what felt like a 45-degree angle, although I am sure it measures no more than 42 degrees. From there we climbed higher still. They could have made a killing selling oxygen masks as we trudged with the pilgrims up to our fortieth-row seats. This structure was four Buffalo Bowls stacked toward the heavens like bricks in the Tower of Babel. Never had I been a member of such an awesome congregation, 72,000 souls exhaling a wide, throaty roar under a haze of industrial lighting, cigarette smoke, and central Texas humidity. The band entered to wild applause, three hundred members strong, marching crisply in orange and white uniforms topped by white cowboy hats and accompanied by the world's biggest bass drum. They were followed on the field by the world's biggest Texas flag, which, unfurled, stretched its single-starred red, white, and blue glory from the goal line to midfield. Every autumn, on five special Saturdays, this spectacle happened under the watchful eye of the world's biggest live mascot, a 1,200-pound longhorn steer named Bevo, all being prologue to Texas beating some poor opponent like a rented mule. Texas loves a winner.

This was college football the way the big boys played it. On that night the Longhorns thumped Utah State 61–7. And the Texas fans were not at all happy about the seven. A sophomore fullback named Earl Campbell— "the Tyler Rose"—rumbled forty yards for one of the touchdowns. I had no clue that I was watching a legend in the making. But I did know that big-time college football would become my calling. This was my game.

The big-time teams played on television every Saturday and eventually trumped my interest in the family's old school. In retrospect, that a televised anything held a young boy's interest over a live experience was a shame. But the Buffs couldn't compete with Notre Dame, USC, Alabama, Oklahoma, Nebraska, Michigan, Ohio State, and certainly not with the Texas Longhorns, my very own guys. So it was as a fourth-grader in the fall of 1977 that I begin to stalk the afternoon paper delivery boy. Our hometown of Amarillo maintained the anachronistic tradition of both a morning and afternoon paper long after most cities of its size. This was a very good thing. The Associated Press national college football poll never made it into the Tuesday morning edition, but by the afternoon it magically appeared. Many cynics believed that the *Amarillo Daily News* simply reprinted the morning content in an afternoon edition to sell twice as many papers. I knew this to be false. Somewhere in the middle of the news building on Tyler Street there worked a dedicated junior sports editor who took the time to update the day's scorecard with all of the late game results and the fresh AP poll, which I would turn to immediately after the delivery boy handed me the paper in what became a weekly ritual. There, perched at No. 1, would be the Texas Longhorns, the team I had seen with my own eyes play in their huge cathedral of a stadium two years before. Someday, I knew, I would return. In the meantime, the Horns were running roughshod over the college football world behind Earl Campbell. The senior tailback would win that year's Heisman Trophy, the first Longhorn ever to do so. The 1977 Longhorns unfortunately lost the national championship to Notre Dame in that January's Cotton Bowl. I was not sophisticated enough at the time to actually blame God for this. I should have; it was Notre Dame after all. But I let it go. Next year is always the best year for college football fans. I now had something to look forward to every Saturday in every fall of my life to come.

Americans may celebrate the New Year in January, but they mark time by Septembers. After the winter solistice and the end of bowl season, we hibernate in warm basketball arenas through the cold months, then depend on the quiet cadence of baseball to get us through the summer heat. After a lazy summer, work settles into a regular rhythm and a new school year starts; some kids leave home for kindergarten, others for college. Parents cry under both circumstances. Thankfully, back-to-school means that the eight-month gestational cycle of football comes to a fruitful end. The games begin and the stakes slowly rise.

Nothing compares to the arrival of football. Individual basketball and baseball games are not events that require a week of preparation and anticipation. If you lose a basketball game, a chance for redemption comes in the second half of the season. Lose a football game and you wait a year to get back on the field with your rival. There is no turning back, and few second chances. In a college football season there are a mere dozen games. The true fan relishes every one, relives it long after it has passed, regardless of whether the memories bring pleasure or pain, and then turns all too soon to waiting for the next cycle to begin.

This cycle requires faith. My own faith was built in the Christian tradition, which has a full liturgy of waiting. Advent consists of four weeks during which the hope of the Messiah's birth lies just beyond man's reach. Lent lasts forty days that grow darker and darker before the great dawn of resurrection and life where all rejoice. This was my family's tradition. My mother was the most faithful of all of us. She would never confuse religion and college football, which made her a better—or at least more disciplined—person than her youngest son. Not only did I blur the line between faith in God and football, during some moments of my life I wholly obliterated it.

Christian patience and discernment carries one only so far when a national title is on the line. I first reminded God of this in 1983 when my grandmother had suffered through a fall of failing health. That season the WT Buffaloes couldn't win a single football game. Audrey didn't have much to give them that year. She died that January, just after the New Year. I guess the losses could have killed her, but it was more likely the cancer. A few days before Audrey died, the Longhorns again lost the national title in the Cotton Bowl, this time to Georgia on a cruel special teams blunder. In the bloom of my rebellious adolescence, I suspected that God was mocking me.

"What's the matter with you? My grandmother's dying."

"Lots of grandmothers died over the holidays."

"Texas was an eight-point favorite."

"That's all well and good, but it doesn't explain why you skipped church on Epiphany."

This started a tradition of the Texas Longhorns not winning the national title and of God not being particularly helpful in them getting there. Nevertheless, the University of Texas had secured my lifelong loyalty. The Longhorns did this by winning almost every game I watched them play. During my adolescent years, Texas won thirty-seven, lost nine, and tied one. Texas does love a winner.

By the time I got to Texas as an official member of the student body, however, the world went black. Texas started to lose about half their games. The Longhorns played lousy football while I attended school in Austin from 1985 to 1990. They continued to lose as I went away to graduate school and kept losing when I returned to Austin to start life as an adult. But the losing didn't matter; I would no more leave the Longhorns than my mother would abandon Frank Kimbrough or Jesus. I believed in Texas. Like all the other members of the Longhorn faithful, I had no doubt that Texas would again ascend to the mountaintop to claim the national championship.

I didn't realize that it would be such a long wait. Texas football lived in the shadow of—some would say under the burden of—a man named Darrell Royal, the head coach who led the Horns to national titles in 1963, 1969, and 1970. Some of us didn't count the title in 1970 because it was handed out by United Press International preceding the 1971 Cotton Bowl, which the Longhorns lost to Notre Dame. I was clearly too young to blame God for that one. In any case, the title drought had stretched to fifteen years by the time I set foot on campus and twenty years by the time I graduated. Coaches were hired, then fired. Expectations were raised, then dashed. The Texas mediocrity cycle continued to churn.

The Longhorns were thirty years past their last national championship by the time they lured to campus the man who would finally break the cycle. Mack Brown had turned the University of North Carolina—the ultimate basketball school—into a college football power. Oh, what he could do with the resources and tradition of Texas. Mack worked fast. The millennium dawned and with it came a renaissance of Texas football. By the fall of 2001, Mack had assembled all the pieces. Texas started the season with a roster littered with future NFL players and a No. 5 ranking; I knew that this would finally be the year.

What I didn't know was that this would also be a painful fall for my favorite college football fan. My mother was sick. Cancer had claimed my grandmother years before and now was bearing down on the next generation. As the Longhorns scaled new heights, my mother slowly descended. Mom would silently endure; the woman who used to hold my hand as we climbed the stadium steps at Kimbrough was now unable to accomplish the simplest of tasks without pain. She saved this news until the Thanksgiving holiday had ended. The Longhorns were 10-1 and ranked third; a shot at the national title was right in front of them. She called me on a Sunday afternoon and quietly relayed to me that pancreatic cancer was closing the book on a wonderful life. I rested my chin on the receiver.

"Are you okay?" she asked. I wasn't.

"Yes."

Mothers always know when their children are lying, but instead of calling me on it, she changed the subject to the Christmas season ahead. She stopped midsentence and asked if I remembered the first Advent candle and what it represented. Of course I did.

"Hope."

"Why don't you try and remember what that means?"

Mom would have no more football seasons. I had no choice but to live them for her; I hoped that I was up to the task. Trying to remember what hope meant, I started a conversation with God.

"Texas really needs to win the national championship."

"Really? And what will your gift to the world be?"

"I dunno . . . grace, charity, generosity of spirit . . ."

"Such things are already required of my people. Read Micah 6:8."

"I know, but they're very difficult for me at the moment."

"I understand."

"Oh, and in football."

"Come again?"

"The national championship in football, not one of those swimming and diving ones we always edge out Stanford to get. Can I give you a year?"

"Is this really what the candle of Hope means to you?"

I knew better than to answer. One year was a very reasonable time-table. That simply wasn't worth debate. A better question was: How did I get to the point in my life where I would try to cut a deal with God over a college football team?

That's a long story. It involves the counsel of an old man, two great women, raising three boys, Mennonites singing, night games in Lubbock, Texas, a scrappy gamer of a quarterback, a man with a golden left arm, and, finally, a small boy from the south side of Houston named Vince.

At every step along the journey, I always believed that the Texas Longhorns would be national champions. It was just around the next corner, or maybe the next one, or maybe the one after that. I learned about patience and commitment, about ebullience and exasperation, about fatherhood and faith.

This is one fan's story.

Part 1

THE BEGINNINGS OF FANDOM

1

THE BUFFALO BOWL

*West Texas State University
vs. Wichita State University*

FRANK KIMBROUGH MEMORIAL STADIUM, CANYON, TEXAS, SEPTEMBER 30, 1978

"Throw it to Spencer."

For two solid years this was my mother's constant cry from our seats at the Buffalo Bowl. Reggie Spencer was Mom's favorite player. Spencer, number 7, was a long and lean split end from Fort Lauderdale, Florida. To Mom's credit, he *was* always open. The West Texas coaching staff often didn't notice this, being much more conservative than Mom. Running between the tackles, sound defense, solid special teams—don't do anything crazy. Hurling the ball downfield to a speedster like Spencer rested outside of their comfort zone. The buttoned-down approach wasn't necessarily a bad strategy given that most WT signal callers couldn't throw feed to starving birds. Tully Blanchard, who still holds the WT records for fumbles lost and interceptions, had the most successful professional career. But not as a quarterback. He became a cult hero on the pro wrestling circuit.

"Throw it to Spencer."

Mom's lungs were unrelenting. She had no tolerance for the Buffaloes failing to take advantage of an obvious mismatch. My grandfather was in the next seat over and agreed with Mom's strategic assessment, he just didn't vocalize it. Wichita State was loading up the line of scrimmage to stop the Buffalo running game. This left Spencer free to find openings in the defense, either dragging across the middle with defenders unable to keep pace or going deep into the zones the Wichita State safeties had vacated.

"Throw it to Spencer."

Usually the Buff coaches wouldn't take this advice. Spencer only hauled in twenty-one balls during his senior campaign, which led the team, but it wasn't exactly a wide-open offense. The occasional moments of brilliance—a diving 27-yard touchdown catch against Colorado State comes to mind—were secondary to number 7's role as a downfield blocker. Mom, of course, didn't let the coaching staff off the hook and kept up the constant refrain:

"Throw it to Spencer."

Mom was in particularly good voice on this night. She was a woman of great faith who transitioned seamlessly from the Holy Spirit to college football, believing unimpeachably that she had a direct line into the offensive coordinator's headset. God to Mom to the booth to the field to the quarterback to Spencer. Touchdown. That's how it played out in her mind; she was undeterred that Reggie Spencer had been a decoy all his years on campus.

"Throw it to Spencer."

And then the Buffaloes did. Dad and I rose from our seats in the east-side red chairback section to watch the trajectory as a Buff quarterback I scarcely remember let loose an uncharacteristic tight spiral down the West Texas sideline. Spencer was all alone and probably shocked.

Touchdown.

Well. It would have been, but the ball fell right through his hands. He headed to the sidelines knowing he wouldn't get another chance. An audible groan went up from the stands. Except for Mom. She had only one thing to say, which she articulated loud and clear.

"*Catch it*, Spencer."

My stoic grandfather even laughed out loud at that one. The Buffs eventually lost the game 38–37, but it was hardly Reggie Spencer's fault. WT's last five possessions ended fumble, fumble, interception, missed field goal, fumble—a fairly average day at the office during a 3-8 season. The loss didn't matter much to my game companions. My grandparents and parents were never fair-weather fans. This was their school, for better or worse, and all of us would return in seven days to watch the Buffs be shut out by North Texas State, 35–0.

Football was part of our family from as far back as I can remember—not just for our family, but for most families in the Texas Panhandle. The only thing more important to the people of the high plains was faith in God. Taming and settling this arid and remote swath of America required great confidence in the Creator.

God clearly lived in the Panhandle. Although some referred to this country as godforsaken, that couldn't have been true. The Ogallala aquifer had to have been God's doing; who else would put a roaring underground river under a desert? Once the people figured out how to drop a straw into it and turn the wheels of their giant irrigation machines, they thrived. The small-town economies evolved from subsistence farming to mechanized agriculture to cattle to energy—the last evolution occurred only if the city fathers had the good sense to build their particular village on top of an oil or natural gas field, which could make you rich in a hurry. Not every community was so fortunate, but most towns had a cattle feedlot, a farmer's cooperative, a grain elevator if they were next to a rail line, a rodeo arena, and a church. In the smallest towns, the Baptists were the only game in town. Larger communities might accommodate the Church of Christ or the Methodists. Regardless of denomination, you could prosper here. The land was already perfect for raising cattle for a nation of beef eaters. When they discovered oil and natural gas on the high plains, we really had something. God was good to us.

He also gave us football. With football came an attitude about the game that sustained rural Texas through good times and bad. Though this obsession was made of man, the good Lord always got three minutes over the public address system at each town's high school stadium under the Friday night lights. The moment of prayer bonded communities together for a quiet moment, but its power couldn't compare to the emotional entanglement between town and team. Generation upon generation, season upon season, the ecclesiastical devotion of the masses infused the night air as sweet as the smell of cut grass. The annual prelude would happen every August at back-to-school time when the local bank printed up and distributed business cards with the season schedule and a catchy slogan along the lines of: *It was heaven in '57, back to state in '58!* For there was once a time when the high school kids of rural Texas played the game better than anyone. My father and grandfather were a part of this cultural fabric, both of them good enough to play college ball for WT. While all college football fans talk about "their guys," for my grandfather and father this relationship was not vicarious. The Buffs really were their guys, part of a line of WT players that could not be severed, stretching back almost to the turn of the century.

I knew much of this history because it was constantly retold in my grandmother's kitchen before every home game. The Jones family pre-game ritual commenced among the harvest gold appliances and the huge L-shaped formica table my Uncle Frank had built to accommodate up to twenty-five dinner guests. The old kitchen brings to me fond memories, but never of the food. As grandmothers go, Audrey Emma Jones was a pretty lousy cook. She was one hell of an entertainer—a bold extrovert before her time who fed off the energy of others—just beware what was on the plate, especially the pan-fried breaded T-bone steak. My brother Sam always commented that he didn't know when he'd seen an innocent piece of meat punished like that. Grandma Jones could have

Mitchell and Audrey Jones, 1925. *(Jones Family)*

taught the British a thing or two, but no one dared complain. For starters, Audrey Jones was an imposing 5'10" with enormous sinewy hands that could have made Floydada High School a major power had it occurred to anyone to let women play basketball in the nineteen oughts. The first time my grandfather held her hand he was convinced that he had found his lifelong partner, not out of some tender moment, but a practical one. The young football coach had a mental picture of large sons wreaking havoc on opposing offenses. That she seemed capable and willing to use those mitts to strangle the life out of any poor snake that dared sneak too close to the house only added to the romance.

Grandad and Grandma Jones met when they were students at WT in the early 1920s; it was called West Texas State Teachers College then, and both of them were aspiring educators. It was in the education building that Audrey Watson first set eyes on the slight and studious young man with the wavy brown hair. She had no idea that he was star on the football field.

My grandfather's picture hangs in the Texas Panhandle Sports Hall of Fame. "Bulldog" Jones, nicknamed because of his temperament, was a 5'9", 155-pound pulling guard. He was also blind as a bat, waging desperate battles against much larger men he could barely see. Sportswriters used to joke that he had no idea what he was up against. His first step was quick and sure, and he had the leverage of a wrestler. But the brains set him apart; he was playing chess with his opponents and always knew the right moment and place to assault some poor linebacker, who would seldom see the tiny truck that ran him over.

In the fall of 1923, the drugstore in Canyon rendered the Buffalo starting lineup in candy before the season opener. Sitting in the front window was a perfect chocolate eleven. The linemen were represented by big walnut clusters. Each man's name was printed alongside in block letters. The only exception was the right guard, who was represented by the tiniest chocolate peanut the proprietor could find. The peanut was labeled on a small card that read: JONES. This was a real hoot, the good people of Canyon being easily amused in the 1920s. My grandfather, however, was enraged by the slight. The following Saturday at the Tri-State Fairgrounds field in Amarillo, his opponents felt Bulldog's rage. He whaled his frustration out on any player who dared venture close enough to him to be hit. The "peanut" joke resulted in a full day for the opposing training staff, my grandfather having delivered at least one broken nose and bruises and contusions too numerous to catalogue.

"Bulldog" Jones (center, without helmet) taking someone out. *(Jones Family)*

When his playing days were over, he took his bachelor's degree in psychology and threw himself into coaching with the same warrior's rage and chess master's mien. A 1919 tome called *Inside Football* written by Major Frank W. Cavanaugh was crucial to his development as a young coach. Bulldog and Major Cavanaugh were cut from the same cloth. He gave Grandad nuggets like this, from page 133:

The end must impress his advantage of position upon the tackle by his perpetual shifting; causing him all the worry and mental uneasiness possible in a man of probably superior weight and strength, just as, in the wilds of Africa, the smaller, more tenacious, more active, vigorous and vicious animal has his chance to wear down the larger brute.

Having been a small, tenacious, active, vigorous, and vicious animal himself, Bulldog Jones had found his coaching bible and quickly turned the moribund program at Canyon High School into a winning squad known for fearless defense and daring offensive game plans involving the exotic and unusual forward pass. Their execution was unparalleled. Perhaps this was great coaching, or perhaps these young men were terrified of ever disappointing Coach Jones—they would be the first in a long line of men who could be reduced to quivering wrecks by the narrowed eyes and furrowed brow of the Buffalo legend. He eventually turned this intensity toward academia, taking his graduate degree in psychology from the University of Oregon and returning to the WT faculty to become a beloved eminence, building and molding three generations of Panhandle men and women. Even after he was appointed dean of men, he continued to teach undergraduates in the colleges of education and liberal arts until, at age seventy, he was forced to retire by a shortsighted act of the Texas legislature. He never forgave them, any more than he forgave the First Baptist Church for dismissing him as a Sunday school teacher for a variety of heresies, not the least of which was his insistence on independent thought and a philosopher's approach to the scriptures. He never did cotton to the Elmer Gantrys and the weak of will. My grandfather had great faith in God; it was man who left something to be desired.

The Bulldog I knew as a child had mellowed with age, a man of letters and student of the classics who held court in Audrey's kitchen on a variety of topics. Football was always on the agenda, but the old man knew a fair amount about basketball, as well; he even took one Canyon Eagles squad to the state semi-finals. But my informal education didn't stop at sports. The book of Job might be interspersed with a lesson on trigonometry or his beloved Plato. He instilled in me a love of *Cyrano de Bergerac* and convinced me that I should read *The Brothers Karamazov,* which he claimed was the greatest novel ever written but I could never finish—I don't know how Dostoyevsky could keep his own characters straight, much less expect me to. One summer I took a class on Shakespeare's later plays at WT. When I mentioned the syllabus to Grandad he insisted I take his money and go buy a copy of the complete works. Didn't need one, I said: We had three at the house. Bulldog gave me his disapproving look—gentle and understanding, but disapproving nonetheless. He explained that I needed my own. For Shakespeare was a clean slate on which the reader records his thoughts; no one but me would underline the same passages, or make the same notes in the margins. I took his money and bought the book. And for a summer of lunches, I was one of his students. He always wondered why Shakespeare's most miserable characters always got to give the most touching speeches. He and Audrey both had a soft spot for the underdog. That may be why they loved their daughter-in-law so much.

My mother, Reba Killian, was 5'3" on a tall day (claimed 5'4" but it was a lie) and took less crap from anyone than even Audrey Jones did. My grandmother initially didn't welcome my mom with open arms; Audrey never really believed anyone was good enough to marry my dad, her first born, whom she simply called Son, which must have long irritated his younger brother, who went by Marshall. Eventually, though, Audrey and Reba became fast friends, due mostly to Audrey's figuring out that Mom was just as tough as she was. Mom's character was forged early in life; she always held a memory of being lined up with her siblings and switched for chasing the family cow around the yard during the Depression, an offense that could cost a poor family a day's worth of milk production. They were lucky to even have a cow. Audrey knew that life and admired Mom for rising above it. Both women possessed a keen sense of social justice, great faith in Jesus, and an unerring ability to sniff out hypocrites.

My grandmother may have been hostile and mean-spirited to those who deserved it—pity whatever poor bastard traveling salesman ever came to the door—but she would always defend the weak and downtrodden. During the fifties and sixties, she noticed more and more Hispanic kids entering her fifth-grade class; they would come through the porous Texas border to find work in the farms and ranches and feedlots. Some of these were second- or third-generation Texans, but many were migrants who didn't speak a lick of English. There was no such thing as bilingual education at that time, unless you were fortunate enough to land in Mrs. Jones's class. Audrey spoke fluent Spanish. More importantly, she demanded the Anglo kids respect "her little Mexicans." Patronizing, yes, but the trips to their homes to make sure they had warm clothes and enough to eat were genuine gifts of Christian love, and everyone in Canyon knew it. To Audrey, the politics of immigration were a distant afterthought to the care and education of children and families.

My mother, like Audrey, loved unconditionally. She learned growing up that life was never to be taken for granted. Mom learned some of these lessons as a young adolescent working at a carbon-black plant—an unpleasant relic of industrial America originally built before the promulgation of child labor laws—in her hometown of Pampa. Her goal was to earn enough money to eventually go to Texas A&I University in the Rio Grande Valley. She was the first person in her family to go to college, but her money ran out after a year, so she returned to the Pampa oil patch and worked in her father's shop. We all called my Grandfather Killian Daddy John. He was a slender and easygoing man who had a love of Roi Tans and Red Man and a remarkable memory for auto and machine part numbers. Daddy John was the best parts man around, and his ability to do math in his head was passed down to my mother, which made her a crack student.

Mom was still only eighteen when she went back home after a year at A&I, having graduated from Pampa High as a sixteen-year-old salutatorian two years before. She returned needing a year of wages plus fifty dollars she borrowed from my Aunt Bobbie for tuition. Then she was on her way again, this time never to return to the oil patch. West Texas State was her ticket to a new life, which she pursued with relish and no small amount of guts. It was brazen enough for her to actually go to college, but to major in chemistry and assume a woman's place was in the workplace made her a screaming radical long before it was cool to be one on a college campus and, actually, at WT, it never was cool to be one.

The most uncool Baptist Student Union was her base of operations. Church was never far away—worship on Sunday, Bible study on Wednesday night. That's where she met my dad, a fellow chemistry major and Baptist. He began to court her—unsuccessfully. Mom must have turned him down a half-dozen times. When she finally said yes, she "late-dated" him, leaving the Canyon drugstore soda fountain early to have dinner with another boy going off for the army the next day. But something must have clicked that night, because Mom went out again the next weekend with my introverted father, who regrettably had inherited little of Audrey's spark and sharp tongue. He relied instead on a gentleness and kindness that belied his size and disposition on the football field. He did lean toward the handsome side; his high school picture resembles a young Kurt Russell. Mom said she married him because he made her laugh and my siblings and I assumed she meant intentionally. One of my father's great moments in life was when he was elected King of West Texas High School. Upon taking his seat on the makeshift throne during a school assembly, he backed the large chair straight off of the back of the auditorium riser, leading to a spectacular crash. Only his pride was injured.

Mom and Dad married upon leaving WT and their adventures begin.

They moved to Galveston, where my father finished medical school, then to Detroit. Dad told great stories about the night shifts at Detroit Receiving Hospital, where he once sewed the nose back onto a barroom brawl victim; he wasn't sure he did it right and always wondered if it held. Dad had a series of jobs in Kansas, but eventually they returned to Amarillo, the largest city in the Panhandle. We were a family of six by then, my brother David was the oldest and my first hero, Molly was the big sister who always looked out for me, and my brother Sam became my lifelong friend. Mom and Dad referred to my siblings as "the big three." I was a midlife crisis bonus baby, separated by eight years from the others. It gave me a chance to be both the youngest and, when Sam moved out, to reinvent myself as an only child.

Our family had a great life in Amarillo. Dad's practice thrived; Mom continued her education and eventually became the collections curator for the local art museum. The family's faith life was entrusted to the red-brick and well-manicured Westminister Presbyterian Church, which provided a much more moderate and undisciplined upbringing than my mother's life with the Southern Baptists, although we always did enjoy the traditional blood-sport competition of "beating the Baptists to Furr's Cafeteria" upon departing Sunday worship. A kind and benevolent former college football player named Howard F. M. Childers was the pastor at Westminster. He became my spiritual guide, and his son Ben a close friend. That Reverend Childers had played ball for the hated Texas A&M Aggies was a flaw in his character I simply forgave; I believed that was the Christian thing to do.

Away from church, our sacred devotion was to the West Texas State Buffaloes, giving my mother and her children plenty of opportunities to cheer for the underdog at the Buffalo Bowl. There is no more serious public manifestation of an American college than its football team. You can call that a symptom of a nation's misplaced priorities if you want, but it's also the truth. We couldn't disconnect the Buffalo football squad from the university, and we couldn't disconnect the university from the Jones family. My grandfather was WT: The university even affixed his name to the biggest building on campus, a men's dorm called Mitch Jones Hall.

Our family never missed a home game during the 1970s. This was the last golden age of small-college football, where everyone played in the top division of the National Collegiate Athletic Association. There were haves and have-nots, to be sure, but that never stopped my family from feeling like WT was part of something bigger than just the small-time Missouri Valley Conference. The Buffs had a couple of Sun Bowl victories to their credit and had even produced two star tailbacks in the National Football League: Duane Thomas and Eugene "Mercury" Morris, both products of the 1960s when a fiery coach named Joe Kerbel had WT right on the precipice of big-time football. But they could never sustain that success. After Kerbel's departure in 1970, the Buffs settled into the mediocre play that I remember from my childhood. Economics eventually betrayed WT—a small college trying to play big-time football wasn't a winning proposition. As television became more and more of a driving force in the college game, the Buffs slid with many other schools from the mighty NCAA Division I-A down to I-AA, then down to Division II.

Regrettably, the family's interest waned as well. By 1980 my brothers and sister had already gone away to their own college destinations. I stayed behind, still in junior high school, by this time a locked-and-loaded Texas Longhorn fan with little interest in the Division II tilts down the road in Canyon. I was a teenager and had better things to do than follow a small-time conference. Not only did I not miss the Buffaloes, I was both too young and too Protestant to feel guilty about it.

The Buffs may not have needed one more adolescent voice in the crowd, but they must have missed my grandmother terribly. Audrey had always been the driving force behind our trips to Kimbrough. By the time I was a teenager she had stopped attending the home games at all. Her replacement knee bent at about a fifteen-degree angle on a warm spring day; you could forget climbing the stairs to our seats on a crisp fall evening. And without Audrey, well, it just wasn't a Buffalo football game.

Mom and Dad didn't make many of the games without my grand-parents. They weren't the only ones: attendance waned to the point that some nights perhaps 2,000 folks were rattling around the 20,000-seat stadium. It felt like a high school play-off game between two small towns; the size of the crowd did anyway. The difference is that during a Texas high school play-off game, each person in the crowd lives and dies with every play and wrings every last bit of emotion to support their hometown boys. The high school play-off games in Kimbrough had a much better atmosphere than the Buffalo crowds delivered.

Mom was the best fan among us, yet I am not even sure she missed the atmosphere at Kimbrough, especially since she and Audrey could no longer cheer the Buffs together. She was, of course, never without War-ren Hasse's call on the Buffalo radio network. Hasse was from Pampa, and Mom knew the family. He always worked alone and had a smooth delivery on the play-by-play, a baritone with just a touch of nasality that aped the affectless tone of the Midwestern broadcaster. Very few people knew that he got his start in Wisconsin. He affected a slight Texas twang, which assured anyone within radio listening distance that he was, indeed, one of us. Hasse was background noise on a lot of fall nights; I say background noise, but as soon as I was convinced no one was listening, the Buffs would make a great play and my mother, perhaps touching up the baseboard paint in the family room, would break her estimable concentration and let out a "Way to go, Buff-a-lows!" She re-mained the unconditional football fan and I never bothered to change the channel. We would listen through the postgame show and Warren would give way to the *Ruby Lewis Show* on KGNC. Ruby would go back to the standard soft favorites programming, but always managed to slip in some extra Ray Charles or Nat King Cole. It may not have occurred to anyone in Amarillo that Ruby Lewis was black. Perhaps they just enjoyed Dionne Warwick too much to give it a second thought. Dionne and Ruby Lewis became our family entertainment and the seats in Kimbrough sat sadly vacant.

Audrey's kitchen was vacant as well. I remembered this place as the warmest room in the world when I rolled Hot Wheels cars along the floor as Grandma Jones made pancakes. The jigsaw puzzles, the Monopoly games, the large family dinners, Buffalo pregame—I was trying to remember where it all went. The family no longer gathered in her kitchen before Buffalo football games, or much of anything else. The crazy arts and crafts projects, the trips to the Tri-State Fair with her grandchildren to watch the animal judging, the huge Thanksgivings, they all seemed like a different lifetime. I still remember the first Christmas that the giant picture window in the kitchen wasn't painted with some Rockwellian holiday scene—Grandma used to use tempera paint, my mom would help her. The paint covering the huge six-foot-by-ten-foot glass at the back of the house signaled the coming of the holidays. Now not only was the window not painted, there wasn't even a tree in the living room. One by one the touchstones of my childhood with Grandma Jones slowly faded into the crawl spaces of the big house on Fifth Street. Sometimes you would catch a glimpse of our great matriarch, but it never lasted. Audrey was getting sick. She was a tough old bird, but cancer doesn't care. Cancer's the Devil. And the Devil kept this formidable woman in a hospital bed on Christmas Day, 1983. Night begin to fall fast for Grandma Jones.

The last time I saw her coherent was on that Christmas day. She asked me quietly to be one of her pallbearers. Audrey had six grandsons and figured it was just the right number. Her big wonderful hands were pockmarked with black spots and they were barely robust enough to close around my own. The IV needle looked like it might poke straight through them. It was the first time in my life someone died whom I actually loved. I was sixteen.

I had few regrets about Audrey leaving me. My immaturity might be one explanation: Did I lack the realization of how much she had meant to me? No, that wasn't it. Regret is a funny thing; we have no need of it when we know exactly how special something was when we had it. As I left First

Audrey's picture window at Christmas. *(Jones Family)*

Baptist with my sobbing grandfather on the only day I ever saw Bulldog cry, I understood. Grandad's heart was broken, for his lifelong partner was gone. For not one day in the life of Mitch and Audrey Jones had either of them doubted that they had profoundly changed each other's lives.

Bulldog Jones once wrote:

I do not want to go backward unless it is to pick up things extremely valuable that I overlooked. And ultimately that would mean going forward. Can we ever know backward from forward?

We let Audrey go, and with her we left behind many memories of childhood and the West Texas State Buffaloes. But I often go back there to feel her embrace. I can still smell the oil heating to just the right temperature on her well-worn stovetop at that exact moment when pancake batter collides with cast iron and fills the kitchen with the smell of life.

And I still carry with me West Texas State's last amazing feat, an extremely valuable day in 1980. It happened in a place called Stillwater, Oklahoma. Maybe I overlooked it at the time, but in hindsight, it was the best day I ever had as a college football fan. Can we ever know backward from forward?

2

STILL WATER

West Texas State vs. Oklahoma State University

**LEWIS FIELD, STILLWATER,
OKLAHOMA, SEPTEMBER 13, 1980**

True college football fans are not allowed to switch teams. Your allegiance is what your allegiance is, end of story. While I may have "left" the WT Buffaloes for the Texas Longhorns, it wasn't as if the Buffaloes were replaced—augmented, perhaps, but never left behind in the sense that I severed my attachment to them. The Longhorns and Buffaloes lived in different worlds, and by 1980 the Buffs were simply marking time before they would be left out of big-time college football altogether. WT was trying to compete with the major colleges with only thirty-seven scholarship athletes, with private donors picking up the tab for perhaps a dozen more. The big boys regularly had over a hundred in the days before the NCAA imposed the eighty-five-scholarship maximum. Few chances remained for poverty-stricken WT to make its presence felt on a national scale. Unfortunately, one of those chances would result in

31

a spiritual crisis for the Jones family, or at least for my oldest brother, David.

College football dwells as a spiritual anchor in the hearts of the faithful. If there is one thing we are sure of in life, it is in our allegiance to the Texas Longhorns, or to the Florida Gators or Yale Bulldogs or Furman Paladins, or whomever else—especially in our own stadium. True fans ascribe mysterious forces to the outcomes of games played on these sacred grounds. I was always convinced that Episcopalians were such natural college football fans not because most of them went to college but because they have a deeply instilled sense of sacred tradition liberally spiced with arcane and imponderable pageantry no different than game day on any given fall Saturday in the South. The Episcopalians also have all those great cocktail recipes. I may simply be voicing my own jealousy. The Presbyterians didn't do pageantry, or cocktails, for that matter. Thankfully, this did not get in the way of my spiritual life away from the church, honed as it was by the West Texas State Buffalo faithful and steeped by my great pilgrimage to Austin and the cathedral of the Texas Longhorns.

While I arrived at my spiritual attachment to the Longhorns quite honestly, it was not an inevitable event. The first college man in the Jones house was my brother David. I was only seven when he packed up his pale yellow Pontiac Grand Prix and headed off to Oklahoma State. He chose State because he "liked their math department." Whatever that meant. I think he probably was tired of touring colleges, had some buddies headed to Oklahoma State, saw that Stillwater was one of the world's great college towns, and, oh yeah, the girls were hot. That's what I think. It mattered not, but I vaguely remember my first trip to Stillwater. In the interest of full disclosure, my first taste of big-time college football may have been at Oklahoma State in the fall of 1974, not at Texas the following year. But I don't remember that experience very well. Lewis Field did not make an impression upon me the way Memorial Stadium did. It did not help that Lewis Field was named not after a man of athletic greatness, but rather a former dean of veterinary medicine, Laymon Lowery

Lewis. Perhaps, even at a young age, I understood that Lewis Field hosted 45,000 folks cheering a mid-tier Big Eight Conference squad perpetually playing in the shadow of Big Brother U: Barry Switzer's Oklahoma Sooners, arguably the finest college football team of the mid-1970s. That was all fine and good, but it was not Austin, where 72,000 cheered the Longhorns, the cock of the walk in the Southwest Conference with our three national titles under Darrell Royal and a team capable of standing toe-to-toe with the hated Sooners every October. Perhaps I knew the difference between the big time and the Big Time. It didn't hurt that Texas was Texas and I was a Texan.

In 1977, the Longhorns spent most of the season at No. 1 and Earl Campbell won the Heisman Trophy. Oklahoma State went 4-7, and their underappreciated tailback, Terry Miller, finished second. No team really threatened my love for Texas after that. Except for West Texas State, who would always hold sentimental rank, even when they ceased being an active rooting interest. But that was just it: West Texas and Texas

Earl Campbell won the 1977 Heisman Trophy, the first in University of Texas football history. *(University of Texas Athletics)*

would never compete head-to-head in anything. The Buffaloes had outstanding bowling and rodeo teams and no doubt would have left poor Texas in the dust in any team roping competition, but such a contest damn sure wouldn't have been on national television.

My brother David was not so lucky as to keep his allegiances separated. His fateful collision with old family loyalties came when Oklahoma State hosted West Texas State at Lewis Field. We made some allowance for his predicament: Everyone in our family was well aware that this was purely a pay-to-play game. That was when a big conference school would guarantee a certain sum of gate proceeds to a small-time school that needed the dough. It kept schools like WT financially viable—for a while anyway—and guaranteed a win for the home team. No one really expected for David to be on the spot.

My family left Amarillo after lunch on the Friday before the game to drive to Oklahoma. I was thirteen; Mom and Dad loaded the car and picked me up from school, pulling me out of Davy Crockett Junior High before afternoon classes—football was an excused absence in the Texas Panhandle. All of us looked forward to WT playing in a large venue, but we knew the Buffs' limitations. The graduation ceremony for David's class a few months before probably brought more excitement to Lewis Field than would the overmatched Buffaloes. The Buffs could be counted on to play hard, but this was a very solid Oklahoma State squad. The 1979 Cowboys had finished the year with five wins in their last seven games; the only losses were to No. 3 Nebraska and to No. 7 Oklahoma. OSU returned seventeen starters for the 1980 season. A team could build on that, especially one coached by the head man in Stillwater, the talented young University of Arkansas product, Jimmy Johnson. Seven years later, he would coach the Miami Hurricanes to the NCAA title. For an encore, he would win a pair of Super Bowls with the Dallas Cowboys. The odds were not with West Texas, although that didn't dissuade Mom. I still remember the conversation she and Dad had in the car. Dad, ever the diplomat, was concerned about her game-day enthusiasm around David's wife, Ellen, a loyal

OSU alumna. Ellen was a natural fit for the Jones family ever since she and my brother had started dating. However, she had never seen my mother at a football game, certainly not one where they were cheering for opposing teams.

"We really need to be polite during the game."

"What do you mean by that?"

"Let's just not get carried away rooting for the Buffs."

"Go butt a stump."

I've never heard anyone else use this particular expression. It was pure poetry coming out of Mom's mouth, never failing to leave Dad at least temporarily speechless. He did his best to recover.

"Ellen's never been to a game with you. We're their guests."

"It's a football game. Ellen has her team and I have mine."

Mom called it correctly. David's marriage to Ellen was no accident, for she possessed all of the character traits of the other female role models in our life. Audrey and Mom loved Ellen's toughness and felt David desperately needed her. Ellen had once disenrolled from Oklahoma Christian College—Reba Killian style—because she didn't feel it was a challenging academic environment. She enrolled instead at State. This would not have pleased her father, the redoubtable country veterinarian and Church of Christ elder Dr. Charles Kelsey—had she bothered to tell him anyway. Which she hadn't. I was not particularly concerned with her standing up under the pressure of intense Buffalo fandom, especially when her team was liable to beat the ever-living country-cousin crap out of the Buffaloes and pull their starters by the middle of the third quarter.

We all enjoyed several laughs at the Buffaloes' expense in the hours leading up to the game. Guessing things like how many touchdowns the Cowboys could score before halftime. We were real comedians. I certainly got the joke because I had already requested an excused absence from Saturday morning seventh-grade football practice. Coach Anthony, an OSU grad, teased me about who I was going to root for and informed me that it wouldn't really make any difference one way or another. My expectations were established.

The kickoff was a brutal midafternoon slot. You could count on a 90-degree September day in central Oklahoma, but this particular day hit 100. If it was 100 in the stands, then that meant the temperature on a synthetic playing surface in the bowl of a stadium was closer to 110. In response, Oklahoma State came out in their road white uniforms, figuring it would keep the players cooler. I didn't know whether the summer wardrobe was real coaching genius on OSU's part. I doubted it. Yes, the Buffs would be uncomfortable, but weren't you somehow ceding the moral high ground by not wearing your own home colors? West Texas wore their dark maroon home jerseys. It was odd. I expected to see the road whites, which I had never seen before; I hadn't attended a WT game on the road until now. The Buffs looked exactly the way the Buffs were supposed to look.

As a young high school basketball coach, my grandfather once took Canyon High School to the state play-offs and found that his Eagles sported exactly the same uniforms as their opponents. Bulldog and the opposing coach settled the matter with a coin. Canyon lost the flip and donned the white practice jerseys of the small college hosting the play-off game. The Eagles then proceeded to lose, but not by much. Grandad always attributed the final margin to the split second of doubt his players must have had trying to remember throughout the game what color was what. Years after the fact, he continued to second-guess himself over such a strategic blunder, noting that, at the very least, both teams should have switched jerseys.

I wondered if the Cowboy coaching staff might have the same regrets some day. WT took the field with relish and played inspired football. State played sloppily, putting the ball on the carpet several times in the face of the Buff's defensive pressure. I would like to think that some of that pressure came from the tiny volume machine sitting next to me. My mother only said two words when the Buffs played defense. But she said them on every single play: *Get him*. That's not how it came out. This is how it came out:

GIT HIIIIIIIIIIIIIIIIIIIIIIIIIIIIIIIIIIIIIIIIIIIIIIIIIIIIIIIIIIIIIIIIIIIIIIIIIM!!!!!!

Mom was at her best when the final M was punctuated by a big Buffalo hit. She would exhale in perfect synchrony with the wind being knocked out of the opposing player. On this day, the Buffs flew to the football with reckless abandon, dominating the line of scrimmage. Mom got louder with each play. We were surrounded by OSU students and alums who, like good fans, knew to be quiet when their team had the ball. Mom's screams in this vacuum could probably be heard in Tonkawa. I responded the only way a thirteen-year-old could: I joined in. Perhaps in some families it would be the mother's responsibility to put the lid on an obnoxious adolescent. But today we were allies. Both against the Oklahoma State faithful and against my father, trying his best not to be associated with us by pretending to examine the game program with an intensity he usually reserved for medical journals.

The Buffs led 6–0 after their first two possessions ended in field goals. In contrast, Oklahoma State's first two possessions had ended with a blocked punt and a lost fumble. To add insult to injury, after scoring on a short touchdown pass to push the score to 13–0, WT attempted— and recovered—an onside kick. The game was still in the first quarter and the Cowboy return unit responded by throwing up their arms in frustration, like a kid complaining "no fair" out on the playground. WT didn't score after the onside, but they kept the ball away from the Cowboy offense as a wave of unease swept through the State crowd. Playing a team who decides early on that it has absolutely nothing to lose is a dangerous and unsettling proposition for the favorite. Play-for-pay or not, the Buffs hadn't read the script. The hayseeds in the maroon jerseys didn't particularly care about the stadium crowd, or the Big Eight conference, or the point spread or Laymon Lowery Lewis, the former dean of the college of veterinary medicine. They came to play a football game and they were outhitting and outhustling the Cowboys at every snap.

The Cowboy offense got off track in the second quarter and the Buffs clung to a 13–11 halftime lead. Surely superior talent and the locker-room adjustments of a big-time coaching staff would turn the game in the Cowboys' favor. We knew the Buffs had gotten every break to this point. Oklahoma State would slowly wear down their visitors and coast home in the second half.

That's not what happened. The Buffs returned from the locker room and continued to make every play. When a promising Cowboy drive was thwarted by an interception by reserve Buffalo safety Greg Houlette, a kid our family knew because he had been my counselor at Camp Summerlife the previous June, the outcome seemed to take on a certain air of destiny.

At this moment, I was graced with a firsthand view of the power of childhood connections. It happened when my brother David completely took leave of his senses. Forgetting his current allegiances, the diploma on his wall, the years of friendships and experience forged at Eskimo Joe's and the Hideaway, his loyalty to his teammates on the OSU rugby team, the upsets, the disappointments, the 1976 Tangerine Bowl, and the spouse sitting in the seat to his right, David begin to cheer for the Buffaloes. It started small. A faint "Yes!" after a successful Buffalo play. It slowly grew to not only cheer Buffalo success, but also unseemly, giddy reactions to Cowboy mistakes.

David stood and cheered when WT's tailback, Danny Clark, scored a third-quarter touchdown to make it 20–11. He let out a frustrated sigh when a bad snap caused the WT punter to retreat to his own end zone and take a safety, cutting the lead to 20–13. He sat on his hands when State—his alma mater—scored a fourth-quarter touchdown to close the gap to one, but went delirious when the Cowboys failed on the two-point conversion.

Ellen didn't find this turn of events either humorous or touching, but David couldn't help himself. Deep within him, there remained a latent allegiance to West Texas, just as infants can recognize their mothers' voices, college football fans remember their roots. David had returned to his spiritual home. The Buffaloes welcomed him back in a warm embrace that stretched from Lewis Field all the way back to pregame meals in Audrey Jones's kitchen, proving in the process that perhaps blood is deeper than Stillwater. By game's end, my father had on his hands a rebellious wife, a wiseass teenage son, and a newly minted graduate traitor in imminent need of marriage counseling. At least Dad had an ally in Ellen, with one difference: Deep in his heart, he, too, wanted the Buffs to win, and more than any of us. He was just polite about it.

When the clock hit zero, our family was fully bound together in Buffalo bliss. The only thing missing was Audrey.

West Texas State University 20, Oklahoma State University 19.

Mom insisted we stay for the playing of the WT alma mater. Dad was too tired (and happy) to argue.

> *Over boundless reach of prairie,*
> *Over rolling plains,*

"This doesn't hurt Oklahoma State."
"It's not even a conference game."

> *Over cliff and crag and canyon,*
> *Alma Mater reigns!*

"First games are always filled with mistakes."
"We beat Arkansas next week and no one will remember this game."
"It was a fluke."

David tried every argument on the long walk out of the stadium to repair the damage wrought by his fit of temporary insanity. Ellen wasn't buying. We had no choice but to respect her for that. She was a true and loyal Cowboys fan with her own allegiances and she wasn't switching sides; the victorious demonstrations of her in-laws would not compromise her commitment to Oklahoma State for the sake of family peace.

We had borne witness to the last great thing West Texas State would ever do on a football field. It was also the last football game my mom and I would ever attend together. I didn't know either of these things as my family walked across the subdued OSU campus after the Buff upset. What I did understand was the precarious position of my oldest brother. He was stuck between a new life with a wife and a job and his whole

The Jones siblings, David (left), Sam (right), Molly, and Adam (center).
David could have avoided much trouble by going to Texas with the rest of
us. *(Jones Family)*

future before him and the desire that afflicts us all to be kids again. For
one afternoon, David was a kid again; the only thing missing was a quick
slide down the hill behind the concession stand at Kimbrough. My mom
must have enjoyed this; mothers always like it when their kids come
home. I didn't fully comprehend Mom's delight as the September day
turned to dusk, but I would some day. Fatherhood was in my future and

so was the delight in sharing the gift of college football with my own son. One day, far away, there would be a moment—if only a brief one—when my own son might indulge me in memories of childhood, his and mine both.

The one thing I did know on this day, I learned from my oldest brother: no matter where life took me, I would always have the Buffaloes. And Mom and I would always have 20–19.

3

THE BIG TIME

The University of Texas vs. the University of Missouri

Texas Memorial Stadium, Austin, Texas, September 21, 1985

Why the federal government built Interstate 27 escapes most folks with even a passing interest in where their tax dollars end up. A direct, four-lane divided superhighway connecting Lubbock to Amarillo couldn't have been essential to national defense. The road isn't even an *inter*state at all; it starts in Texas and ends in Texas, 119 straight miles from the population center of the South Plains to the population center of the Panhandle. A traveler trying to make it to Kansas then must choose another route, typically U.S. 287 through Dumas, another hour and a half through rangeland, cattle feedlots, and small towns before he escapes the vast boundaries of the Lone Star State.

It had been five years since the epic West Texas Buffalo upset of Oklahoma State and I was now a freshman at Texas, on the way home for Christmas after my first semester. Interstate 27 provided comfort to the kids of the remote plains who traveled the five hundred miles south to the big state university in Austin. Once you hit I-27, you were almost home. You had already made your way out of Austin and through the hill country of Lampasas and Goldthwaite, up an imperceptible grade to Brownwood, where, true to its name, the trees begin to disappear and oil and cotton fields took over. At Coleman, the self-proclaimed friendliest town in Texas with twenty-two churches—the chamber of commerce claimed this right on the billboard where the Lions Club and Rotary noted their meeting places—anyone who knew the back roads could cut across ninety miles of State Highway 153 to Sweetwater. Under almost no circumstance would a driver be tagged for speeding here. In the twenty years I drove this road I can't even recall seeing a single cop other than the occasional sheriff, who likely had better things to do than to chase down speeding teens with stickers on the back window proclaiming their love for Texas or Texas A&M, Texas Tech, Tarleton State, or Abilene Christian or a dozen others. The greatest danger was to take a bend in the road too sharply and come grill to grill with a Gleaner combine whose mass couldn't possibly confine it to the safe shoulder. Year after year, I survived the farm machinery gauntlet on Texas 153, exiting at Sweetwater and taking the long drive through the cotton fields that separated Snyder and Lubbock on the vast South Plains. The railroad tracks ran right along beside you through the state's agrarian past as you climbed the Caprock Escarpment to the higher plains. There was an Allsup's convenience store outside of Snyder that sold awful coffee and the deep-fried burritos that brought back memories of grade school cafeterias. The burritos just sat there, foil wrapped and comfortable, waiting for a friend to free them from the prison of the warming tray. I obliged more often than not.

Six hours out of Austin, Lubbock appears, the only city in the five hundred-mile stretch between Austin and Amarillo. The home of Buddy Holly and the Texas Tech Red Raiders, Lubbock was the farthest outpost of the old Southwest Conference, the only chance to watch big-time college football for hundreds of miles in any direction. You picked up I-27 here and made your way north to the Panhandle. Most Texans actually believe the Panhandle starts in Lubbock, but this just isn't so. Panhandle natives distinguished the geography with vigor, insisting *their land* begins north of the Red River, where cotton gives way to cattle and the nasty weather fronts from the Rockies get a clean shot at engulfing the entire high plains in a blizzard at a moment's notice. I-27 split the difference. The south end stretches out of Lubbock past the cotton gins of Abernathy and Hale Center, but by the time you arrive at Plainview—a big town roughly halfway and with one hell of a fine high school football tradition—the giant Producers Grain Corporation elevator and rail terminal indicate the start of cattle country, where cottonseed presses give way to the feedlots of Tulia and Happy. The next stop was Canyon, which meant Amarillo was only about fifteen minutes away. But my spirit was already home by then.

Driving into the December dusk, my 1978 Pontiac Bonneville crested a small rise in the highway and the West Texas campus came into view. My eyes always scanned the city and focused on Mitch Jones Hall, our family's eight-story concrete legacy. Did the men who lived in Jones Hall even know that my grandfather was still alive? Still huddled with Uncle Frank among his books and memories in the big red house a few blocks from the campus? I always wondered what Grandad and Frank were doing, if they were even awake. Frank had moved into my grandfather's house a year after my grandmother died. The company helped the spirits of both, but Grandad must have missed Audrey every night as the sun went down. He would probably welcome a surprise visit from a grandson, and the thought to go see him always crossed my mind, but I never acted on it. I look back on this inaction with great regret, choosing my own convenience over the chance I might bring some happiness to two old men. But I was full of rationalizations: the interstate bypassed Canyon just like it bypassed every other small town along its Panhandle route, I would have to exit the highway and Bulldog and Frank were probably asleep, and soon enough we would all be around the Christmas dinner table anyway.

Those thoughts fermented as I skirted Canyon and drove past the light stanchions and parking lot of Kimbrough; the bowl of the stadium was invisible, since it sank straight into the Panhandle landscape. The memories really began to flood at this point—a torrent of images from Audrey's kitchen and of being wedged into my seat listening to Mom sing the alma mater in the beautiful soprano voice honed by years of Baptist choir practice, of cigarette smoke and stale popcorn and the grassy hills behind the concession stand that I used to slide down as a kid, of Reggie Spencer breaking free in the open and Warren Hasse on KGNC as Grandad would hold a transistor radio to his ear to hear the play-by-play so he could follow the substitution patterns as he watched the game with the strategic eye of the fine coach that he was. These things were crystal clear. And so was the furnace of a day in Stillwater when Mom and I shared a memory of the Buffs' last great moment.

The shocking Buffalo victory over Oklahoma State was the last time they shocked anyone. My childhood heroes delivered to me that almost perfect memory, but the Buffs would slowly fade away. Like the giving tree in the children's book, I had played on the hills of Kimbrough and had traversed the rows and columns of its seating sections. I had climbed the branches of Buffalo football as high as could be climbed. And now I drove past that treasure of childhood in silence, coming home to the team I left behind. I left the Buffs behind for just cause, in my mind. They had been abandoned in my search for big-time football. Now I was returning home from my first semester at the University of Texas, where big-time football lived. Or so I thought.

Truth was, the big time just wasn't all it was cracked up to be. Why the Texas Longhorns chose my freshman year in college to begin the worst stretch of football in the program's history was beyond me. The honor of cheering for a topflight football program was a perfectly legiti-mate reason to choose a college, and I figured they owed it to me—it was in the brochure. That's why I went there. My sister Molly had gone to Texas to become a chemical engineer and she proved a talented student with a joyous spirit; brother Sam arrived in Austin a bookish hipster with a passion for music and literature who eventually took a degree in English when he wasn't taking in an unending series of long nights immersed in the thriving punk culture of Club Foot and with the aging hippies at the Armadillo World Headquarters and Soap Creek Saloon. Both of these choices were fine, but I chose Texas for co-eds and Longhorn football. I rejected academia when I declined Rice's offer to enroll at midterm. Rice had an aggressive recruitment process to backfill the huge number of academic washouts the pressure-packed intellectual environment created. I passed and headed to Austin. How much fun could Rice be? The school was both hard, and, if you dared wander east of campus, you were in the middle of a Houston urban renewal project. But above all else was the Owl football squad. They played horrendous football and did so in an oversized 70,000 seat stadium that was never more than a quarter full. No thanks.

Arriving in Austin, on the other hand, initiates you into a great college football culture. The guys who suited up for the Longhorns were students just like me. The whole campus was electric. To walk down Speedway through the heart of the campus was to be carried along in a flow of humanity I hadn't seen since my trip to Texas Memorial Stadium as an eight-year-old. Thousands of men and women from every corner of the state, the country, the globe, ready to make their mark in life. To live to the fullest, to take risks, to fall in and out of love—this campus intoxicated far beyond its capacity for alcohol consumption, which was formidable. My heart was full. This would be my place, full of more possibility than my parents ever dreamed of in Canyon, Texas.

The waiting for my first season in the student section drove me to distraction. The Kickoff Classic between Brigham Young and Boston College inaugurated the 1985 college football season on August 31. The first full week of the season was on September 7. Due to a scheduling quirk, Texas was idle that day and also the following Saturday. My first Longhorn season started a full three weeks in, on September 21. During that awful wait, the trivial matters of buying books and going to class interfered with priorities such as scouting out Mexican food joints, record stores, bars, and any opportunity to interact with a limitless population of beautiful women, most of whom had little time for a skinny freshman from Amarillo who couldn't even crack the starting lineup of his thoroughly average high school basketball team.

September 21 arrived and my tickets and confidence were secure. The pageantry was just as it had been in 1975. A huge buzz swept through the crowd as the Longhorn band took the field. The Lone Star flag was unfurled, "The *Eyes of Texas*" sung in unison. Everything was perfect. Then the game began and something was terribly wrong. For only the third time since 1958, Texas had been left out of the AP preseason poll. Most observers opined that the disastrous end to the 1984 season—a 55–17 loss to Iowa in the Freedom Bowl—combined with the graduation of the last of the defensive stars from the great 1983 team, would limit the Longhorns' effectiveness. The AP voters were correct; this was not a great football team, but something grated at me far beyond the average performance on the field. The stadium wasn't right. Not only did the artificial turf shimmer a bizarre Day-Glo green under the lights, Memorial Stadium included a feature I had not remembered as a child: a huge running track circled the field to accommodate the UT track team and the famous Texas Relays. While this guaranteed Austin a secure spot on the world track and field circuit, it was lousy for football. From the student section, an interested fan was too far from the field to make a difference on a crucial play. Worse, there weren't nearly enough fans interested in the game. The section was awash in idle social chatter and the unmistakable smell of Jack Daniel's flowing out of hidden plastic flasks and into thirty-two-ounce Cokes. It rendered the game a secondary pastime. Texas wasn't sharp, and their fans didn't seem interested in pulling them through, giving them that extra shot of adrenaline to raise their level of play. Audrey Jones the great fifth-grade teacher and football fan would have been tempted to slap the kids in front of her upside the head and tell them to pay attention.

My date was part of the problem. If college dating is a staging ground for eventual marriage, she was out of the running for the Jones family

Christmas card by the end of the first quarter. The pretty brunette from the Houston suburbs, whose name escapes me, could have been a perfect cross between Donna Reed and Audrey Hepburn and she would have had no shot at Reba Jones's approval. She asked numerous times how many yards were required for a first down. Compounding this error was a continued cross-examination of my goals and dreams, likes and dislikes, and her genuine interest in me as a person, all while a football game was obviously going on right in front of us—she had to have noticed this. We didn't have a second date, and the Longhorns would not have a second chance to give me a passionate display of top-notch football in my debut as one of their own. Texas beat Missouri 21–17 in a forgettable game. The faithful hoped beyond hope that Missouri was better than advertised, but they were actually worse. Mizzou would lose ten games that season—their worst in history. Playing Texas to within four ended up being the lone highlight for the miserable Tigers.

Having been a generally good kid in high school, I had many firsts in college. Being under your own supervision with unlimited access to booze broadens one's horizon considerably, even if they did raise the drinking age from nineteen to twenty-one during my freshman year. That couldn't take away the spontaneous road trips, the fast friendships, the making out while shoehorned into a single dorm room bed while trying desperately not to wake up a sleeping roommate, taking in Austin's magical essence under a starlit night while the great Stevie Ray Vaughan played on Auditorium Shores, being battered in the mosh pit at a Ramones show at the Back Room on Riverside Drive, first love, spring break, Barton Springs, and the sunset over Lake Travis—take your pick, all of these experiences lived up to my expectations. All of them but my first trip to the student section of Memorial Stadium. I couldn't help but think that an entire freshman class had been robbed of that experience.

Mom and I needed to have a long talk about the state of Longhorn football when I arrived home to celebrate the Christmas of 1985. I didn't bother to mask my disappointment with the game-day atmosphere.

"They're probably spoiled," she observed.

"Spoiled? You mean the players or the fans?"

"The fans, of course. You can never believe that the players are not giving their best efforts."

"Yeah, well, that's what I'm afraid of. They are giving their best efforts, they're just not very good."

"Maybe you need to be a better fan."

Moms have an innate ability to get under their children's skin. That is an inarguable fact of life. *Maybe I need to be a better fan?* Maybe the Longhorns need to play with the same passion that I bring to the stadium. But to Mom, being a fan had little to do with excellence on the field of play, which was easy for her, since her team had never won anything. Had I desired this, I would have gone to Rice. The tyranny of the underdog would not get in the way of my search for the big time.

Mom consistently exhibited a number of unhelpful personality traits during her life. She was full of grace, she forgave easily, her faith was unyielding . . . and I understood none of these things sitting in the kitchen performing mental exercises to strengthen my capacity to arrive at a better state of "fan-ness." If that meant loving a team unconditionally while watching them underperform and lose week after week, then I wasn't buying. The West Texas fans did this, but what choice did they have and, for that matter, what expectations? Their potential rested in finishing third in the conference and upsetting Tulsa every once in a while. Fine. But was it too much to ask for the University of Texas to live up to its reputation as a college football power?

Little did I know that I would be humbled by a very long wait. Mom understood this and was trying to do me a favor. She never loved West Texas for the football team; she loved her old school because you never get back that magical time in your life called college and she knew what it meant to her and had lived in the moment every day since she had collected her sheepskin and walked off the campus. I liked the past better, and waited for it to return in the form of Longhorn dominance. At the moment, the past seemed impossibly distant, but actually the Longhorns were at the top of their game not eighteen months before I arrived on campus. The 1983 season had taken the wind completely out of the sails of the good ship Texas.

The 1983 Texas squad played defense like no one had ever seen. Once the Horns had a lead, they simply sat on it because the other team had no chance to get into the end zone, their morale crushed and spirit trampled by a Longhorn D that saw ten out of eleven starting players eventually drafted by NFL teams. This impenetrable wall, led by Tony DeGrate on the defensive line, linebacker Jeff Leiding and the incomparable Jerry Gray in the defensive backfield, produced Texas wins over three members of the AP Top 10—Auburn, Oklahoma, and SMU—in the first six weeks of the 1983 season. An impressive start, even by Texas standards, but not impressive enough to overcome college football's unstoppable force: the 1983 Nebraska Cornhuskers.

The Cornhuskers put on a show of their own, and even Texas fans would admit that Nebraska's was the more entertaining. The Cornhuskers played solid defense, but it didn't really matter how many points they surrendered. Nebraska bombed teams into submission—fifty points, sixty, seventy—it was like watching Jerry Lewis update the telethon tote board on Labor Day. Quarterback Turner Gill ran the offense with Heisman Trophy winner Mike Rozier in the backfield and All-American end Irving Fryar split wide. The trio operated behind what may have been the greatest offensive line ever assembled. Big Red locked down the No. 1 spot in the AP, and Texas locked down number two. Not another team in college football could do a damn thing about it.

Oklahoma State, of all teams, almost came to the aid of Texas. Nebraska traveled to Laymon Lowery Lewis, D.V.M. Field with the intention of stomping the Cowboys like so many roaches in the kitchen. Problem was, the Cornhusker offense never really clicked that day. Nebraska fumbled five times, losing four of them, including one where the typically reliable Rozier let the pigskin slip out of his grasp at the Cowboy one-yard line. Big Red managed only fourteen points on the afternoon and needed a desperate end-zone interception of Cowboy quarterback Ike Jackson on the last play of the game to preserve their 14–10 win. Most observers chalked this up to a seasoned team making the clutch plays and winning on a day when they had not played their best football. Hogwash. This result was payback. College football karma weaves a complicated web. My brother David's defection back in 1980 must have cost the Cowboys perhaps the biggest home win in their history. If not, then surely it was my own delight in the Buffalo upset that triggered God's disdain for taking pleasure in another's misfortune, with the punishment doled out on my Longhorns. God, of course would have none of this.

"You're really going off the rails here."

"What?"

"I know what you are thinking. I had nothing to do with Jackson throwing a pick in the end zone; he simply doesn't have the arm strength to complete that pass. He has other gifts that you will never see."

"I never—"

"Enough. You need to get ready for church. Reverend Childers is speaking from First John on the fundamentals of Christian love. Try and pay attention this time . . . By the way, karma is not something you believe in."

And so Nebraska held on to the top spot. After the hiccup against Oklahoma State, five out of the sixty AP voters switched their No. 1 votes to Texas. These were obviously five men of deep insight and strong spiritual formation, men of courage and character. But they were not enough to get the Longhorns to the top and later would prove their lack of integrity by returning all but one of their votes to the Nebraska column by season's end.

Neither Nebraska nor Texas would lose in the regular season and, in a just world, that would have cemented a showdown of epic proportions. College football, however, is not such a world. There is no real play-off to settle these issues on the field. Texas, the Southwest Conference Champion, would meet its obligation as the host team at the Cotton Bowl in Dallas, where they would play the Georgia Bulldogs, ranked seventh. Nebraska, the Big Eight Champion, took their traditional place in the Orange Bowl against the somewhat unknown Miami Hurricanes, an upstart program ranked fifth.

What happened next was the worst day in Texas Longhorn football history. January 1, 1984, brought the Longhorn defense to the Cotton Bowl ready for a fight. They slugged, clawed, kicked, and shoved the Bulldogs all over the field, just like they had mistreated every other offense during the run of 1983. The Texas offense just couldn't cash in—they managed no touchdowns, even though they camped out most of the game in Georgia territory. Texas led 9–3 on the "strength" of three Jeff Ward field goals. It wasn't pretty, but it was enough. Georgia was certainly not going to score, not without some help anyway.

Unfortunately, help arrived. Fearing a fake punt late in the game, Texas coach Fred Akers inserted defensive back Craig Curry into the Longhorn punt return formation as an up back to guard against a potential pass as Georgia faced a fourth and seventeen. Curry was a fine player, one good enough to play four seasons in the NFL. He had made countless great plays in a Longhorn defensive backfield that featured two first-team All-Americans, Gray and cornerback Mossy Cade. Curry was the kind of dependable and underappreciated contributor who separates championship football teams from pretenders. Any coach in America would want Craig Curry on his roster, and for four years Longhorn fans had cheered and loved Curry. And then they didn't. Curry's life changed in the four seconds it took for a punt to cross midfield and slowly descend into Texas territory. The senior safety couldn't hold on to it and two Bulldog players overwhelmed Curry, coming up with the football at the Texas 23. A visceral *"Dammit"* echoed in the Jones family room that resulted in a look from my mom, but no other reprobation. She was full of grace and understood that the unseemly language of her sixteen-year-old was justified given the circumstances. My second dammit came when Georgia found the end zone three plays later. To this day, Georgia fans commemorate the 1984 Cotton Bowl with a humorous exchange that—for them—never grows old:

"What time is it in Texas?"

"Ten to nine."

Curry should have been celebrated as a member of the greatest Longhorn defense ever assembled and should have worn his "T-man" status as a varsity letter winner proudly for the rest of his life. Instead, because of a coaching decision, or the Cotton Bowl wind, or a slippery ball, or a simple failure of hand-eye coordination, or fate, or karma, or grace smiling upon the Georgia Bulldogs or maybe just because them's the breaks, Curry became the greatest goat in Longhorn history. He would join the millions of Longhorns fans waiting for the next national title: a title that wouldn't slip through the grasp of a single player on a single play on football's biggest stage. College football was a cruel place.

Texas fans were further tortured later that night as the invincible Cornhuskers lost in the Orange Bowl to Miami. With the score 31–30 in favor of the Hurricanes, Nebraska's Tom Osborne went for a two-point conversion to settle the issue, even though playing for the tie would likely have secured the national title. In an instant Osborne cemented himself as a man of courage and integrity (or impracticality and stupidity, depending on one's viewpoint) and, as Turner Gill's pass fell harmlessly to the turf, cemented the Miami Hurricanes as the next great power in college football, a grave sin considering the egotistical swagger and bad behavior the 'Canes brought to the field, leading them to become the most despised team in college football. Miami would win five titles over the next two decades; Nebraska would win two of their own and exorcise the demons of Osborne's fateful Orange Bowl decision. Texas, however, would slowly fade away. I would witness the whole pathetic mess up close.

If I needed to be a better fan in the fall of 1985, then the Longhorns were mostly to blame. The boys in the burnt orange and white had raised these lofty expectations. Wasn't it fair that they live up to them? Meanwhile, back on the high plains, my childhood team—the one that never could live up to my standards of big-time football—started excelling in my absence. The natural order was now reversed. Austin was darkened by a passionless shadow of Longhorn tradition while the good people of the Panhandle were joyously celebrating unprecedented success at Kimbrough behind a series of 300-yards-passing outings by Buff quarterback Tod Mayfield, a kid who Texas never would have even thought about recruiting and was now lighting up the sky above the old Buffalo Bowl. Mom the great fan deserved this. She and Dad loved the Mayfield show. They knew the kid's father—naturally—Gene Mayfield, who was a long-time Buffalo coach for many of the mediocre seasons of my childhood. But the Buffs weren't mediocre anymore and they were playing in front of 14,000 who collectively poured rivers of emotion into Buffalo football while their 72,000 big-school counterparts in the state capital could manage only a trickle. Tod Mayfield provided our family one last hurrah for Buffalo football and proved that a lot of folks in Austin needed to be better fans.

The big time didn't live in Austin anymore, but life wasn't a complete mess. I was still a part of a great university tradition and even got to interact with the players occasionally. I remember meeting Longhorn linebacker Ty Allert at a party and thinking the banded sleeves on his polo shirt would cut off all circulation to his biceps, which were roughly the size of cantaloupes. Thank God I didn't spill a beer on his date. Eric Metcalf, the great Longhorn scatback and kick returner, sat across from me in English class. He was polite and soft-spoken and looked completely normal. Of course, I never challenged him to a footrace across the South Mall. There were others, and their presence did make you feel like they were your guys, just like the 1924 Buffs were Bulldog's guys. You couldn't help but pull for them. The problem was that you wanted them to be better. You wondered where the glory went, whether your faith in Longhorn football was somehow misplaced. Or maybe Reba Jones was right and your lack of faith as a fan led directly to shortcomings on the field.

These shortcomings built an entire lost-cause mythology around Texas football, and it had been growing since 1969, the last time the Longhorns were the undisputed national champs. Nowhere did this essence overcome you more than in a tiny shack on Martin Luther King Boulevard called Bert's. Bert's served up barbecue a couple of blocks from campus and the ribs were especially tasty—if you could get them. Demand always outstripped supply and you had to go early. Other than the obligatory 1985 season-schedule poster with pictures of the Longhorn seniors, the entire place was a shrine to 1969. Bert didn't even deign to include mementos of 1970, when Texas claimed the United Press title but then lost in the Cotton Bowl and was denied the AP crown. Technically, 1970 was a national championship, but it was not undisputed and thus was not on exhibit in this smoke-stained and beef-fed time capsule.

One visage peered out of the dozens of pictures on the paneled walls above all others: Saint Darrell. Coach Royal had led Texas to all three of her national titles. He was the colossal figure of Texas football. A living legend, he walked the streets of Austin enjoying the kind of adoration only Jesus and Willie Nelson could match. To meet him was a religious experience. He stands ramrod straight, tall and slender like the great quarterback he once was. His eyes sparkle, and he has a quick smile that puts everyone at ease. He may be the most approachable legend I have ever met, so humble you would think he was once the coach at the junior high school down the street, not the greatest figure in the history of Texas football. Royal's great teams created the mythology of Bert's, and real life would recommence when the Longhorn football team once again closed the deal. The Cult of 1969 would dine on brisket and sausage and ponder when the next savior would come. This was my kind of cult, and Royal was the patron saint. Little did I know that I would be a member of the Cult of 1969 for more than twenty years, dating from the day I first set foot on the Texas campus.

Texas ended the 1985 season a respectable 8-4, but the magic was gone. The team floated around the bottom of the AP Top 20 for most of

The Jones Family in 1969, the last time Texas brought home the national title. *(Jones Family)*

the year, but the end of the season was miserable. Our state rivals, the Texas A&M Aggies, were a dynasty under construction, led by new coach Jackie Sherrill, who most Longhorn fans believed was about as dirty as a redneck outhouse. The Aggies demonstrated just how big the talent gap had become between the two state schools in a 42–10 throttling of the Horns on Thanksgiving. This was not a good omen. Texas had traditionally dominated the series. A win on Thanksgiving was as predictable at the Jones house as Audrey's rhubarb pie. (The difference was that I actually had a fondness for Longhorn victory and the only thing that rhubarb pie offered was proof that West Texans raised during the Dust Bowl would eat just about anything.) Texas would lose every single game of my college years to Texas A&M. After the Aggie disaster in '85, Texas was relegated to the Bluebonnet Bowl in Houston and promptly lost to Air Force, 24–16. The team we had all watched come within a muffed punt of winning the national championship was now losing to a service academy in a bowl watched by dozens of interested viewers. This, again, is not what I had signed up for.

The bottom fell out in 1986 as Texas won five and lost six and fired head coach Fred Akers. The regents turned to favorite son David McWilliams, who didn't exactly set the world on fire by winning eleven and losing twelve in his first two seasons. His major claim to fame was staked during the 1988 season when he led the Longhorns to a 66–15 loss to the Houston Cougars, who turned the affair into a controlled scrimmage to practice their run-and-shoot offense. Fortunately, because I had taken a semester off, my eligibility had not run out, and in 1989 I returned to Austin for a fifth autumn of Longhorn football. This time, McWilliams appeared to have righted the ship with five wins in the Longhorns' first seven games, including back-to-back wins over fifteenth-ranked Oklahoma and a stunning upset over seventh-ranked Arkansas. My faith returned as I crammed into the end-zone section of Memorial with an incredibly loud contingent bent on destroying the confidence of the Texas Tech Red Raiders. Turns out I had a great view of Tech receiver Tony Manyweather sprinting right into the end zone with the winning touchdown, setting the ball on the end line a mere fifty feet or so from my seat, and I swear on Audrey Jones's grave the son of a bitch looked right up and smiled at me. Texas football was not "back."

At that point, McWilliams was no more in control of the Longhorn destiny than a hot air balloon pilot in a typhoon. Texas went to Houston to be bludgeoned 47–9, and two weeks later lost to Baylor on Thanksgiving weekend, at home no less, 50–7. The Baylor game preempted the traditional Texas A&M season-ending tilt because the Aggies were subject to one year of NCAA probation that did not allow them any television appearances. (We were right about Jackie Sherrill's recruiting practices.) It was of small comfort that the annual loss to A&M happened on December 2, away from the prying eyes of a television audience. Needless to say, there was no bowl invitation for the 1989 Longhorns. More surprising, McWilliams kept his job. I couldn't bear to watch this show. Armed with a bachelor's degree and having no interest in a real job, I chose graduate school and headed to Duke University in Durham, North Carolina, which presented an academic challenge with no chance of being interrupted by anything resembling Big-Time College Football. Goodbye, Austin. Farewell, Cult of 1969.

Perhaps I would be a better fan some other day. Spending my entire college years watching the Texas Longhorns play some of the worst football in their history had exhausted me. Austin faded into the background as I climbed the Caprock one last time in the summer of 1990. I needed to gather my things and turn right to head east down Interstate 40 and out of Texas for the first time in my life. Leaving Texas is a scary thought. It was possible that I would never come back, that never again would I drive past the Buffalo Bowl at twilight or sit at my grandfather's kitchen table. Texans often find it hard to believe that a world even exists beyond their borders. Now it was time to explore it. Maybe the Longhorns would get better while I was gone.

4

BULLDOG EASES ON OUT

Duke University vs. Rutgers

WALLACE WADE STADIUM,
DURHAM, NORTH CAROLINA, SEPTEMBER 4, 1991

Bulldog Jones needed to talk to me about Wallace Wade. This discussion demanded my attention even more than his famous lecture on man's grace as displayed by Shakespeare's characters in *The Tempest* and *The Merchant of Venice.* In the former, Dean Jones noted, Caliban the Savage gave the most touching and sympathetic soliloquy in all of Shakespeare, and in the latter, grace came from the reviled Shylock, the moneylender, who reminds the audience that all of us in this human experience see and hear and hurt and bleed the same, leading the heroine Portia to take pity and proclaim the quality of mercy droppeth from heaven like a gentle rain and blesseth both those that give and receive.

The savage and reviled alike held a soft spot in the heart of my grandfather, probably because he had spent years and years with them on both his football fields and in his office as the dean of men, where he would sometimes expel a reprobate from the campus knowing full well that the boy would return from working the feedlots and farms with a new appreciation for his education. His maturity and discipline would follow suit. This is how Bulldog built men. He had faith in them. This is how they became his men and why they would never forget him. He told story after story of these men and the things they would go on to accomplish; sometimes these stories were repeats and sometimes he would uncover some new material. But the stories of men reviled and redeemed were not part of this morning's syllabus. Today's subject was college football, and the topic was the great Wallace Wade.

Bulldog met Wade at a coaching convention long ago and had always held him as a beacon of what was right in the world. Wade was a legendary football coach; he had won three national titles at the University of Alabama, building the foundation of one of the game's great powers long before anyone had even heard of Bear Bryant. Then, at the pinnacle of his profession, Wade left Tuscaloosa for Durham, North Carolina, to take the coaching job at Duke. This made zero sense, my grandfather explained; Wade could have built an almost unmatchable legacy of college football greatness. Forget the three national titles, Wade could have won ten at the helm of the Crimson Tide. But Wade, like Bulldog Jones, was made of different stuff. He loved Duke's gothic campus and its academic tradition. He was a gentleman scholar who insisted that he not only coach the football team, but also be responsible for the men's physical education department. Unheard-of. These were not the actions of a big-time college football coach, but rather the eccentricities of a pompous intellectual too good for a public university like Alabama. The public couldn't decide whether Wade simply burned out in the pressure cooker of Alabama football or whether some private arrangement with the Duke administration brought him a king's ransom. Neither of these things was true. Wade simply followed his heart.

Bulldog paused at this point in the story and looked at me. Convinced that his youngest grandson had his full attention, his silence spoke.

"You're paying attention to this, right? These stories I tell in this kitchen fade away, but character endures. Faith, hope, resilience, integrity. Love. These things endure."

He had a penetrating gaze from underneath his ever-present flattop. Never had I encountered someone who could convey sternness and gentleness at the same time, even through glasses that had become thicker and thicker. Bulldog never could see worth a damn, but that didn't keep him from having vision. His eyes would narrow and his brow would furrow in lecture mode, but a faint smile would accompany this action: "Yes, I'm serious and demand your attention, but don't be afraid. The world is a wonderful place and you will figure these lessons out for yourself someday."

I held tight Bulldog's countenance, wanting to believe that no one but me was privy to that day's particular wisdom flowing from his end of the huge formica table that Uncle Frank had built.

We exchanged this moment and Bulldog got back to football. Wade, to the surprise only of those who did not understand him, made sleepy Duke a national power. He led the Devils to within a whisker of the national title in 1938 and again in 1942. Then he stepped down again, this time to fight World War II. The story impressed upon me why Wallace Wade was my grandfather's hero, but it also reminded me of why Bulldog Jones was mine. From the moment he stepped on a football field as an undersized offensive lineman, either too blind or too stubborn to know he didn't belong, my grandfather lived life on his own terms, more so than anyone I would ever know. He was the voice of authority and respect for three generations of men and the font of institutional wisdom for a small college on the plains. They really didn't make them like him anymore.

Grandad was my personal embodiment of what it meant to live with integrity. For him to be proud of me on this summer was barely within my comprehension. But he was proud that I held a degree from the state's flagship university and that Duke had accepted me. Someone had to take over my education, for he was growing old and soon there would be no more lessons at this kitchen table. As his youngest grandson headed east, he knew that I would be in a safe place, graced by the spirit of Wallace Wade.

Heading east on I-40, someone from the plains will eventually become claustrophobic. You start with perfect peripheral vision on straight and treeless highways. Oklahoma introduces a few rolling hills and some actual vegetation. There are real trees in Arkansas and, very slowly, they start to crawl closer to the highway's edge. Eventually, the open landscape completely disappears, making a Panhandle native uneasy. Unease gives way to phobia as you work your way through Tennessee. Driving its 450 miles from west to east requires almost an entire day and approximates driving in a closet. The trees come right down to the shoulder of the highway, exactly like the stands at Memorial Stadium should have encroached on the field and made Longhorn opponents claustrophobic, except for the damn running track that kept the real fans separated from the action. Without the blue food-gas-lodging courtesy signs on the interstate pointing out the next Stuckey's or Red Roof Inn, you would be completely lost in Tennessee. Seeing the horizon line your entire life and then having it taken away is disorienting. This pine tunnel might as well have been the Florida swamps for the number of westerners who have no doubt simply disappeared between Memphis and Knoxville; by the time I got to North Carolina, I felt an urgent desire to find the nearest radio tower simply to scale it and look around. Reaching Durham, following one last pine-lined street and negotiating one last blind curve, I finally came face-to-face with the majestic Duke Chapel. "Chapel" is a misnomer; the massive gothic cathedral opens up in front of you as you leave the forest wilderness for the civilized lawns of the university. The front bell tower looms straight up into the heavens. Duke might as well erect an enormous sign that simply says GOD LIVES HERE. I believed it.

Duke was my second chance at college; Texas and its 50,000 students were an extension of high school. Duke looked like the campus in all of those coming-of-age movies they used to make. The grounds suggested some mythical titan had gathered up all of the beautiful gothic buildings

Duke Chapel: God Lives Here. *(Sam Jones)*

from Oxford, rearranged them, and dropped them right into a perfectly maintained landscape surrounded by gardens so lush you completely forgave the unseemly thought that tobacco money paid for every last plant. This academic bulwark sat right in the middle of the American South, although the regional flavor was sometimes hard to pick up. The students came from all over, with a huge contingent from the Northeast and California. Everyone wanted to come here, which resulted in a diverse, cosmopolitan feel, on campus anyway. Off campus, you were definitely in the south.

"Stawch in thu shuutz?"

I'm sorry? The dignified proprietor of my neighborhood cleaners glanced back at me; she looked a bit like Audrey and certainly had the same bearing, which indicated that fools were not especially tolerated. Somewhat put out that I had not paid attention the first time, she cleared her throat of a lifetime of too many Virginia Slims and clearly repeated herself with her eyebrows raised over the tops of her glasses as if to note that this was the last chance for me to listen. My being raised with dozens of drawling relatives helped me translate: "Starch in the shirts?"

"Yes, ma'am, light starch please."

And so Durham's rhythms went. The winding tree-lined back roads were the last bastion of mom-and-pop gas stations run by friendly and genuine people—almost without exception a jar of pickled pig's feet sat on the counter and pictures of Ronald Reagan and Richard Petty often looked over the cashier's shoulder. This contrasted with a campus life interacting with graduate classmates from all the great football powers: Harvard, Penn, Trinity, Pomona, Vassar, Williams, Davidson, Emory, and a whole host of other Ivies and liberal arts colleges dedicated to the humanities and the unerring ability to get their alums into the graduate school of their choice. Communing with big-time football fans took a great deal of effort here, which allowed me both to concentrate on my studies and eventually to become immersed in a different experience altogether, for there was one grand show that united all: basketball season.

The Blue Devil cagers and their extraordinary coach, Mike Krzyzewski, brought far more students to Duke than any recruiting campaign or *U.S. News & World Report* ranking could ever generate. They played in a tiny band-box field house humorously named Cameron Indoor Stadium. Ah, but these were real fans. My mother would have been beside herself with joy as a Duke basketball fan. The students always got the best seats—crammed into bleacher seating right next to the floor, sometimes four or five short feet from an opposing player inbounding the ball under a withering barrage of invective. The season ticket holders were consigned above the bleachers in the permanent stands, literally separated from the undergrad riffraff by a brass rail protecting the balcony. The fans were attentive, knowledgeable, unruly, loud, and incredibly disruptive of the opponent's train of thought. If one could impart all this to the Texas student section (and get rid of the running track), then we would have something. Nothing could make you fall in love with these fans more than an elegant cheer directed at their archrival:

> *Go to hell, Carolina, go to HELL.*
> *(clap, clap)*
> *Go to hell, Carolina, go to HELL.*
> *(clap, clap)*

Genius. The Duke students dispensed this helpful advice to the North Carolina Tar Heels in a light singsong that made the message even uglier. These were my kind of fans, condemning an opponent to eternal damnation and not feeling the least bit guilty. This was an insult dipped in sweet southern cream and even accompanied by joyous hand claps. Reba Jones, being something of a straight arrow and raised in the Christian tradition, might have found this unseemly. But Audrey would have embraced these people fully. The students back at Kimbrough Stadium easily could have coaxed my grandmother into a rousing version of:

> *Go to hell, Hardin-Simmons, go to HELL.*

The whole family would relish not only the irony of Hardin-Simmons being a Baptist college, but be further amused by the looks of horror enveloping Bulldog and my father as Audrey joined the chorus. Big-time athletics really missed something great when Audrey Watson fell in love with the young football player and pledged her eternal love to West Texas State.

Duke basketball cured all ills; it brought needed stress relief to over-worked and overachieving undergrads who would camp out for weeks in shantytown Krzyzewskivilles just for the honor of being crammed in below the brass rail. The Devils lifted the spirits of graduate students who were getting their first taste of the big time and, for one graduate student in particular, delivered in big game after big game, just like the Texas Longhorn football teams of the late 1980s did not. Duke won the NCAA basketball title both years I was there and didn't lose a single home game. It left me confused that a small private university could accomplish such feats when the flagship institution of the great state of Texas with its limitless resources could not.

As great as the Blue Devils were, two things worked against them. First, they were not "my guys." Second, they played the wrong sport. Basketball lacks football's emotional intensity; there are too many games for any single contest to be a life-and-death struggle. You always get a second chance. Lose a heartbreaker in college basketball and you could always regroup and run the tournament table at the season's end. Lose a heartbreaker in football and your heart really broke. There were no second chances to be had.

Eventually, I found the football stadium, which wasn't easy. Wallace Wade Stadium was just as Bulldog had described it: Coach Wade's name-sake is a jewel. Settled on the edge of the campus and surrounded by pine trees, the stands were built into a natural ravine, which reminded me of Kimbrough. The quality of football was roughly the same. Only about 30,000 can fit into Wade Stadium and that's about 15,000 seats too many on most Saturdays. The faithful come to watch one of the worst teams in the NCAA's top division. When I say "faithful" I mean

Reba Jones faithful; the Duke football boosters had to love unconditionally. During my first semester, I joined the faithful to watch an outstanding Virginia Cavalier squad drop fifty-nine points on the hapless Devils. Duke did not score. It did not matter to the most loyal—a band of brothers and sisters called the Iron Dukes, named after the famous 1938 Wade-led Duke squad that was scarcely scored upon. The Iron Dukes cheered for a team with few prospects simply out of love for a place that nurtured them the way West Texas embraced the Jones clan. How much more difficult to sit in these half-empty stands than to enjoy the bounty Coach K's warriors always brought to the hallowed ground of Cameron.

Wade Stadium couldn't have changed much since it hosted the Rose Bowl in 1942. The fear of Japanese attack had moved the huge gathering away from the West Coast. Duke lost that day to Oregon State, 20–16, even though Wade's last Blue Devil squad—before he went off to fight himself—was heavily favored. A small plaque commemorates the affair. Otherwise you can barely tell that Duke had ever hosted a big-time college football game.

That, of course, did not dissuade some of my classmates from making the most of Duke football. Rutgers was visiting, which would be at least a competitive matchup, if not an inspiring display of gridiron talent. The semester had barely started, so our academic burdens were light, and it was a perfect late summer morning in the Carolinas. We would put together a group of experienced tailgaters and make a day of it. Assembling this squad from a corps of intellectual grad students was not easy, but we did field a passable contingent. My roommate Rich Clinch was a burly and seasoned Cleveland Browns fan who brought some rust-belt attitude. Kevin Warmath was an all-state Colorado high school football player who left behind actually playing big-time football (for SMU, the team Texas fans referred to as Southern Money) because he was smart enough to transfer into Brown. Dave Hepenstal—who simply went by Hep—went to tiny Hope College in Michigan but grew up under the influence of the mighty Michigan Wolverines the same way the Longhorns owned my allegiances. Garrick Francis was a local kid made good who loved his hometown North Carolina State Wolfpack, but left them behind for Penn. The five of us and a few curious classmates would surely bring the Blue Devils a rare victory over the Rutgers Scarlet Knights, a team with less football pedigree even than Duke.

Clinch decided the morning called for Bloody Caesars, a northern twist on the Bloody Mary—I took particular fascination in the ingredient Clamato, heavily favored by Canadians as the right complement to vodka, but ignored by most of the southern world for whom it would never occur to mix tomato juice with desiccated clam parts. The specifics of the mixture did not stop our little band from imbibing several quarts of the concoction. When faced with a one o'clock kickoff, you really need to go ugly early; otherwise your team may lack a well-lubricated fan base for the early start.

Duke, of course, would need all the help they could get. The Iron Dukes, as enthusiastic as they were, were seriously lacking in numbers. At the University of Texas, friendships have dissolved and divorce decrees amended to account for possession of prime tailgating spots, some of which have been held for years by fans who think nothing of arriving on a Wednesday for a Saturday kickoff. The Duke experience differs somewhat. Students may camp out for days to assure a spot in the Cameron bleachers, but in the grandstands at Wallace Wade the seats are literally given away, if anyone bothers to take them. We—and by we I mean a band of transient graduate students with no prior allegiance and certainly no financial commitment to the university—set up shop in adjoining parking spaces no more than thirty yards from the stadium entrance. After finishing the dregs of the Clamato, we crossed the street, showed our student IDs, and basically had the run of any set of hundreds of vacant seats. Regardless, I was in a college football stadium. I knew what to do.

The contest was a fair fight on paper, but the Scarlet Knights proved to be no match for our newly embraced Devils. Our mercenary contingent cheered from the first kick of the ball, enthusiastic and devoted and as attentive as we could be, given that most of us were drunker than a boiled owl. Duke quarterback Dave Brown, who was a legitimate NFL talent, threw the ball around at will and led the Devils to a 42–22 win in front of the Iron Dukes and five hammered graduate students who made all the difference. We all loved Duke a little bit more at the end of the day.

Honoring Bulldog's request that I search out Wallace Wade, combined with the familiar cheering for the underdog in a half-full stadium built into a hillside served as a comforting reminder of my youth, but I still had Texas on my mind. Much to my astonishment—and perhaps right on schedule—the Longhorns got surprisingly good. All I had to do was leave the campus and the 1990 Texas squad responded with their best season in years. Surprising the college football world, they opened the season with a road win over Penn State. No real fan trusts the result of a first game; openers can be harbingers of great things, but they can also be flukes won at the expense of an overrated opponent. This opener was no fluke. The next time out, the Horns outplayed Colorado most of the night only to drop a tough one to the Buffs, who pulled it out in the fourth quarter and won 29–22. The faithful had no idea at the time that Colorado would go on to win the national championship. As for the Longhorns, the 1990 squad wouldn't lose another game, upsetting fourth-ranked Oklahoma and clobbering Arkansas before going on the road and winning at Texas Tech. The Texas defense reminded some of the great '83 squad, but this team actually scored points in bunches behind a stout offensive line and a deep collection of talented receivers and backs.

At this point, any real fan would be pleased. True to my mother's criticism, naturally, I was annoyed. Texas drinking the magical football serum while I was two thousand miles away must have been some sort of sick joke, no different than seeing an old girlfriend looking spectacular after a breakup just to remind you that your stupidity knew no bounds. Come on, God, must the mocking continue?

"Texas is fantastic. Where is this coming from?"

"Isn't Duke Chapel a magnificent place?"

"Texas—"

God interrupted. "'All creatures of our God and King' fills me with joy on a Sunday morning. What a wonderful creation of man it is."

"You didn't hear a word I just said."

God seemed to care more about a dead British composer than he did about the living, breathing Texas Longhorns. He certainly knew—being omniscient—that disappointment inevitably derailed each promising Longhorn season. That was my suspicion anyway; the Horns couldn't possibly be this good under McWilliams, who was no better than a 5-6 coach riding a hot team playing over its head. We would find out soon enough.

Texas hadn't defended the University of Houston's run-and-shoot offense effectively since its inception five years before, often leading to embarrassing losses in which the Longhorn secondary proved incapable of covering anything more dangerous than a cold casserole dish. Cougar High—Houston's nickname born out of Texas snobbery directed at what most considered a commuter school—had our number, and their jackass of a coach, the arrogant and unpleasant John Jenkins, delighted in this knowledge. Characterwise, Jenkins was the anti–Bulldog Jones; in 1990 the Jackass had assembled his finest team. The Cougars were ranked number three and would travel to Austin for a nationally televised night game, which brought the risk of being humiliated from coast to coast in a time slot where there were few other games to distract the nation's attention. All eyes were on Austin, and here I was, trapped in basketball country.

Sometimes great fans transcend the limitations of television. When you park yourself on the sofa, the stadium environment coming over the airwaves from hundreds of miles away washes over you. Even on a lousy television set, college football can make you jump out of your seat and pump your fist and shout and curse and carry on as if the players can hear you; if you lose your emotional attachment to the guys on the field, they will certainly lose. Your imagination fully captures a stadium scene that you have no more firsthand knowledge of than an art critic does the mind of Picasso. Picasso would have been a college football fan; the collective mass of the faithful creates art, a loud, boisterous passion that millions cannot live without. On this my mother and I would have certainly agreed.

This artful transcendence always happens in the Southeastern Conference, Bryant-Denny Stadium in Tuscaloosa, Alabama, and their despised cousins at Jordan-Hare in Auburn, Arkansas's Razorback Stadium, which Texas fans referred to as "Fayette-nam," Tiger Stadium's Death Valley at LSU, Williams-Brice at South Carolina, Ben Hill Griffin Stadium—The Swamp—in Gainesville, Florida, playing between the hedges in Athens, Georgia or in front of over 100,000 at Neyland Stadium at Tennessee. All of these scenes threaten to blow up your television set; one more decibel of white-hot southern noise and your living room would turn into a shower of sparks and flying pieces of metal and plastic amidst the pizza boxes and beer bottles.

Texas rarely rose to this level, never quite arousing that passion of the Old South. Maybe Texas held itself aloft in the grandiosity of being Texas, or maybe the pain of defeat never roused Texas to venegeful fury the way it did their Civil War comrades in the deeper South. Or perhaps college football wasn't the only game in town and the success of the corporate titan Dallas Cowboys interfered with our total immersion in the college game. Whatever it was that made Texas fans hold something in reserve, it didn't diminish the passion on Saturday, November 10. The Houston Cougars walked into the emotional equivalent in Memorial Stadium of 80,000 angry villagers wielding pitchforks. Not being one of the 80,000, I settled for an off-campus party where the hostess promised me that a television would be dedicated to my bizarre public school fascination with the gridiron exploits of immensely talented kids to whom it never would have occurred to go to Williams or Vassar. And so a group of genteel and sophisticated grad students watched me pump my fists and let out a guttural *yes* every time a Longhorn defender punished a Cougar receiver with a nasty hit, which happened on nearly every play. Led by the savage headhunter safety Lance Gunn, Texas released years of frustration and pounded the Coogs into submission, beating the holy hell out of their Heisman-hopeful quarterback David Klingler and intercepting him four times in the process. Only some garbage-time touchdowns by Houston made the score a respectable 45–24, but the national television audience knew that this one wasn't close.

The Cougars were the last undefeated team in the NCAA that season until the Horns took them to the woodshed. This would be one of those college football years where a one-loss team could win the national championship. My guys had a shot. They climbed to number seven in the polls, then to five and finally, after their first win over Texas A&M in seven very long years, the AP poll on December 3 voted Texas number three. The newly crowned Southwest Conference Champions would play college football's current barometer of excellence, the Miami Hurricanes, in the Cotton Bowl on New Year's Day and I was not about to miss it. Texas needed an impressive performance in Dallas to disband the Cult of 1969 against the team America loved to hate.

The semester ended and I plotted logistics on my plane back to Texas. As luck would have it, an old Longhorn alum down the street from my parents' house had a pair of Cotton Bowl tickets. He gladly parted with them, having no intention of leaving home during the holidays to see the game live. I was in.

The future of college football showed itself that New Year's Day. It started just fine; overcast and cold conditions forced my date—a knowledgeable football fan this time—and me to bundle up for the drive to what some people would refer to as "the wrong side" of Dallas, where the Cotton Bowl sits. The neighborhood surrounding it receives substantial income from football fans paying five dollars to park a car in someone's front yard; wondering whether or not your car would be there when you returned added to the excitement. It was a great day for football, but upon taking our seats, the ugly spectacle of the new Jumbotron television screen at the Cotton Bowl ruined part of the appeal. Instead of listening to the Longhorn Band, the fans were subjected to endless highlights of Cotton Bowls past interspersed with advertisements apparently targeted at the hard of hearing. The future also included a fixed CBS camera scaffold directly in front of our seats. Sitting low and in the middle of the field, this obscured our view of all action between the 40-yard lines. The rolling-track sideline camera managed to obscure the rest of the field, positioned strategically between our seats and the line of scrimmage on almost every play. We would have to depend on the oppressive Jumbotron for instant replays. But we were in the stadium, braving the elements and with the chance to say "I was there" in countless bars when talk turned to the Longhorns' 1990 National Championship Season.

The future also came in the form of the fourth-ranked Miami Hurricanes. Their brash taunting and dancing in the stadium tunnel had become de rigueur for the modern college football team. Seventy thousand mostly Longhorn partisans prepared to scream until their lungs bled in an effort to shut the 'Canes up. Miami's vision of football held no appeal for us. To hell with the future.

The present, regrettably, was worse. Miami returned the opening kick all the way to the fifty. On first down, as our section craned our necks around the midfield camera, a view of a badly thrown football came into view. Miami's quarterback, Craig Erickson, had thrown a sideline hitch route and the Longhorns' All-American safety Stanley "the Sheriff" Richard jumped the pattern. Texas would start this game with an interception return for a touchdown and all would be right with the world. The Longhorn Band had already raised their instruments to break into the fight song when the Sheriff lost his grip and the ball bounced off the Cotton Bowl's aging Astroturf.

In everyone's life, there are moments of clarity and insight. Had I been in my grandfather's kitchen at this moment, he would have dialed up his lecture on "pride goeth before a fall." Today's syllabus taught the

Longhorn Faithful what it meant to accept reality and put hubris aside. Miami had just made the only mistake of any consequence that they would make the rest of the day. Texas failed to make the first of many plays that were required to compete with the stoked-up and confident Hurricanes. The sleet began to fall right on cue, adding physical discomfort to the emotional misery of all in attendance as the Cotton Bowl was treated to the ugliest display of football since the birth of Amos Alonzo Stagg. Miami didn't just beat Texas. Miami throttled Texas 46–3 and added insult to injury by committing sixteen penalties for a whopping 202 yards. The referee's microphone cut right through the freezing rain, interrupting the action roughly every fourth play.

Personal foul, roughing the passer, fifteen yards. First down, Texas.

Unsportsmanlike conduct, excessive taunting, fifteen yards . . .

And on it went, providing a sound track of Miami indiscretions, none of which Texas took advantage of. By the end of the game, the refs had to make up new penalties just to keep up with the visiting miscreants.

Kicking the home team right in the nuts just when their fans thought they were good again, fifteen yards. First down, Texas.

Colorado and Georgia Tech shared that season's national title, but Miami probably would have beaten either of them. Being beaten by the best would have been some consolation, had Texas made a game of it. Or perhaps the flameout would provide some resolve for next season's Longhorns to prove to the world that they weren't a fraud, a one-trick pony living a dream season where they got every break possible.

Texas couldn't sustain the success of 1990. They opened the 1991 season ranked fourteenth and went downhill from there. An opening loss to Mississippi State, coached by our old friend Jackie Sherrill, now out of the NCAA compliance doghouse and willing to take over at a school that sat in the dregs of the SEC and apparently had no moral turpitude clause in its contract template, sank everyone's hopes for a return to excellence. The Longhorns finished 5-6 and reassigned favorite son McWilliams. Time to start over. Again.

Another forgettable season by the Longhorns allowed me to polish off my master's thesis with little distraction. The Duke basketball squad tried to make me feel better by racking up another national title on the hardwood. Duke issued me a graduate degree in public policy and Texas called me home. I had left my state two years before wondering if I would ever return; I now knew that there was no other place for me. Many of my classmates stayed east and started an exploration through the maze of power and prestige in our nation's capital. But the rhythms of Washington, DC, though invigorating, didn't appeal to me. Not only did I lack a passion for federal government, there was absolutely no guarantee of adequate Longhorn football coverage. Cramming my life into the dependable 1985 Honda Accord, I pointed it west, hung a left at Little Rock, and headed to Austin.

This would be the first time in my life I was truly alone, dependent on no other but myself. I remembered Grandad sitting in his kitchen listening, eyes closed, to my brother Sam reading to him from Ecclesiastes. The great tragedy of my grandfather's aging was that his failing sight prevented him from reading without effort. Sam recognized this and recorded many of Grandad's favorite works, speaking clearly into an old RadioShack tape player. Bulldog listened to Sam's rendition of Ecclesiastes a thousand times. The words came to me as I drove back through Tennessee.

For everything, there is a season, and a time for every matter under heaven: a time to be born and a time to die; a time to plant and a time to pluck up what is planted; a time to kill and a time to heal; a time to break down and a time to build up . . .

God has made everything beautiful in its time; also he has put eternity into man's mind, yet so that he cannot find out what God has done from the beginning to the end.

What would God do next?

College football provides spiritual nurture and a healing presence for thousands. While I clearly embraced this provision, never did I

The 1924 Buffalo Seniors, from left: Roy Golden, Mitchell "Bulldog" Jones, Grady Burson, and Odus Mitchell. *(Jones Family)*

believe the game would deliver any tangible benefits. But in January 1993, college football got me a job. The Texas legislature was working through its postelection turnover and I had an interview with the new chairman of the prestigious House Committee on Appropriations. Rob Junell was a charismatic lawyer from San Angelo with almost impossibly bright blue eyes that looked stolen from Santa Claus, for they made Junell appear as if he was always two thoughts ahead of the other guy, which was usually the case. More important, his short stature and the beginnings of a middle-age spread belied his greatness as a college football player, an undersized and intense linebacker for the Texas Tech squads of the late sixties. Bulldog Jones loved players like Rob Junell.

It never takes much for college football fans to strike a bond, even in a job interview. My prospects for employment improved once we dispensed with my academic credentials and took a side route through Texas Tech football history. After my brief expository remarks on E. J. Holub's claim to being the toughest player in Southwest Conference history, followed by a discussion of legendary Tech halfback Donny Anderson's running style, the interview was a walk in the park. We could have talked all day and would have, except his increasingly annoyed committee director noted that the interview slots were backing up and she gave the Chairman the "enough already" look. Junell caught the glance from the edge of his seat where he was enthusiastically talking up Tech's prospects for the next fall. He embarrassingly eased back in his seat, remembered what our purpose was, and thanked me for coming. Halfway out the door, he called out to me: "Oh, you're hired. Can you come back tomorrow?" And so I began as a legislative budget analyst assigned to the state's education budget, which included the funding for the massive University of Texas System but, regrettably, gave me little sway in its decisions to hire and fire football coaches.

I found my footing: back in my college town with a real job, an alumnus ready to make his way in the world. Austin exploded with growth and opportunity during this time. The most famous U.T. dropout of my time, a young entrepreneur named Michael Dell, had turned his side computer business into a corporate juggernaut and a corps of young Dellionaires with stock options began to overtake the aging hippies as Austin's brand name, not that this sat well with everyone.

The new Texas football coach didn't sit well either. John Mackovic had a cool exterior and an NFL pedigree. He was a noted offensive genius with equal reputations for organization and, regrettably, not getting along with his players. He was buttoned-down and genteel and a noted wine connoisseur, the anti–Darrell Royal. Mackovic fit Texas football culture like a Hasidic Jew at a Southern Baptist Convention. No one cared, as long as Mackovic won, and he did undo some of the damage from the neglect of the McWilliams years, slowly making progress through an initial two seasons where the Longhorns were at least competent most of the time and the recruiting began to improve. But he also built a team centered around offensive firepower and ignored the Texas tradition of solid defense.

No Texas lead was safe during the Mackovic years, and this drove the faithful crazy. The Longhorns had their moments—a 10-2-1 season in 1995 and a shocking upset of Nebraska in the inaugural Big 12 championship game in 1996—but some of the losses were noxious, repulsive, and sad. Somehow during his tenure, Texas managed to lose to Rice. There are lions and Christians in the college football hierarchy. The Rice Owls are the Christians, trotted out for the amusement of the Roman populace to be eaten by the likes of the University of Texas. The Rice squad of 1994 played as if the Christians had stuck their fists right down the lions' throats and forced them to choke (which Texas did often behind a defense that held up about as well as a colander full of water). After the humiliating 19–17 end result, the first Rice victory over Texas since LBJ was president, the Texas fans embraced Mackovic with the same enthusiasm that Americans embraced the metric system.

Disappointments aside, we tend to remember our salad days in a glowing light. For me those days stretched a solid ten years from the time I set foot in Austin as a college student through my life as a single professional without a care in the world. During this time, the Texas Longhorns played pretty sorry football. They couldn't replay those seasons; the record would always reflect that my devotion led the Longhorns to nothing but mediocrity interspersed with the tease of greatness just often enough to keep me in the fold. But ten years without a care in the world and nary a crisis is a gift no sane person would reject. Maybe I didn't need the Longhorns during this time. But these days would end.

Dad called one day in the summer of 1994. His voice was quiet and clear and sounded like peace. My grandfather had died and it was time for me to come home. Was Dad okay?

"Yeah, I guess so." He spoke from the end of a very long journey accompanied by relief at the destination. How was Grandad? Were you there?

"He was fine. Didn't eat much the few days before, just asked for a little water every once in a while. His blood pressure dropped during the day . . . He just sort of eased on out."

Eased on out. That made sense. If ever old age was a cause of death, then this was it. Grandad lived a life without vice; rose early, swam well into his eighties: dined on bran cereal and water most nights. The Jones men lived forever, but the further Bulldog got from Audrey, the more he faded into life's background. He spent most of a year at Palo Duro Hospital on the edge of his beloved Canyon; you could see Jones Hall from its front lawn and the empty plains stretched endlessly out the back. He seemed to sink into the covers and become smaller and smaller with each visit.

Bulldog Jones was ready to go. He was tired and his body betrayed him by not knowing when to quit. My last few visits with him would end when he dozed off. Then my father would always remind me to wash my hands on the way out the door—there was no breaking this habit he acquired in medical school.

Dad was the great caretaker. I would watch him take care of my grandmother and then my grandfather and my Uncle Frank. His dedication and love knew no bounds. Had he not been a doctor he would have been one of the world's great nurses, coaxing even the most difficult patients into finishing a glass of Carnation Instant Breakfast to keep their strength up; Dad believed the powdered and vitamin-packed Carnation had special fortifying powers. For almost two years Dad drove to Canyon every afternoon after work to care for his father and to return his love to a town that blessed him like a gentle rain.

My Uncle Frank didn't quite get all of this. Frank was ninety-one and didn't always track so well. The day after Grandad died we asked Frank if he wanted to go "see Mitch." He wasn't sure what we meant, but he knew he didn't want to go, thinking he would go see him some other time, not comprehending that Mitch's time was gone. The night before the funeral, Frank finally told my father that, yes, he did want to go see his brother. Dad called Mr. Brooks at the funeral home. Of course he would accommodate the Jones family. He met Dad at the door, helping him with Frank's wheelchair and escorting him to the viewing room. Frank stood up and Dad held him steady as he peered into my grandfather's face. Frank told Dad of how all the generations seem to run into each other; he had a vivid memory of his own father's funeral and wondered if Grandad didn't look just a little like my great-grandfather, Samuel. He remembered the old men of his youth and the children who took their place and now a generation would change again. My father was on the verge of tears when Frank rested his hands on the edge of the casket and lowered his head to give his brother one long last look. Frank said nothing, peering in with the intent of someone trying to understand. He slowly raised his head and turned to my father, giving voice to the clearest and most deliberate thought of his ninety-one years.

"Is that my suit?"

My father furrowed his way to the deadpan expression of a man who doesn't know whether to blink back laughter or tears. He finally smiled at his ancient uncle. No, Frank, it's not your suit. Satisfied, Frank sank into his wheelchair. It was time to go.

My mother led the Jones family into First Baptist the next day. Standing and turning in my front-row pallbearer's seat to watch the processional, I saw Mom's smile—the light that guided my father through his life. Mom didn't do somber, only joy. Joy at a life that had touched so many, a builder of men, a man of word and honor. Joy celebrating the greatest West Texas Buffalo of them all. This joy filled the room, all the way to the back of the sanctuary where the men of Mitch Jones Hall stood honoring a man who, to them, was merely a picture in the lobby. They joined in the singing of the WT alma mater as a living legacy to the ferocious pulling guard whose spirit inhabited their home.

My father and grandfather. *(Jones Family)*

Bulldog Jones was ninety-four, the same age as Wallace Wade when he died. My life would never be the same without him. When I went back to the house, I found the book Grandad had authored a few years before: *We'll Remember Thee,* an early history of West Texas State. Each of his grandchildren had received a copy. On the inside cover of mine, there was a note.

To Adam—
Our youngest grandson whose early versatile successes have made me known as Adam's grandad—and reminds us that the good life moves ever forward.

Grandad Jones

The relic safely tucked away in my bag, I thanked God for this good life and recalled a moment of grace. My father drove me to the airport, mostly in silence. As I caught Dad's driver's-side profile, I noticed that his age was starting to show. A generation was changing hands again. What could I possibly do in life that would compare to the legacy Dean Jones had left behind?

I found an aisle seat on the plane, closing my eyes and thanking God for my grandfather.

"Those college men at the back of the church didn't even know my grandfather, but they came anyway. They didn't have to do that."

God understood.

"Your life will be marked by thousands of kind acts that someone didn't have to do."

The plane went wheels up as I wondered what the good life held in store.

5

A PARTNER IS BORN

*Texas vs. the University of
North Carolina*

THE SUN BOWL,
EL PASO, TEXAS, DECEMBER 30, 1994

While I still thought about Bulldog in the fall of 1994, eventually I moved on to the mundane human tasks of making a living and paying the bills. From there I would move on with surprising speed to starting a family. Just after the 1994 Sun Bowl ended, I found out that I would be a father. I wasn't prepared to be a dad, maybe no one ever is. God does not make these decisions in accordance with your time lines and I am fairly convinced that somewhere out in the ether children choose their parents, not the other way around. The news was unexpected, but it was not unwelcome. It was a boy. The sonogram rarely misses boys. Without benefit of hindsight I had no idea that this player-to-be-named-later would become my favorite football fan. That he would take my mother's place. That he would be my little man. I knew nothing of this. You never do.

I was out in the world for the first time, my apartment in a cool neighborhood in the shadow of downtown, and my job paid me well enough to largely do whatever I wanted whenever I wanted, which included mostly drinking, dating, and going to Texas sports events, not necessarily—but quite often—in that order. My life as a single was not exactly like meeting a future spouse at the Baptist Student Union in Canyon and having a Coke. Nothing like it, actually. Austin is a city of late nights and rock and roll and Mexican food in the morning as a salve to nasty hangovers. The Continental Club, Liberty Lunch, and the Hole in the Wall laid down a blistering sound track—heavy on guitars—that made me feel young and alive in the coolest city in America. Sunday nights at the Continental Club, the reigning hot guitar player in town—a title just as revered as Longhorn starting quarterback—would take the stage. Junior Brown was retro cool in his Stetson and western suits, but his playing was cutting edge; the guy's hands blistered the fingerboard in a staccato rat-a-tat like a pinball careening among the bumpers. The Continental's tiny stage could barely contain him.

I spent many Sundays crammed into the dark smoky room on South Congress with the rest of Junior's weekly congregation: a motley collection of rednecks, punks, bikers, young hipsters, and those, like me, trying to forget that they had to work in the morning, which was often accomplished in the Monday haze of too many Shiner Bocks and memories of cigarette smoke that had somehow crept into your pores at night while you tried to catch four or five hours of sleep. Having seen enough of this show, God presented me with the sobering prospect of fatherhood and my first stab, albeit unsuccessful, at marriage. That was my life away from college football. On the gridiron, there was a Sun Bowl to play.

The Sun Bowl, which occupies the lower bowl tier, doesn't merit a prime-time viewing slot, or even a weekend kickoff. This was a low-grade showcase for a depressingly low-grade Texas football team. This edition kicked off early Friday afternoon on December 30 when most folks are off work, but a random collection of the luckless has to make the world turn, however slowly, between the two holidays. A new job and a lack of vacation accrual left me luckless. I only had one escape: sick leave. Stomach flu's always a good option—could be serious if you needed a two-day break, or it could just be bad seafood and you're good to go twenty-four hours later. Best thing is nobody really wants the details. So I lied to my employer. College football demanded it.

On this day, I saluted the pregame show with a bottle opener and my first Bass Ale of the afternoon and ordered a pizza. The beer and pizza went down well with a Longhorn win; even though the 1994 Horns underachieved and disappointed all year, they salvaged the bowl season behind the great running back Priest Holmes. Of course, we didn't know Holmes was great at the time. He ran for four touchdowns against North Carolina that day, then suffered a terrible knee injury and was barely heard from again until he rehabilitated himself and became a perennial All-Pro in the NFL. Had I known how the story would end I would have enjoyed his Sun Bowl star turn even more. But you never know how the story ends, and the Sun Bowl was just a bad consolation prize anyway. Even West Texas State won the Sun Bowl once, back in 1962. I have proof.

The winner's watch from the 1962 Sun Bowl—a gold-plated Timex in a faux-leather cardboard box from Feder's Jewelers in El Paso—rested comfortably in a top drawer right next to all the pairs of socks I could never distinguish between—black and navy—when I was in a hurry and trying to get to work at a decent hour. A place of honor to be sure for such a humble timepiece. Nineteen sixty-two was not the age of Rolex armaments paid for by deep-pocketed alumni and television largesse. But it was special to me. Even though I was the youngest child, Bulldog handed me down the watch partially because of my precocious fascination with the game he loved. That and the likelihood he had forgotten the damn thing in his own sock drawer and hadn't uncovered it until my two older brothers were long gone.

The watch represented Bulldog's final triumph in football. Forty years past his last lick in a leather helmet, Dean Jones, he of the psychology department and the faculty lounge, won a fierce fight as WT's faculty representative to the NCAA. It all started with an innocent recruiting violation in the summer of '62 that needed reconciling. If you were recruiting the Texas Panhandle in the early 1960s you could cross the top-flight talent right off the list. If they were the best, then Texas and Oklahoma would slug it out for their services, and if their daddies had any stroke at all then Southern Methodist and Texas Christian would be right behind them. Texas A&M got theirs, typically Aggie legacies and farm boys who had no love for Austin and Dallas. Texas Tech would enroll the rest. That still left some good football players from some hard-to-find places. Buffalo coach Joe Kerbel was pretty good at finding them, and his won-loss record proved it. But it made for some interesting decisions: the harder it was to find a player in rural Texas, the more likely you were to find a package deal with a teenage bride. And that's where WT found trouble. Hotel room for a recruit? Fine. Hotel room for a recruit's wife? Clearly out of bounds. This circumstance must have made Bulldog's fairly prominent ears turn beet red. Here he was at the dawn of the age of whores and hundred-dollar handshakes among the big boys in the grand old Southwest Conference and his little teachers college out on the plains that never hurt anybody and certainly never paid cash money for someone to play football was being nicked for a nine-dollar hotel room for a *married couple.* Explain yourself, West Texas State University.

And so Dean W. Mitchell "Bulldog" Jones did. In his heart he wanted to explain how the world really worked to the starch-shirted curmudgeons on the Infractions Committee. He instead chose restraint and apology. Appealing to their love of learning and the opportunity for a better citizenry, he preyed on their sense of true love among young people and the chance of a college education for the underdog. Should a publicly subsidized room and bath jeopardize a young man's future? It wasn't his mistake; it was the university's. And what of the child bride? Were we to leave her out on the street? Can you really punish a hard-working farm boy and his loyal teammates for the sins of an ignorant administrator? And then Bulldog went biblical on them.

"I say to you gentlemen: What the good Lord has brought together, let not the NCAA cast asunder."

They bought it. The Buffaloes were slapped on the wrist. Probation would not deny them their destiny. West Texas State 15, Ohio University

Dean Jones: "Let not the NCAA cast asunder." *(Jones Family)*

14: Sun Bowl watches for everyone. Bulldog Jones got his. And it all enabled the Buffaloes and Longhorns to have one small thing in common.

The 1994 Sun Bowl ended and I called to check in on dinner plans; the woman in my life had not bothered to call in sick simply to watch Longhorn football with me.

"You're what?"

Comprehension was not my strong suit. Her news would change my life as a football fan. I was going to be a dad.

Zachary Peace Jones was born the day before the 1995 Texas-Oklahoma game. Had I been a total son of a bitch, I could have been in Dallas at the game. A friend had offered me tickets two days before Zach's birth. I would like to remember seriously considering it, but I didn't. I wasn't a total son of a bitch, my Protestant upbringing had the better of me and Zach's middle name was no accident; I hoped desperately that he would be the Peace that passed all understanding. He was, in a way. There's no question in my mind that an important paternal connection formed as I watched him peacefully sleep while the Longhorns blew a big lead and allowed a pretty terrible Sooner squad come back and forge a 21–21 tie on a muted hospital television. He felt my frustration.

Zach was my shot at reliving the great experience of father, son, and college football stadium. We started our own traditions watching mediocre football together, just as my mother and father and I had with the hapless Buffs of the early 1970s. The difference being that, some day, I knew, the elusive national championship so cruelly snatched away in 1977 and 1983 would return to its rightful spot in the Longhorn trophy case. I was faithful enough to believe that Zach would not spend his childhood lamenting defeat.

Zach saw the Longhorns up close for the first time at the close of the 1997 season, the end of the line for John Mackovic. An early season rout at home at the hands of UCLA by the ridiculous score of 66–3 sealed the deal. The only thing worth watching was Ricky Williams. A dreadlocked free spirit from San Diego, a wickedly talented tailback, and the best player in the entire nation, Williams was trapped on a three-win, six-loss squad. Dispirited and embarrassed, the Longhorns showed little fight and little heart. Since there was no question that Williams, then a junior, would be gone to the NFL the next year, I had to make sure my two-year-old could one day look back on his life and say, yes, I did see Ricky Williams carry the football. Unlike my first experience at Memorial Stadium, there was no magic, just a very cold and rainy November day. Zach and I bundled up the way my father and mother and I did twenty years before at Kimbrough. Tickets were easy to come by; we sat in the end zone and Zach slept in my arms as the clock ticked down on a meaningless 45–31 Longhorn victory. The faithful said goodbye to Ricky Williams.

Or so they thought . . . for Ricky wasn't finished in Austin. After the board of regents thankfully dismissed Mackovic, they, perhaps unwittingly, set Texas back on the path to greatness. Texas hired the losing coach from the 1994 Sun Bowl, North Carolina's Mack Brown. Brown earned his reputation as a rising star by leading the ultimate basketball school to back-to-back ten-win seasons on the football field. He did it the old-fashioned way: by convincing great football players to come to school at North Carolina. Brown could talk a dog off a meat wagon. His sideline coaching was inconsequential, and somewhat suspect actually, but he always put the best players on the field. It was Brown who persuaded Ricky Williams to stay for his senior year. Brown's Longhorns got good, and they got good fast. The Giant that was Texas football had awakened.

While the Longhorns ascended, I slid. Zach's mom and I were in a marriage that had never really worked. We pondered our separation right after Ricky Williams collected the 1998 Heisman Trophy and the surprising Longhorns thrashed Mississippi State in the Cotton Bowl. That was the last football game I watched in the big house in the suburbs. It sold in three days, and the divorce went wonderfully. The judge looked at the assembled parties, asked if we had read the document, signed it without waiting for an answer, and returned to her lunch. Chicken salad if memory serves.

It was time to make my own chicken salad. Step one was to seek refuge. In the summer of 1999 my sanctuary ended up being an eight-hundred-square-foot condo on Bellevue Place, right up the road from Memorial Stadium and across the street from the Posse East—it was East not because there were multiple Posses but because the original one in West Campus had burned to the ground—a joint in which I had spilled a lot of beer during my college life. I had a lot more to spill. I was home with Truman, the burnt orange and white Brittany saved from the Town Lake Animal Shelter. Truman was the last link to my past life. When we sold the house in the suburbs, we had arranged to place Truman at the Humane Society, where he could find a loving home. This lasted a couple of weeks, before I inquired about him one afternoon from the depths of my postdivorce depression. Truman had been adopted, but it hadn't worked out and the family had returned him. I raced out the door to get my dog back; I desperately needed him. Noting on my deed restriction that pets were not allowed in the Bellevue Place complex, I took great pains to hide him as if he were a hirsute Mafia informant on the lam. For several months, I rose before the sun to walk Truman out of sight of anyone who looked like they might have been a real grown-up. I eventually solved the problem by getting myself elected president of the homeowners association. It was a major sacrifice, but life without Truman was unbearable. He kept me company during the nights when Zachary was now sleeping under another roof. Truman and I settled into being bachelor roommates and, since custody was split right down the middle, Zach joined us on alternating Sunday, Monday, Tuesday, and Wednesday, Thursday, Friday, Saturday blocks. Unless it was game day. Game days were Dad's days. Always.

Our first game day together saw the resurgent Longhorns host the North Carolina State Wolfpack in the 1999 season opener. All the old pregame electricity lit up Longhorn Nation. The opening-day crowd filled old Memorial to the brim and exploded when Tour de France win-

Partners: Zachary Jones and Truman. *(Jones Family)*

ner and Longhorn fan Lance Armstrong rode his bike to midfield to drop off the game ball. The pageantry was back. It was 1975 all over again, except now I was the parent and it was my son who would never forget this scene. This was not the depressed version of Longhorn football that lulled Zach to sleep on that rainy day when he was two. This was alive. He would feel it, revel in it, remember it. This was the do-over. My life needed one, and it would start with college football. Of course, just when I thought the Longhorns would deliver . . .

North Carolina State blocked three Longhorn punts that night and turned two of them into touchdowns. The Longhorn comeback fell short in a 20–16 defeat. So much for electricity. Zach boarded my shoulders for the trudge home. We were both exhausted and couldn't fall back on the reserve adrenaline of a Longhorn win. A block from the house he wanted to get down and walk. We held hands and he looked up at me.

"Dad, did the Longhorns score more points than the Red Wolfpack?"

Apparently I had work to do. I put Zach to bed and opened the upstairs windows as a thunderstorm was rolling over Austin. The rain started to fall. On television, weather radar kept track of the slow-moving yellow and orange blob creeping across the Hill Country and into the calm green of Travis County. I listened to the storm outside and watched the boy sleep. With the television completely orange and the thunderous mass right on top of us I lapsed into silent prayer.

"Three blocked punts? Are you kidding me?"

"Excuse me?"

"What I mean is, here I am, trying to be a good guy, and they can't win the damned season opener?"

"Didn't you enjoy the day with your son?"

"Not as much as I could have."

"He doesn't care who wins. Maybe it would be good if you didn't care so much?"

I thought maybe it would be good if God took college football a little more seriously.

All in all, this was not a bad life. Zach learned the appreciation of a good cheeseburger and *SportsCenter*. We would hang out at the Posse on Wednesday, have dinner and watch whatever was on, baseball, college basketball, the NBA. We would never get too far into the game of the night because we had a child's bedtime to accommodate. By the time Zach was five we would go next door to Double Dave's Pizza and shoot pool. I figured he would need these skills in college. At six, I taught him about point spreads. Slowly I became accustomed to the life of a single dad. And it was a good life.

The Horns helped considerably by playing solid football, very good at times, but never quite at championship level. After the loss to North Carolina State, the 1999 squad climbed as high as eighth in the polls before a late season skid left them at nine wins and five losses for the year. Mack Brown was slowly returning Texas to prominence. His improving young team helped make the postdivorce year bearable.

One Sunday morning, Zach snuck downstairs ahead of me and I heard him turn on the television set. He was hooked on *Scooby-Doo*, a harmless diversion that would give me fifteen more minutes in the sack. When I rousted out and went down to join him, there were no cartoons on the screen, only *SportsCenter*. I tried to engage Zach in conversation and got nothing. I thought it was a precursor to the preadolescent years when boys quit speaking, but it was deeper than that. As I gave conversation one last shot by asking him if he wanted me to make pancakes, his four-year-old patience finally ran out.

"Dad," he started abruptly, "I'm watching the highlights."

I was raising a college football fan. Whatever other deficiencies I may have had as a parent, a failure to imbue my son with an appreciation for the finer things in life was not among them.

Zach, Truman, and I spent the last evening of 1999 together in our small encampment just up the street from campus. On a night when people all over the world went to great lengths to welcome the new millennium, I settled for homemade spaghetti and cartoons, for the love of a young boy and a faithful bird dog. Zach drifted off around ten and I carried him up to bed. I called Mom and Dad and assured them that my life would be just fine, that the world would not come to end on this night, literally or figuratively. I thanked them for all that they had ever done and told them I loved them before I hung up the phone. It occurred to me that three very good things were keeping me afloat as the century came to a close: Mack Brown, the Posse, and a four-year-old Longhorn football fan.

6

SOONER NATION

Texas vs. the University of Oklahoma

THE COTTON BOWL,
DALLAS, TEXAS, OCTOBER 7, 2000

My love of college football was born in Oklahoma. Long before West Texas gave the Jones family a lifetime of education and cheering for the underdog, Oklahoma gave the world Mitch Jones and Audrey Watson. My grandparents endured the Dust Bowl with thousands of other Oklahomans; it never occurred to their families to move to California. They did have the sense to eventually come to Texas, which hardly shielded them from the Great Depression. In Audrey's case, this was a doubly bad decision. My great-grandfather, J. E. Watson, held a parcel of land in northern Oklahoma right next to the Cherokees. He jumped at the chance to swap it for some rich farmland in Floydada around the turn of the century and that's how my grandmother became a Texan. Nothing wrong with that, except J.E. didn't have much formal schooling, least of all in geology, so it never crossed his mind that the slick bastard who made the trade had no intention of farming the land in Oklahoma, since it sat right on top of about a million barrels of Cherokee crude. The Indians weren't the only ones screwed out of it. The Watson Lease still produces. Someone unrelated to me still walks to the mailbox and picks up a royalty check every once in a while. The Watsons chose subsistence agriculture over copious wealth and didn't even avoid the Dust Bowl doing it. Perhaps this choice built character.

My great-grandfather Samuel Jones built many of the houses in Altus, a small town close to where the Red River separates Oklahoma from God's Country. Bulldog explained this to me during one of the many days I would take him to run his errands. His eyesight cost him the freedom of driving but gave me the gift of wisdom as a teenager. We would have long conversations while taking a tour of the optometrist or the drugstore or maybe a department store if he needed a new shirt or jacket. Grandad and Uncle Frank both became very accomplished carpenters building homes right alongside their father, starting from about age fifteen. Before that, Grandad made his way selling *The Saturday Evening Post* at the train station. He must have mentioned this to me a dozen times and I always thought he was kidding; it sounded like an indulgent set piece thrown in to round out a biography.

Sunrise. A young boy calls to passengers in a smalltown train station offering The Saturday Evening Post *for a nickel . . .*

No sense in calling him on it—he was the most honest person I knew—I just never bought it. You could imagine Norman Rockwell setting up an easel by the tracks and painting Grandad's picture. Better were the football stories. They increased in violence and vulgarity as I got older. Bulldog had no interest in protecting a teenager from the realities of the world; our afternoon man-to-man conversations were a far cry from playing with cars on his kitchen floor while Audrey made pancakes in animal shapes at the stovetop.

"Did I tell you about my worst moment as a coach at Canyon High School?"

He hadn't. Even if he had I would have let him repeat it in the hope that some new detail would emerge. These stories always had a point, even in the retelling. Today's lesson was about being young and full of vinegar and the trouble it can lead to if you can't contain yourself. He began the story as I pulled his ancient Delta 88 out of the Sav-On Drug parking lot.

One of Grandad's cornerbacks with a maddening reputation for athletic brilliance combined with a lack of work ethic kept getting beat on a quick hitch, leading to easy first downs for the opponent. Bulldog called time-out to confront the lazy schoolboy. Before he could get a word in, the player told Grandad that the opposing receiver was pushing off and that someone needed to talk to the referee about it. Coach Jones considered this advice from the young charge before him and thoughtfully offered some advice of his own, at football-coach volume.

"What you need to do is to shut up, quit telling me how to coach, get your thumb out of your ass and cover the sonofabitch."

It wasn't exactly Shakespearean; and Bulldog let it fly during a rare quiet moment, allowing hundreds of parents and children a glimpse into the kind of person the good Christian board members of the Canyon Independent School District had hired to lead and nurture the town's young men. Had he not already been a local legend, Mitch Jones might well have been fired on the spot. But he didn't even get a reprimand. This was the famous Bulldog Jones after all. Where did the young boy who sold *The Saturday Evening Post* learn such language anyway? Oklahoma.

Oklahoma also gave Texas Darrell Royal, which we appreciated greatly. He grew up in Hollis, which is only one county west of Altus and within ten miles of Texas. A small tectonic shift or a large tornado would push Hollis right across the border. It's so close to the homeland, in fact, that Royal's picture hangs in the Texas Panhandle Sports Hall of Fame right alongside Bulldog Jones's. We always figured he was one of us. Long before he saved Texas football, Coach Royal had been an All-American quarterback and defensive back at Oklahoma. Ironically enough, Royal's first step toward Longhorn deification came against his alma mater in 1958 when he knocked off the second-ranked Sooners, then riding a forty-seven-game winning streak.

A whole string of coaches at Texas were dismissed for a number of reasons—McWilliams's lack of experience, Mackovic's arrogance, and Akers because the damn crackers down in Georgia still think it's ten to nine in Texas—but the biggest sin of all was the sin of not being Darrell Royal. Not being Darrell was a crushing weight, and it got heavier the farther Texas got from 1969. Mack Brown felt it just as intensely as had any of his forebears. Brown made Texas a winner very quickly, but to disband the Cult of 1969 and take Texas to the promised land? No one really knew if he was up to that task. Surely Brown knew that millions of people held a deep spiritual investment in Texas football. Especially the divorced dad and his young son hanging out at the Posse on Wednesday nights in the shadow of what was now called Darrell K. Royal–Texas Memorial Stadium. The one thing that stood in Mack's way seemed to be an insurmountable impediment. Oklahoma.

Explaining the depths of hatred and contempt Longhorn fans have for the University of Oklahoma requires a philosophical knowledge possessed only by sages and mystics. Possessing none of that myself, the best way to describe it is found in the purely Texan saying: "I wouldn't cross the street to piss on a Sooner if he was on fire." This hatred manifests itself on the second Saturday of each October during the State Fair of Texas when an enormous horde of burnt-orange Longhorn fans converge on the fairgrounds from the south and are met by a horde of crimson-clad Sooners. The two collide at a neutral site—Dallas is roughly equidistant from Austin and Norman—for one of college football's best days. The midway of the fairgrounds is crowded shoulder to shoulder with humanity, which shuffles around in small herds under the gaze of a forty-foot animatronic cowboy. Big Tex welcomes visitors to the State Fair and encourages them not to litter. The recorded voice is supposed to resemble a Texas rancher's twang, but actually sounds like a garbled overdub from a Japanese horror movie. People always use "under Big Tex" as a guidepost for meeting friends, forgetting that "under Big Tex" leaves you in an open courtyard about forty yards across crammed with five thousand people expressing their hatred for one another. Good luck finding anyone in that mess. I never took Zach to the Texas-Oklahoma game; it was the perfect place to lose a kid.

Oklahoma as Redneck Apocalypse was the Texas vision of the state: an ugly and desolate place where gap-toothed mothers chased their dirty children through bar ditches. The Oklahoma vision of Texas conjured arrogant silver-spoon-fed namby-pambys who would cry upon being hit in the mouth by a Real Goddamn Football Team. Like any great melodrama, all of this was overblown, but such rational thought is impossible when you are walking the midway with a noontime buzz and eyeing the standard-issue OU fan in all of his J. C. Watts midriff-cut fishnet Sooner jersey, Wrangler jeans, pie-plate-sized belt buckle, gold chain, mullet haircut, and handlebar-mustached glory. Texas fans held common currency that Oklahomans—my own family excepted, of course—were trailer-dwelling, nose-picking mutant love children resulting from an illicit affair between Pa Joad and Lulu Roman from *Hee Haw*. We called their state Mobilehoma.

Any day you get to send these people home as discouraged losers is a great day to be a Texas fan. Two years before, Texas had throttled Oklahoma 34–3 behind an unstoppable Ricky Williams, who dedicated the game to the great Doak Walker. Walker had won the 1948 Heisman Trophy playing for SMU and was the reason the Cotton Bowl was called "the House That Doak Built"—the city fathers had to expand the stadium's capacity to accommodate the crowds the old Mustang teams would draw to Fair Park. Walker befriended Williams in the off-season after the Texas star had won the Doak Walker Award, which went to the nation's best running back. They were quite a pair, the grand old man from the golden age of college football and the young Californian with the untamed dreads, and they became quite close. Tragically, Walker died two weeks prior to the Oklahoma game. Ricky felt the loss deeply, and so it was that when he emerged from the Cotton Bowl tunnel he had donned Walker's number 37 in place of his usual 34. Upon scoring his first touchdown, Williams tapped the number on his chest and pointed to the sky. I wept openly, as did every other person on the Texas end of the stadium possessing a living, beating human heart.

For an encore, the 1999 Longhorns, sans Williams, broke the Sooners' hearts with a 28–17 come-from-behind win led by Major Applewhite, the poster child for gritty Texas quarterbacks. The Longhorns had a long tradition of scrappy quarterbacks, the kind who possessed "intangibles" as opposed to remarkable athletic skills—guys with "guile" and "moxie" and lots of other euphemisms for "Why the hell did Texas even recruit this guy?" Texas fans embraced these quarterbacks because it gave them a rare opportunity to cheer for the underdog, which was next to impossible when you were fielding teams permanently ensconced in the AP Top 10 with future All-American players at every other position on the field.

The faithful loved Applewhite. He was a winner who wrung all he could out of his limited physical skills, a coach's kid with a great feel for the game and all the other adjectives dear to the Longhorn heart. It didn't hurt that he bore more than a passing resemblance to Opie Taylor from the *Andy Griffith Show.* No one much mentioned that Major Applewhite was actually from Louisiana.

For years, Texas had thrived on underappreciated quarterbacks who managed the game, didn't make mistakes, and led their team to victory. For Mack Brown to recruit a five-star quarterback would go against that tradition, but that's exactly what he did. Brown wasn't about gamers; he was about having an overwhelming talent advantage at every position on the field. And so Brown proved his mettle as a salesman by persuading New Jersey's Chris Simms, the bluest of the nation's blue-chippers, to forsake the University of Tennessee and come to Austin. Simms was the anti-Applewhite: blond and blue-eyed, 6'5", a magic left arm, and an NFL pedigree—his father Phil had won a Super Bowl for the New York Giants.

All of this would have been fine except for a case of food poisoning. The morning of the 1999 game against Texas A&M, Applewhite found himself doubled over in a vomiting mess. The freshman Simms would have start against the rival Aggies on their own turf and not just in any game. This was the Bonfire Game. A few weeks prior, twelve A&M students had died while working on the huge stack of wood for the annual Thanksgiving bonfire. The stack collapsed and brought down in heartbreaking fashion the grandest of A&M traditions. The tragedy touched both campuses: A&M and UT had a shared history and friends and relatives and lovers traversed between the two campuses for generations. The week before the game, Texas held a memorial for the Texas A&M students on the steps of our great tower. I walked the few blocks from my condo to the campus and arrived at a packed South Mall, full of hundreds of Longhorns and Aggies alike. How easily I could have been on the other side.

On my walk home, I thought of all the Aggies that I knew, especially my old pastor, Howard Childers. He was my spiritual mentor, one of the men I held in esteem almost equal to my grandfather. No doubt he was sad for his beloved school that night. I was sad with him. I didn't see how I could watch the coming football game without some decidedly mixed emotions.

Texas never should have played this game; it was the worst of no-win situations. Nevertheless, I made the trip to College Station, and as I trudged up to my seat in the nosebleed section, I overheard the rumors working through the crowd: Applewhite was sick; the superstar freshman would have to take over. There would be unbelievable pressure on Chris Simms to deliver; this was his moment. He lived up to it for a while, throwing bullets all over Kyle Field and staking the Horns to a halftime lead. The Aggies responded in the second half, mixing coverages to confuse Simms and taking a 20–16 advantage. A miraculously recovered Applewhite then entered the game but could not lead a Texas comeback. The Aggies secured what just might be their most precious victory. No one would ever know what the outcome would have been

Major Applewhite on the headset: the scrappy
gamer. *(University of Texas Athletics)*

had Simms been allowed to finish what he had started. Applewhite returned to start in the Big 12 Championship and the Longhorns were run
out of the stadium by Nebraska. Texas accepted an invitation to the Cotton Bowl, and not only did the Arkansas Razorbacks embarrass a lackluster Horn squad, Applewhite went down with a knee injury. Not
convinced of Applewhite's full recovery, Brown made Simms the starter
for the 2000 season. In picking the Golden Boy over the Scrappy Veteran
he might as well have kicked someone's puppy. Into this controversial
mess stepped the 2000 Oklahoma Sooners.

Texas entered the game ranked eleventh and would have been higher
except they were upset at Stanford, partially because Mack couldn't decide which quarterback to play. Oklahoma was ranked tenth, and most
thought the game was a toss-up. It was the first game in years in which

Chris Simms: the prize recruit. *(University of Texas Athletics)*

both teams were ranked, and the tickets were tough to get. I only secured one by agreeing to be a bus host for the Texas alumni association's morning charter to Dallas. The requirements to be a bus host are to be reasonably entertaining, to make sure the bus leaves Dallas with the same number of people it arrived with, and to occasionally encourage an inebriated alum to leave the other passengers alone and sleep off his drunk on the way back to Austin. Having been a camp counselor, this was not much of a stretch for me. For a shot at a Texas-Oklahoma ticket, I also would have happily power-washed the bus and sanitized the back bathroom after a full day of accommodating beer-soaked football fans.

Rain clouds parked on top of Dallas that day. Typically Texas-OU is a sun-splashed scorcher; the Texas climate has no respect for October. On this day, the drizzle never stopped. The fairgrounds, instead of being divided evenly in burnt orange and crimson, were pockmarked with yellows, olives, and a variety of camouflage patterns on ponchos fished out of the trunks of cars or purchased on the fairgrounds from price-gouging entrepreneurs that made OPEC sheikhs look reasonable. The damp and cold brought back memories of the awful Cotton Bowl against Miami, but those memories faded and excitement returned upon hanging a left at the midway and coming into full view of the cradle of Texas football. This was heaven to me.

The Cotton Bowl looms straight up in white concrete, a beautiful art deco monument to all that was good. COTTON BOWL is helpfully printed on the side in green block letters, as if you needed the reminder. There was no reason to build wide pedestrian spaces and accessible restroom facilities in the 1920s when the old place was built. The Cotton Bowl hasn't really been updated since then, which results in anxious fans being hemmed in by humanity as they make their way up the ramps. This layout is to a claustrophobe what the upper deck back in Austin is to an acrophobe. As the shoulder-to-shoulder river of perspiration carries you along, you pray to God that the wave will eventually deposit you in your seat. The bowels of the stadium are dark and cold, but when you break their grip and emerge from the tunnel to see the green expanse of field unfold beneath you, you're breathless. The uncontainable emotion you fell upon entering Texas-OU makes your heart burst. Great things happen here. Legends are made. For the past fifty years, Texas-OU has been an elimination game in the race for the national championship. Three times in its history Texas had won against OU in October and returned on New Year's Day to secure the national title. Wedged into your seat, with barely any leg room and an arduous trip to get any concessions or relieve yourself, you had to be a great fan here. The Cotton Bowl was the most stunningly intimate stadium in the country, and it offered only one creature comfort—college football. And even that pleasure was taken away from you if your guys lost. Your existence was either glorious or miserable three hours after kickoff, and only the fates knew which. Either way, the losers had to drive home. This was the beauty of the neutral site tradition, and there was nothing else like it.

Applewhite started this one off for the Longhorns, and I staked out the standing room in front of my drenched end-zone seat ready to watch the next chapter of the legend. My joy was short-lived. The Oklahoma Sooners took it away by forcing Texas to start with a miserable three and out possession. The Sooners drove the ball the other way for a touchdown. Then we repeated the same sequence. 14–0, Sooners. Oklahoma was driving for their third touchdown when Texas cornerback Quentin Jammer leapt high to intercept a pass in the end zone right in front of my seat. *Yessssss* . . . No, a yellow flag sat in a puddle on the end-zone turf and brought further dejection. Though I would never admit this to an Oklahoma fan even under threat of death, Jammer had clearly pushed off and was flagged for interference. OU punched it in to make it 21–0. I am not really sure how it became 28–0, but I remember 35–0 very well—that's when the Golden Boy, replacing the ineffective Scrappy Veteran, hit Sooner linebacker Rocky Calmus right in the chest on an out pattern and Calmus brought it back 41 yards for the fifth touchdown of the half. Regrettably, there was a sixth touchdown before ennui settled in on the Sooner sideline and Texas scored before intermission to make it 42–7.

I chose to dishonor the Jones family code of fandom in the third quarter. Joined by thousands of Texas fans, I huddled in the adjacent International Food Pavilion, a beautiful warehouse structure that allowed fair patrons to sample overcooked chicken tandoori and soggy beef Wellington in a culinary homage to the diverse ancestry of Texans. Did I mention they sold beer there? The four-dollar drafts served in plastic cups made even the best of fans forget that they had left their heroes to fend for themselves and chose the comfort of bad beef Wellington and alcohol over the honor of staying to the bitter end of a 63–14 blowout and singing "The Eyes of Texas" while enduring the taunts of the thousands of mutant trailer-dwelling redneck invaders on the opposite end of the stadium. Being the good bus host that I was, I encouraged myself to sleep it off and not bother my fellow passengers. We arrived home past midnight and I took the short walk to my condo, where Truman gave me the canine version of my mother's "where have you been?" look from high school. I mercifully let the Brittany out to pee and chase night birds. Has my life as a fan come to this? A drunk divorced dad walking his dog in the middle of the night while pondering the worst collapse in Texas history?

It was obvious that Texas had hired the wrong savior. Mack Brown could recruit lights out, and he was a refreshing change from the pompous Mackovic, but Oklahoma's young genius, Bob Stoops, brought energy and fire and his blood ran cold. Stoops hated Texas with the passion we deserved. Mack Brown didn't hate anyone. Stoops spoke with the clipped tones of a confident football coach. Mack had an easy drawl that made you wonder if he was about to offer you a glass of iced tea. Stoops took every perceived slight personally and stoked his team's hatred until their eyes bulged and they foamed at the mouth. Mack kept an even keel and took things in stride as he occasionally joked with the press. Stoops leveraged the victory in the Cotton Bowl into an unparalleled streak of success that culminated in the hated Sooners winning the 2000 national title behind perhaps the finest defense college football had ever seen. This was supposed to be *our* national title season, not the black tale of the forces of evil reaching the summit that the Cult of 1969 only dreamed about. There was only one explanation for this.

Bob Stoops was the Devil.

"Right, Adam, Satan is coaching football at the University of Oklahoma."

Tracking Truman's movements in the darkness of the park, I had not noticed God's presence.

"He's not?"

"Go to bed. And pray for something other than your own selfish fulfillment. Your life can't be about you. It certainly can't be about chasing down the Antichrist as a recreation. It's blasphemous and offensive."

Eventually, my life wasn't just about me and I put aside my resentments and started anew. The Longhorns finished a respectable twelfth in 2000, but the die was cast. The Oklahoma Sooners owned Texas and would block their path to greatness at every turn. I moved out from under the shadow of Royal-Memorial Stadium and found peace in a small

Erin Florence and a new life to come. *(Jones Family)*

house in East Austin and with a girl from East Texas who would change my life. Erin Florence was warm and kind, beautiful of body and spirit. Being a Vanderbilt grad, she understood the big-time football of the rugged Southeastern Conference, but cheering for its worst team left her football allegiances easily swayable to a more hopeful cause. Her agreeing that we should buy Longhorn season tickets together shocked her girlfriends and left me with no choice but to ask her to marry me. She said yes on a perfect Austin night on my back deck. Truman served as a witness. My life wasn't about me anymore, and it didn't even have to be about the Texas Longhorns. Good thing, because college football wouldn't be the most important part of my life when the 2001 season began. And God knows I would miss it.

Part 2

LOSS, AND HOPE

7

ST. GEORGE AND THE MENNONITES

Texas vs. the University of South Carolina

COLLEGE WORLD SERIES CHAMPIONSHIP GAME, ROSENBLATT STADIUM, OMAHA, NEBRASKA, JUNE 22, 2002

We had called Mom in October to tell her that my marriage proposal had been accepted, two weeks after Erin sat through the 2001 Texas-OU game with me, giving her a full tour of the depths of my insanity as Oklahoma ground out a 14–3 win and I ground through a full distillate of colorful language and tequila. Like Reba Killian, Erin was a competitor who was unafraid of my passion for college football, even on days when I was an exceptionally poor sport. She understood loyalty to a cause, which was no accident, given that half her family was made up of Nebraska Cornhusker fans.

A few weeks after our engagement, God had blessed me with appendicitis. Blessed, not because I enjoyed being cut open to relieve pain approximating being beaten repeatedly in the stomach by a baseball bat, but because Mom and Dad came through Austin to see me on their way to a medical convention in Houston and spent a full day with Erin while I recuperated. It was the last day I remember my mother firing on all cylinders, and it was a gracious gift. By the time we saw Mom at Thanksgiving, I pretended not to notice that my mother was starting to seem a little bit smaller, just like Bulldog Jones did many years before.

My parents made the extraordinary gesture of driving eight hours from Amarillo to Longview, in East Texas, to spend Thanksgiving with me and Erin's family. There was no way I could have known at the time that my mother had terminal cancer. She certainly didn't tell anyone who was there and, even in private, my father told me that they had not received any test results. I didn't believe this, but I pretended to and tried my best not to look for hints of Mom's illness. Did she shine just as brightly as she always had? Did she look a little tired? Something was missing, but she was a masterful poker player, never giving me the satisfaction of a tell. Faced with the most devastating news of her life, somehow my mother made this holiday all about me. Being a parent, I guess I understood this, but I didn't let myself explore it. This celebration was hugely important to her, and I had no intention of bringing my own sadness and fear to the party. We thoroughly enjoyed a 21–7 victory over Texas A&M the day after Thanksgiving, and it didn't cross my mind that Mom and I would never again watch a game together. God hid this realization from me, an act of divine grace perhaps.

When Mom told me over the phone that she had cancer, Thanksgiving was a dim memory. I wanted to climb through the phone or get on a plane or get in my car—anything to let her know that I would never leave her. She told me instead to take care of my own family. My parents were always very clear. When I had become an adult, they let me know that I didn't owe them anything and they didn't owe me anything. The agreement was a present that should be given to all children; it leaves no room for past recriminations and puts you in complete control of your own future. But I never could quite believe it. I owed her everything.

I finally saw her again two weeks later as I pulled into the driveway in Amarillo for the Christmas holidays. My mom shuffled out to the car

with her arms outstretched. She lived her whole life with her arms outstretched, no reason to stop now. Her hands touched Zach first and then
embraced Erin. She finally got to me as I walked around from the driver's
side and into the house to celebrate Christmas in her house. The house
smelled like home, a mixture of Christmas pine, the morning coffee, and
the slight aftersmell of the Amway cleaner that Mom had bought in bulk
for years. The house did not smell like cancer; the Devil was confined to
the corner of the garage and not allowed in this house, for this was a joyful time. For one December afternoon, everything was right with the
world. I never did explain the candle of hope to Zachary, even though
my mom had asked me to do so. I just wasn't that good of a father. I did
know—theoretically anyway—that no matter how dire the circumstance,
the world would be good again; that was God's promise. The intervening
weeks had given me time to try and sort out my mother's inevitable
death. But I hadn't come to the point of faith at which one is certain that

Zach, Mom, and the smile her grandkids always brought. *(Jones Family)*

death does not constitute a final victory over God's people. Some day, perhaps when I understood it and believed it myself, I would explain this to Zach.

Mom sat in the corner of the living room and watched her grandchildren gather in her house. The early winter sunshine through the windows reflected Mom's old glow: the smile that guided my father through life. She looked like she hadn't a care in the world and would relish every moment of her last Christmas.

Texas, true to its nature, had blown a perfectly good shot at the national title in the fall of 2001. Mack had finally chosen Chris Simms over Major Applewhite, which didn't sit well with some of the faithful, but the sin was largely forgiven because Texas was flat loaded. After the 14–3 loss to Oklahoma, the Longhorns slowly worked their way back into contention by mounting an impassioned winning streak. They were ranked ninth when Erin said yes to my wedding proposal and made it to number seven when appendicitis hit. We celebrated the Thanksgiving holidays with the Longhorns ranked fifth. When Mom called me with her terrible news, the Longhorns had climbed to third. A few days later the Longhorns teed it up for a night game against Colorado in the Big 12 Championship Game; second-ranked Florida had been upset and a spot opposite the Miami Hurricanes in the national title game was there for the taking. Texas could disband the Cult of 1969 and redeem the disastrous 1991 Cotton Bowl loss against the nemesis Hurricanes; I could bear any sorrow under that circumstance. The emotional heft of Mom's news would lighten: Wasn't joy allowed to play on the same field as sadness? Wasn't college football a fair counterweight to news that lay like a suffocating boulder on my chest?

Chris Simms obviously believed in the healing power of college football. Moments after the championship game kicked off, the Golden Boy had the Colorado Buffaloes right where he wanted them. He drilled a pass to Roy Williams for 21 yards and followed up with Sloan Thomas for 45 more. All-Conference tailback Cedric Benson powered in from the five and it was Texas 7, Colorado 0. Texas had already slammed Colorado 41–7 during the regular season and tonight would be more of the same. Texas held the Buffaloes to a three and out. Simms drilled another 27-yarder to Williams, but the drive stalled. No matter, the Texas defense got the ball back again and Benson got loose for 24 yards to the Colorado 23.

Then time simply stopped. God came to the conclusion that my lack of emotional maturity could not handle such good fortune. The Old Man dialed up the Job package. Floating down from the heavens came a message delivered through the mortal left arm of Chris Simms right into the arms of Aaron Killion—the name couldn't have been a coincidence—a CU linebacker who returned the leather prize 73 yards to the Texas 12. Colorado cashed in to forge a 7–7 tie at the end of the first quarter as the collective blood pressure in the city of Austin slowly rose.

God wasn't finished. Simms threw his next pick one minute into the second quarter and fumbled the ball two possessions later. For an encore he threw his third interception, which Colorado simply returned 64 yards for a touchdown, saving their offense the inconvenience of taking the field. With Colorado in complete control with a 29–10 lead, Brown finally inserted Major Applewhite, who calmly hit flanker B. J. Johnson for a 79-yard touchdown and taunted the Buffalo sideline on his way down the field. The script called for an Applewhite comeback, but the crafty senior didn't quite deliver. It wasn't Applewhite's fault; Mack Brown had violated the Texas scrappy quarterback tradition by trusting the Texas fortunes to a blue-chip Golden Boy from New Jersey. Colorado held on, 39–37. Two points. Haunted by two points.

I thought of those two points at the family breakfast table on our first morning back in Amarillo for the holidays. The game had been over for two weeks, but I was still bitter. My mother broke into my thoughts with an astonishing statement.

"Tough break for the Horns."

I looked up from the paper at my family's kitchen table. Did my mother just say that to start a conversation? Why wouldn't she? We had always talked about the Horns before during the holidays and I knew exactly what she meant.

"Yeah. Disappointing."

"Something's not right with Simms. He's a bit of a flake, isn't he?"

She had watched the game. Right in the middle of the biggest crisis in her life, of doctors and diagnoses and the pain of chemotherapy, she had watched the Big 12 Championship Game. I was incredulous, but I knew she had seen it because "flake" was a term of art for her; it was how she described the undependable, either on the playing field or in real life. She didn't throw it around lightly, not without doing her homework.

I laughed. "I don't know about flake, but he sure as hell can't look past his primary receiver."

"No, but Applewhite can. I love Applewhite."

Of course you do. The scrappy gamer. You always loved the Applewhites of the world; you were one of them. For a moment it was 1974 and a mom was teaching her seven-year-old the basics of football strategy at Kimbrough Memorial Stadium. This was a moment I would never get back. I could only pass it on.

The next morning, I awoke to the sound of my father slowly moving down the hall with Mom. She had almost disappeared into the spacious tent of his winter coat. They were on their way to the car.

"Your mom is confused. I'll call you from the hospital."

Confused was not a diagnosis I had expected from a medical school graduate, but it sufficed. The toxins in Mom's body were wreaking havoc on her brain and destroying her spirit. She didn't know where she was or who she was or why. Had I just seen her last lucid moment? I left my own sleeping child with Erin, filled the Jones family thermos with fresh coffee, and followed Dad.

As a child, I knew this place as High Plains Baptist Hospital, but the huge facade now read Baptist St. Anthony's, a hybrid name formed out of a corporate merger. This seemed peculiar. Half the Baptists I knew thought the Catholics were going to hell, but I guess corporate health care profitability knows no prejudice. Bundling up against the Panhandle winter, I remembered making rounds with my father as a very young child, waiting in the hall as passing nurses smiled at me and touched me on the head while Dad was in a patient's room. Some of the nurses looked familiar to me as they directed me to the intensive care unit, where I found my mom comfortably resting. She looked fine, but she wasn't. Her doctor eventually admitted her to a room up on the sixth floor where she spent Christmas Eve and most of Christmas Day. This brought back memories of my last days with Audrey during the Christmas of 1983. But Audrey was an old woman, wasn't she? Mom was just seventy. It never occurred to me that Mom was an old woman, too, and she had a bad heart that wouldn't win this battle with the invading armies of cancerous cells. Her indomitable spirit was losing a contest with her brittle body.

The holiday season didn't get any better as news came on the morning of Christmas Eve that Erin's grandmother had died during the night on the plains of Nebraska. Grandma Hare couldn't quite make it to the New Year to watch her beloved Cornhuskers play for the national title. Perhaps God didn't want her to see the beating the Miami Hurricanes would put upon them that night. I didn't really know. Erin spent Christmas Day with us and then we woke up in the darkness of the twenty-sixth and took a drive to the airport for my new wife to board a plane to Dallas and eventually Omaha. Saying goodbye seemed to be this year's holiday theme.

Alone in my parents' den, a place I previously associated with loud conversation and children and Christmas toys scattered strategically to impale the heel of any adult who didn't tread carefully in the darkness, I said goodbye to Major Applewhite's career. Texas was in San Diego for the Holiday Bowl against the University of Washington, a far cry from playing for the national championship, but at least they kept me company in my parents' empty house. The mocking continued as the Washington

Huskies did not realize that I was having a really lousy Christmas holiday, nor did they realize that Texas was favored by thirteen. Neither did Applewhite, who threw a couple of early interceptions, including one that Washington returned for a touchdown. Chris Simms couldn't have done it better. Texas trailed 36–17 late in the third quarter. Then Major summoned his last bit of magic. After all, he was always the kid who got the most out of his talent, wasn't he? God and I watched Applewhite go on a ridiculous tear as Texas scored four straight touchdowns to close out an unlikely 47–43 victory.

It was after midnight when I rose from my mom's chair and passed through the kitchen on my way to bed. The family Advent wreath sat on the table. The first candle, Hope, is always a molten mess by the end of the Christmas season since it gets lit on every Sunday during the month. Hope needs to endure; there's a danger that God's people will use it all up. On this night Hope was barely a wax nub clinging to the sides of Mom's old pewter candleholder. But Hope always hangs on, perhaps because it sits next to the second candle, Love. If you light Hope and Love, then Joy appears. Peace follows.

Hope, Love, Joy, Peace. A child sits in the middle of the wreath protected from the cold. On one magical night, Peace lights the child's candle. And that candle lights the world. I thought about candles in the darkness of the kitchen. These candles represented a life . . . *and in that life was the light of men. The light shines in the darkness, and the darkness has not overcome it.* This is what I believed. *And the Word became flesh and dwelt among us, full of grace and truth.* Finally, remembering what I believed, I said goodbye to the bittersweet Christmas of 2001.

Elke was the bartender at the Lone Star Brew Pub at Love Field in Dallas. She always asked me for my ID when I settled into one of the middle stools, which amused me almost as much as trying to figure out why they called this airport watering hole a brew pub when no beer was actually brewed here. Nevertheless, this was my way station between Austin and

Mom and Dad. *(Jones Family)*

Amarillo during the spring of 2002. My new life was in Austin and I was responsible to the people there. But I wasn't done with my old life in Amarillo; I wasn't ready to let Mom go. So I lived an entire spring back and forth, with Love Field the neutral ground in between. From high-tech Austin to corporate Dallas the plane was always packed with MBA mercenaries with laptops humming, many of whom were on a first-name basis with Elke. Connecting in Dallas to go to Amarillo finds you on a half-empty plane with a collection of salesmen and families, often older folks who need to be picked up at the airport and taken to their families in one of the small communities of the Panhandle. Southwest Airlines kept a lot of Texas families together, including mine. In my home city, I was planning a wedding and in my hometown a funeral. This emotional compartmentalization doesn't work, going from melancholy to bliss and back again. However, being a committed college football fan is a better training ground for this existence than therapy. A pity there's nothing to be contested in the spring. The Longhorns were terrific in the off season; Mack was pretty much finished with his rebuilding project and sixteen of the twenty-two guys slated to start in 2002 were NFL-caliber players. The best season is always next season. Problem was, Mom was out of seasons. She wouldn't be part of my life the next time Texas took the field, or when the lights came back on at Kimbrough.

Sometimes I would see Mom at home, where Dad would take care of her, and I would catch little glimpses of who she used to be. One night we watched the Tony Awards, of all things. Mom loved musicals and a particularly offensive one called *Urinetown* won top honors that night. This made her smile; I could see the corner of her mouth turned up on her left profile. I hardly needed a camera to capture such a moment and I very much needed to remember it so that I could hide it away in my mind's eye and bring it out later and show it to the grandsons she would never meet. Her Baptist upbringing instilled in her both a strong faith, which was the goal of the Southern Baptist Convention, and a longing for irreverence, which the church fathers had little use for. Eventually, Mom had little use for the Southern Baptist Convention; she told me once that the problem with fundamentalists was that they often told us what God wanted without actually consulting God on the matter. In times of cultural warfare, a scripture-quoting art curator was the hypocrites' worst nightmare.

As the spring progressed, Mom was more likely to be in the hospital when I went home to Amarillo. She seemed to diminish a bit with each trip I took during March and April. One afternoon, as I sat by her bedside, she started to slowly disappear into the covers and the gray light of afternoon in her antiseptic quarters. Conversation stopped and I became afraid that she was going to ease on out and join Bulldog, finding his company more interesting than my own. Then my niece Elizabeth arrived with her notebook from a senior trip to Florence. Mom sat straight up and the glow returned. She left cancer behind and went on her own vicarious trip to Florence with her granddaughter sitting at the edge of the bed. They went through every page, every note, every drawing.

Each page of the worn-out spiral brought a new expression, and I saved them all, not knowing if I would ever see Mom's face the same way again. Can someone get a day of their life back? Can you reach out and find that special place you used to occupy before your body and mind began to fail you? Through a battered spiral brought back from across the Atlantic, Elizabeth had helped Mom find that place, if only for a moment. For that act of kindness, I will always remember my niece.

My mother showed her resilience by making it through my May wedding. As I heard the strains of "Joyful, Joyful, We Adore Thee" while waiting in the wings, I knew that this was when my parents were supposed to be seated. But they were safely in the living room in Amarillo. Mom couldn't travel, but somehow Beethoven's "Ode to Joy" must have reached her. I could picture her smiling down the center aisle to the same chorus during Bulldog's funeral. This was her theme song, and I couldn't help but think that it would be played at a summer funeral and then it would be my job to smile.

Upon my return from an Australian honeymoon, that funeral was drawing near, and Southwest Airlines took me home one last time.

"Are you afraid?" I asked her as she sat in her chair.

"No." She looked puzzled and let out a surprising laugh, as if I had asked her an obvious question and she couldn't believe my lack of understanding. Reba Jones did not fear death, for it held no final victory over God's people.

"You were the best mother anyone could have had."

She laughed. "No, I wasn't. I didn't have to be."

That was not an answer I expected, but I should have. She needed me to know that I was hardly the kind of person who required some superhuman mothering effort—to know that I didn't really need her, which was something I was not prepared to believe.

"I never did learn to live in the moment, not the way you did."

"You're wrong. You do just fine in the moment . . ."

Her voiced trailed off. We embraced and wept, and I felt as though she would break. That was the last conversation I had with the woman who taught me how to love unconditionally, to live in the moment, to be passionate. To be a true fan. Now all I had to do was to live up to it.

All of the Jones kids gathered around a hospice bed two weeks later. We were all together one last time; I think Mom knew we were there. She died on June 20, 2002. Her life had been quite a ride.

The Boxwell Brothers ran the biggest funeral home in Amarillo. How could they not? This unintentional joke never failed to amuse me, even when I was going to my own mother's funeral. Erin and I slipped in and found Mom in one of the side rooms. The flowers swallowed her up, spilling out into the hall. She was in a plain pine coffin, exactly what she would have wanted to return her body to the Panhandle soil. The only sign of pretension was her favorite necklace, a long chain with a gold medallion that sat on her chest revealing the face of a long-dead British monarch. The Boxwells couldn't have known that this old king was not why she loved this piece of jewelry. I flipped the coin over to the side Mom always favored: a brilliant engraving of Saint George the Dragon Slayer in full fight. George had shoulders squared and his lance pierced the awful beast cleanly. He bore a warrior's confident look. Fearless. Passionate. That's who Mom was. I set Saint George gently back on her chest and walked away, taking the hand of the next great woman in my life.

Erin and I went to Hummer's, a sports bar in which I wasted lots of time as a young man. The Texas baseball team was matched up with South Carolina in the final game of the College World Series. For some reason, probably no more than a hunch, Longhorn coach Augie Garrido inserted little-used outfielder Chris Carmichael into the starting lineup for the biggest game of the season. Carmichael was well liked by the faithful, a fleet and slick-fielding outfielder without much of a bat. This did not stop him, on the biggest stage of his life, from rocketing a three-run homer in the fifth inning to break the game open for the Longhorns. Mom would have loved Chris Carmichael. Texas won its fifth national championship in baseball, two ahead of the football team, and while it was the wrong national championship, I would take it. Deep sorrow, overwhelming joy, all in the same day. It's really one hell of a life, isn't it? I did manage a smile as I entered Westminster Presbyterian for the funeral two days later. I simply thought of Chris Carmichael. And of Saint George, settled silently on Mom's breathless lungs, protecting her and guiding her on her way to a better place.

After the funeral, friends converged on my father's house and each of the Jones children accepted them by staking out a special seating section. My brother Sam and I chose the metal patio table on the back porch, which was somewhat unstable, especially into the evening when the Shiner Bock bottles began to stack up. Any nudge from a leg or an elbow was like pulling the wrong block in a Jenga game and would send a couple of empty bottles over the side, which in our highly stressed state resulted in hysterical laughter. Eventually, my friends dispersed and I took refuge inside. Stumbling into the den, I found it full of Mennonites. The Mennonites were peaceful and loving people. They always appeared during times of trouble and disaster and they never left anyone in need. They were loyal and decent and had the perfect emotional makeup to be great college football fans, except most of them were pacifists. Dad had been the medical director of a Mennonite psychiatric hospital in Kansas, and the people there had become his corps of lifelong friends, particularly a gregarious chaplain named Bob Carlson, who had a personality not unlike my mother. Dad, Uncle Marshall, and the Mennonites were drinking ouzo and Drambuie and laughing out loud in the den, telling story after story. I politely declined their invitation and ended up in the laundry room with Erin and my sister, Molly. Molly sat on the red Coleman cooler filling in the details of Mom's life to her new sister-in-law. The details were interrupted by a sweet sound emanating from the living room, a cappella voices. We all stopped and let them carry us.

What a fellowship, what a joy divine,
Leaning on the everlasting arms,

Reba Killian Jones (1931–2002). *(Jones Family)*

Marshall and the Mennonites were singing in perfect four-part harmony.

What a blessedness, what a peace is mine,

Dad joined in, my brother Sam gently singing into his ear to keep him on key, just as he did at every Christmas Eve service. True to their faith, the Mennonites were both singing with my father and to my father. I had no choice but to join in, for, as the Mennonites sang, what did I have to dread? For what did I have to fear?

Leaning on the everlasting arms.

Looking across the living room, I saw my father's smile. I knew this smile well. It was Mom.

8

MY SEASON HAS ARRIVED

Texas vs. Oklahoma

THE COTTON BOWL,
DALLAS, TEXAS, OCTOBER 12, 2002

God gave me a sign through the U.S. mail. Chris Simms's confident face looked up at me when I tore the plastic mail cover off the August edition of *Texas Monthly*. Dallas Cowboy legends Roger Staubach and Troy Aikman flanked him, trying desperately to confer their own greatness on the fair-haired boy standing between them. The tagline underneath was both trite and profound:

WHY UT WILL HOOK A NATIONAL CHAMPIONSHIP

Why? Because God owed it to me. That's why. I hadn't forgotten my conversation with God on the day of Mom's phone call. God had chosen to answer that prayer with a series of Chris Simms interceptions. But my resentment eventually faded. I was past that disappointment and ready to trust that he worked in mysterious ways (God, not Chris Simms). Now God had delivered to me a sign that 2002 would be the year of Texas redemption. This was not the only sign during the summer of 2002; it didn't escape me that the most valuable player for Texas during the College World Series was relief pitcher Huston Street, whose father James had quarterbacked the last national football championship team and was a revered figure to the Cult of 1969, his picture prominently featured on the smoke-stained walls of Bert's Barbecue. This was all coming together; as the *Texas Monthly* article noted, all the pieces were assembled. Mack Brown's recruiting genius brought together stars like Cedric Benson, Roy Williams, and a nasty offensive line to operate behind. On defense, linebacker Derrick Johnson was a killer, and he played behind future NFL defensive linemen like Cory Redding and Marcus Tubbs. Superathlete Nathan Vasher patrolled the secondary, and he was joined by a freshman wunderkind named Michael Huff. Most importantly, Simms would no longer look over his shoulder and see the specter of Major Applewhite. He would now meet his destiny as an All-American quarterback of the 2002 National Champs.

This foreknowledge of the season to come did not stop me from praying, of course. Christian prayer follows a very standard course. Protestants usually progress from praise to thanksgiving and then to forgiveness. From forgiveness comes intercession—the prayers for the people in your life who need God's help. After Mom died, I skipped through most of these constructs and went for grace and strength, interceding on my own behalf. Before long, I skipped this entirely and went straight to "What's in it for me?" That's not purely a Christian concept, but I bought the philosophical argument that without great sorrow there can be no great joy. Great joy meant watching a bunch of college kids I had never met with TEXAS printed across their jerseys going nuts on a football field in celebration of a national championship. My prayers for strength and grace turned into "Come on man, just once . . . just once can't my guys win the lousy title?" The answer was yes. The time had come.

The voters in the AP poll didn't fully believe *Texas Monthly*. Although thirteen of them—men of courage and integrity—did give Texas first-place votes. This wasn't enough to overcome Miami, who held down the top spot. Nor was it enough to get the second spot, the sulfurous domain of Bob Stoops the Antichrist and his band of violent thugs known as the Oklahoma Sooners. Texas opened the season in third place, and Erin, Zach, and I crammed into Darrell K. Royal–Texas Memorial Stadium—thankfully now shortened to "DKR" among the faithful—for the debut.

Mack Brown hadn't just assembled great talent; he had changed the entire culture of Longhorn football. Where John Mackovic seemed either intimidated by or uninterested in Texas tradition, Brown embraced the past. Old lettermen were welcomed back after being persona non grata in the Mackovic years. Darrell Royal was seen on the practice field for the first time in years. Coach Royal was never really Mackovic's cup of tea, but it was obvious Saint Darrell liked and respected Brown. There wasn't a high school coach in Texas Mack wouldn't happily make time for. This network of football men was the lifeblood of recruiting, and they welcomed Mack with open arms. Brown came by it honestly; his grandfather and father were both legendary high school coaches in their native Tennessee. This familial understanding of the high school game and the relationships Mack built with coaches, players, and mothers—mommas loved Mack—brought great players to Texas, which in turn made Texas a winner again. Mack was doing his part, but he asked much of the fans in return. For starters, show up to the damn game on time. Texas fans were notorious late arrivals with a lackadaisical attitude among far too many old alums and students alike that didn't befit such a great tradition. COME EARLY, BE LOUD, STAY LATE, WEAR BURNT ORANGE WITH PRIDE. It was the least we could do, and the university, which in its proud history has never missed an opportunity to turn a financial profit, made a killing selling thousands of T-shirts with these simple instructions.

We did our part; even the wearing of the burnt orange, which was not an easy sell among the fashion-conscious Texas women. Everyone arrived on time, and while drinking still maintained its grip on Austin culture, it was now a recreational diversion, clearly second to the events

Partners in crime—coming early, staying late . . . *(Jones Family)*

on the field. Mack and his talented charges started a new era for the culture of Texas football.

To keep Mack happy and enable his full evangelical zeal to corral the
best prep talent in the nation for the Texas cause, the regents had no
choice but to expand the stadium to well over 80,000 seats. This building project marked the demise of the running track. The quarter-mile
oval had been a thorn in my side since I was a freshman, and getting rid
of the unnecessary barrier made everyone a better fan. The 80,000-plus
throng now sat right up against the edge of the gridiron, woven of sublime prescription athletic turf sodded carefully over a million-dollar
drainage system. True to form, to replace the track, the university's
deep-pocketed alums simply erected a stadium across the street to keep
their revered Texas Relays. Problem solved.

Texas ripped North Texas 27–0 to begin the 2002 season, and many
fans complained that it wasn't enough. The sluggish Texas offense took

the criticism in stride and bombed North Carolina 52–21, then continued to score almost at will right up to the October 12 showdown with
the Sooners. As Coach Royal used to say, all the games leading up to the
Oklahoma game are only so much clearing of the throat. The Longhorns
needed to prove their worth to the college football world, and they could
only do that in Dallas. With any luck my marriage would survive this as
Erin and I traveled together for our first game at the Cotton Bowl. She
had watched this game on television with me, which was bad enough,
but it was nothing compared to being crammed into the House that
Doak Built with the boisterous and sweat-soaked rabble of short-fused
and volatile Longhorn fans. These were my people, who would bleed
burnt orange if pricked. The Orangebloods were desperate for a win.

The best of spousal instincts drives one to purchase a gift in this circumstance. My wife had brought me through a terrible summer, not at
all fair for a pair of happy newlyweds. The anniversary of our engagement was upon us, and I needed to go all out. Nothing short of Neiman-
Marcus would suffice. I ventured to the epicenter of chic Dallas style and
refinement.

"Sir, what is your fragrance?"

This is what happens when you loiter in Neiman-Marcus for too long.
The beautiful people assume you are in the camp of men with "fra-
grances." My wristwatch was likely worth much less than anything behind the "fragrance" counter and I knew damn well nobody at Blackburn's
in downtown Amarillo ever asked Bulldog Jones about his fragrance.

The young Neimanite didn't wait for an answer. Two quick sprays
front and back of a small card and he handed me Acqua di Parma.

"Tuscan cypress," he explained with an affected half British Empire–
half American prep school intonation. "I'm very pleased to offer you this
Neiman-Marcus exclusive with our compliments."

Erin's gift was a lost cause, but it was some small consolation that I
now smelled like a tree in Tuscany. What a vastly different world than
the Cotton Bowl. Surveying the faces as the escalator descended, I wondered how many of them I would see twenty-four hours from now. Quite

a few, probably. In my fantasy life, the Texas stadium cheer broke out right in the heart of extravagance central.

Expensively coiffed Dallas ladies meeting for lunch: *"Texas."*

Salesmen of indeterminate sexual preference in $2,000 suits: *"Fight!!!!!!!"*

Small army of security guards patrolling the sales floor: *"Texas!"*

Makeover experts in black smocks: *"Fight!!!!!!!"*

"Texas."

"Fight!!!!!"

The roar can be heard all the way to Tiffany's, Brooks Brothers, and Lord and Taylor as the mall shakes with noise. To escape this land of gourmet biscotti tins and $200 ties one needed the company of loud-mouthed redneck football fans, Fletcher's corn dogs and funnel cake, frito pie and enough beer to drown a cat, the sweet smell of freshly scrubbed Greek couples and their rocket-fueled Coca-Colas, maybe even a fistfight in the stands.

The magic was still in that old place when Erin and I emerged from the Cotton Bowl tunnel the next day. The ticket distribution brilliantly divides red from orange right down the middle—not lengthwise, the way polite bowl games are conducted with alums and students sitting behind their own benches and the stragglers mixing together in the end zones, but cut horizontally so that students mix at the fifties on one side and alums on the other. Hostile fans behind both benches and an uneasy peace in the middle. Redemption was in the air and the sound of "Texas Fight" was the clarion call to arms. The school fight song evolved over the years in honor of today's hated opponent. The shouted rally in the middle of "Texas Fight" as written was:

> *Hail, hail, the gang's all here,*
> *And it's goodbye to all the rest . . .*

Texas fans did away with this cornball nonsense early in the school's history and replaced it with:

Give 'em hell, give 'em hell,
Go, Horns, Go!

Texas undergrads quickly vulgarized these lyrics to:

Give 'em hell, give 'em hell,
Make 'em eat shit . . .

But during Oklahoma week all Texans band together in the spirit of the alma mater. Faculty and students, grandmothers and small children, even clergy render the fight song like this:

Give 'em hell, give 'em hell,
OU SUCKS!

The last punctuated syllable rolls like thunder through the bowl of the stadium as the Longhorns emerge from the dressing room. The players enter the field from a single opening in the Cotton Bowl that cuts through the Oklahoma end of the stadium. Texas players are mercilessly taunted and booed as they assemble and break through to daylight, but at midfield the boos turn to cheers and the Longhorns are lifted up by the faithful. The time had come to reverse Texas fortunes, wad up the failures of the past, and shove them right up Bob Stoops's ass. This was *my* season.

Texas knew this. God must have reminded them. Simms quickly lofted a rainbow to Roy Williams for 44 yards to the Sooner one. The Golden Boy himself dived over for the score, and it was seven-zip, Horns. The Texas defense would give nothing to the Sooners and their much-maligned and mistake-prone quarterback, Nate Hybl. Right on cue, Hybl threw a pick to Texas safety Dakarai Pearson. Simms tried to make them pay for the turnover by going long again, this time to an open B. J. Johnson. Texas's chance to break it wide open ended on a brilliant diving interception by Andre Woolfolk, the Sooner cornerback. Damn.

Simms would throw another pick a few possessions later, causing me to breathe a heavy sigh and to talk myself into being satisfied with a 7–3 halftime lead. Then God really intervened. Hybl lofted a ball deep to his left. The Longhorn corner, senior Rod Babers, was on the case, but this one looked like it would fall harmlessly out of bounds. Babers closed. This was going to be one more notch on the passes broken-up column or, if the receiver wasn't living right, Babers might just knock the poor bastard into next week as a reminder for next time. Babers was an exceptional cover corner—bold, fast, hard-hitting, disciplined. You didn't complete many to his side of the field. His hands, however, were less than praiseworthy. Truth be told, Babers couldn't catch ants with sugar water.

Damned if stone-handed Rod Babers didn't pluck the ball right out of the air. Then he turned on the jets the other way. And it was 14–3, Texas.

At that moment, Texas had not only won the game, but there was no doubt that the Horns would be national champs. My long wait was over. I bounced up and down, crushing Erin with the one arm I had around her. The other arm extended to the heavens in a salute to the only person who could possibly have made Babers catch the ball. These emotions were unconfinable. Then Antwone Savage screwed it all up. The OU kick returner torched the typically reliable Texas kickoff team for 81 yards. OU would set up shop inside the Texas 15. In my fantasy life, Savage fumbled the kickoff and Texas went to the locker room up 21–3. Instead, OU would be no worse than 14–6. But I certainly did not account for my heroes being drawn offside on a fourth and three. The mistake would lead to an OU touchdown. Don't even ask about the two-point conversion. The Texas lead was down to 14–11.

Oklahoma squibbed the ensuing kickoff and Texas took over at midfield with one last chance at redemption. Then Mack Brown up and did it. He sent his star quarterback into the game accompanied by his gifted receiving corps. And Chris Simms promptly kneeled on the ball. At that moment, Brown convinced me that he could not be trusted. In the span of a mere two minutes on the game clock, my blood coursed the long distance from an answered prayer to a dream deferred and returned to a heart grown cold. Brown later claimed that he chose not to let the conference's strongest quarterback take a shot at the end zone with the conference's most physical set of receivers to "maintain momentum" going into the half. Horseshit. One could count on one hand the number in attendance who believed Texas had any momentum at all with a 14–11 lead. What you could find were plenty of takers convinced that Brown had exhibited very publicly that he had no confidence in his own guys. Our guys. Bob Stoops, on the other hand, played to win. Stoops owned Mack Brown. Satan owned the 2002 college football season.

The third quarter was notable mostly for Hybl's inept quarterback play and Simms and the Texas offense failing again and again to convert on third down. Texas still had a 17–14 lead going into the fourth, but Erin and I possessed zero confidence. The Texas defense finally broke under the strain. The Oklahoma ground game dominated as tailback Quentin Griffin started to pick his spots on the delayed draw like Dom DeLuise at a half-price deli. Oklahoma 35, Texas 24.

Margaritas and guacamole at the Blue Goose on Greenville Avenue salved our wounds somewhat. Greenville Avenue in Dallas stretches out across the city in an endless oasis drowning sorrow and fueling celebration. The Blue Goose housed a largely Texas crowd, and that was fine with me. By margarita number three my faith in God had been restored. I reminded myself that as recently as last year Texas had a shot at the title despite an early season lost. Yes, that's it. This is a part of the test, God subjecting my faith to a healthy strain to see if I will break, just like he did with the Israelites. Texas can still win out. All may not be lost.

Erin didn't buy any of this. As the night wore on, her criticism and corresponding disgust at the Texas offensive game plan grew more pointed. In true Reba Jones fashion she reconstructed a series of ineffective short passes from the third quarter. Tired of rational explanation, she just sort of let her point trail off and die, shaking her head halfheart-edly. "I mean, what's Mack thinking? . . . The second half was just"—words escaped her—"just . . . just . . . bullshit." She exhaled.

This made me smile. I guessed that somewhere up in heaven it made Bulldog smile as well. My grandfather knew that the right woman was in my life, no doubt about it.

We should have drawn more enjoyment from the postgame margari-tas, for they were the last we would enjoy that season. A few weeks after the Oklahoma game, a blue stripe on the drugstore test strip indicated that our lives would move ever onward with or without the Texas Long-horns. This would be the first of two grandsons my mother would never meet. This one had a shot at being born into a world where the Texas Longhorns were national champs. We had an arduous road ahead, start-ing with a road trip to Kansas State the next Saturday. The Wildcats were very good and the conditions would be miserably cold. Texas had fallen only to eighth in the national polls and we would have a full six days for Mack Brown to grow a pair.

Or was I hoping against hope? Only God knew.

9

FRIGID NIGHTS AND AN UNLIKELY HERO

Texas vs. the University of Nebraska

MEMORIAL STADIUM, LINCOLN, NEBRASKA, NOVEMBER 2, 2002

My grandfather made sure that there would always be a place for his grandchildren—and all of the neighborhood kids, for that matter—to play football. He ensured this by purchasing an entire block in Canyon on which to build the family home. Divided into four sections facing Fifth Avenue, Grandad used the middle two parcels to build his house, complete with a full shop and a garage in the back. Then he added a two-story fort for his grandkids, along with a tree house, a playhouse, and my uncle Frank's old trailer. It was a sprawling place that could be endlessly explored. The two outside lots were left vacant because Bulldog didn't really like to be hemmed in. Eventually he sold one of the lots to his friend Gus Miller, the Buffalo basketball coach. The other one was left empty purely to accommodate the games of childhood. We would play touch football there regardless of the weather. It wasn't exactly pristine grass. If you didn't stay on your feet, you spent the next thirty minutes of your day pulling burrs and stickers out of your jeans and shirtsleeves, but it was wide and treeless and all ours. Some days during the holidays, we would bundle up and play right through a norther, the wicked Panhandle cold fronts that could drop the temperature thirty degrees in a matter of minutes. Chilled to the bone at game's end, we would return to Audrey's kitchen and be force-fed hot chocolate and sweets. Then we would repair to the den and watch football on television, safely protected from the elements.

My childhood at Kimbrough also saw a lot of cold fronts, which came without the comfort of Audrey's kitchen and a warm den. The family would instead persevere under Bulldog's wool maroon blanket with the block WT sewn into it. I always assumed this was his genuine letterman's blanket, but for all I knew he might have bought it at the Buffalo Book Store one afternoon before a November night kickoff. It didn't really matter, the experience stayed with me, crammed between my father, who always sported a black watch cap pulled down over his ears in the back, and Bulldog, who was old school to the end in his muffler and felt fedora. His prominent ears were not intimidated by the violent north wind coming off the Rockies. He had played a lot of football in this weather, and his face took on a ruddy shine on nights like this. We never left early. Even if the snow began to fall, the Jones family occupied the red chairback seats until our guys on the field had finished business for the night and closed up shop.

When you are displaced from the High Plains of Texas and living in the capital city, there is always an autumn moment when you envy the homeland's frozen weather. You switch on the ten o'clock news and the big Texas weather map notes that tomorrow's high temperature in Austin will reach 80, while far north in Amarillo the mercury might get to 36. This moment causes Panhandle natives to reflect proudly on their ancestors of hearty pioneer stock enduring the rugged conditions of the high plains, or some other such mythical frontier hooey. In central Texas, a Longhorn season ticket holder could make it through an entire fall without even getting a jacket out of the closet. For me, this absence of autumn chill was one of the few things missing from the Texas football experience. The 2002 Texas Longhorns would have to compete in some foul weather against some pretty salty competition if they were to salvage the mystical season that the Oklahoma Sooners had just done their best to ruin. Had I not fully believed this to be part of God's master plan, I would have been concerned. The rest of the faithful were. To win in these circumstances required a level of play from Chris Simms that few thought he was capable of. Grandad used to joke that he was a lousy football coach because his stupid quarterbacks did exactly what he told them to do. This was not Simms's problem. His physical gifts allowed him to overcome almost anyone's coaching. Quite frankly, unlike most quarterbacks, including Major Applewhite, Simms could put the football anywhere he wanted to anytime he wanted to. His power and accuracy were so reliable that even under the worst circumstances the ball always went directly where he wanted it to go. Where he wanted the ball to go, however, was a huge problem. Simms chose some destinations that defied all logic. Why the hell did he rifle the ball through double coverage against Colorado in the Big 12 Championship expecting to complete the pass? Simple, because he had done it dozens of times before. His physical gifts absolutely corrupted his decision making. Why abandon the primary receiver when his left arm of gold could complete the pass regardless of coverage? Why indeed?

Because God and I spoke regularly about this, I had faith in Chris Simms; I just wasn't convinced that Simms had faith in Simms. My Longhorn brethren didn't, but they were stuck with him. Texas had to get off the mat after the Oklahoma loss, travel to Manhattan, Kansas, and somehow find a way to beat the seventeenth-ranked Wildcats. Throughout most of the twentieth century, this would have been easy. Kansas State had historically been one of the worst programs ever to field a varsity squad. *Sports Illustrated* once labeled them the very worst football team in the country, which didn't dissuade a coach named Bill Snyder from undertaking perhaps the greatest reclamation project in the history of the sport. The 2002 Wildcats were aggressive and tough, possessing the confidence of a program that had won 87 games over the last nine years. For comparison's sake, State had barely won 87 games in the *thirty-five years* preceding Snyder's arrival. These cats were good. They had an aspect of the nouveau riche about them, not quite knowing how to respond to this success. When they visited Austin on a miserably hot day in 1999 it appeared that someone had made a run on purple coach's shorts at Wal-Mart. What made it worse was that their guys proceeded to kick Texas around our own stadium that day, forcing Major Applewhite into six turnovers in a 35–17 loss.

Zach and I had attended that one. The four-year-old couldn't make it through the first half, and I didn't blame him. We were in the far reaches of the west-side upper deck and I wrenched my knee descending the stairs as we left. We took the painful walk home and watched the rest of the game with Truman in our condo across the street from the Posse. Not yet old enough to comprehend the depressing outcome, Zach wanted to go down to Eastwoods Park and play. This is one of the many problems with children. They are wide-eyed and enthusiastic at times when adults need desperately to sit quietly and ruminate over an eighteen-point home loss. My mother also had this problem. She recovered from Buffalo disappointments quickly. When you loved unconditionally the losses rolled right off your back. Texas Longhorn fans tended not to love unconditionally. We loved a winner. In this regard my mother was right: We were more than a little spoiled.

With knee throbbing, I wondered if it was perhaps time to give up pickup basketball as my lifetime sport. I suspected the pounding had turned my ligaments into shredded wheat, and that meant I would never be able to play with my kids. When the pain of divorce is still fresh, you tend to have defeatist thoughts like this. I gutted up and took Z to the park. He played happily in the sandbox and I pushed him on the swing. Eastwoods was close enough to the stadium that wayward Wildcat fans would walk through our play date on the way back to their cars. Each one wore a smile, having no idea the resentment this fostered in the divorced dad with the bad knee who would have happily pushed anyone wearing purple right into Waller Creek if given the opportunity.

Three years later, preparing for the rematch, I remembered God interrupting this thought.

"Whatever happened to forgiveness?"

"What?"

"You know, the concept that perhaps these people walking through the park don't deserve your resentment?"

"What am I forgiving them for?"

"You place blame unfairly upon them for ruining your day. Maybe instead you should forgive the Wildcat players for lining up and beating this team that you place so much importance on?"

"Maybe I should forgive the Longhorns for playing such lousy football."

"That might be a start. That punt return was a real backbreaker. I made David Allen really fast; he feels my love when he runs."

"Yes, thanks for that."

"Maybe someday you will discover your gifts."

"Maybe."

Remembering God's helpful guidance three years later, I still wasn't sure that I had discovered my gifts. But I did know that we owed Kansas State one, and I wished I could be there in person. Not only was that not going to happen, I wouldn't even see the game live on television. Not realizing the game was a night kickoff, Erin and I had scheduled a dinner celebrating the first anniversary of our engagement. After setting the VCR, we hit Jeffery's, typically a tough table to get in Austin, but it was half empty competing with the Longhorns. We returned home early and Erin succumbed to first trimester exhaustion and went to bed. This left me in no-man's land. I couldn't very well turn on the game in midstream. Doing that would leave me lacking the proper context for understanding what was unfolding. The only solution was to wait until the VCR finished its work, rewind, and watch the game the way it was meant to be viewed. There was at least an hour and a half of waiting ahead of me. Not daring to pass the time watching television, which might provide me with a final score and ruin the ending, I went to sleep and set a midnight alarm.

There are all kinds of great fans in the world. There are those who go to sometimes obscenely expensive lengths journeying to every away game, those who paint themselves in the school colors and shirtlessly mock the freezing stadium air, those who name their pets—and sometimes their children—after famous players and coaches and even a few who would go to the grave in a scarlet and gray casket with Ohio State Buckeyes emblazoned on the side. But not enough credit is given to the fan who, for the sake of temporal purity, would begin a recorded game at midnight on a thirteen-inch television set perched in the corner of a wardrobe while a pregnant wife slumbered beside him. As Chris Simms fired his first scoring strike, a 39-yard beauty to B. J. Johnson to stake Texas to a 7–0 lead, I abandoned the bed and stood for the remainder of the game, my eyes squinting six inches from the tiny screen in the corner. Abandoning the bedroom for the downstairs VCR would have saved me eye and back strain, but that never occurred to me—I would be willing to suffer vicariously for my guys on the chilly Kansas plains.

The game itself was ugly. Neither offense could generate a sustained attack. Texas defensive stars Derrick Johnson and Cory Redding made every play needed to keep the Wildcats away from the end zone. But the Kansas State defense was equally brutal, completely shutting down the Texas running game. The two teams combined for eighteen punts. Just when I thought Texas would never score again, Simms threaded a perfect needle through double coverage and B. J. Johnson pulled it in 53 yards downfield to set up another Texas touchdown. With the score 14–14, Simms led a final drive to put the Horns in position for a go-ahead field goal. It was good. Unfortunately, Kansas State mounted a last drive and had a chance to tie the score with a short field goal of their own. This was when the left hand of God—I was fairly certain it was God, but it may have been Marcus Tubbs, the Longhorn defensive tackle—smote the Wildcats. He batted the kick away and it fell to earth.

It was 3:00 A.M. and I hadn't even bothered to fast-forward through most of the commercials. I collapsed in bed content in the knowledge that Chris Simms, the quarterback my dying mother determined was a flake, had just secured a major road victory and kept alive my special season of 2002.

The win kept the chase alive and set up the next trip to the frozen north. On paper, Nebraska wasn't as good a team as Kansas State. The Cornhuskers had been a juggernaut throughout the 1990s, winning national titles in 1994, 1995, and 1997, but had fallen on relatively hard times. They were nevertheless a fine football team and in their last 74 games had lost only once on their home turf, Memorial Stadium in Lincoln. The one loss was to Texas as Major Applewhite led the Longhorns to victory in 1998 with a huge assist from Ricky Williams, who locked up Texas's second Heisman Trophy with 150 rushing yards on that day. The Husker fans, with a well-earned reputation for being the classiest bunch in college football, applauded Williams as he exited the field, even though their gaudy 47-game home winning streak had just ended. This always presented a big problem for Cornhusker opponents: Their fans were almost impossible to hate. An Oklahoma fan is easy to hate. There are too many instances on the state fairgrounds where a conversation would start with something along the lines of "Your ass is going down, you lousy m—er f—ers!" and any decent Texas fan would respond in kind, going into great detail about the Sooner fan's ancestry and personal hygiene. A Cornhusker would instead start the conversation with "Well, gosh, it sure is nice to have you folks out to Lincoln; it should be one heck of a ball game. Could I get you a beer or maybe a pop for your son?" What was a college football fan supposed to do with that?

When Erin's grandmother had died the previous Christmas Eve, it marked one of my life's great regrets. I never met Grandma Hare, but knew her reputation as a fan. She watched every second of every Nebraska football game. True to her advanced state of fandom, she did this with the television sound turned down and the Nebraska radio call turned up. She capped this ritual by calling her friend Effie at game's end to analyze the finer points, sometimes deep into the night. Two octogenarians staying up late to critique Tom Osborne's game strategy was too rich for words. Having been raised by a number of women just like these, I was heartened to have married into the right family. Adhering to their family tradition, the Nebraska uncles and cousins helped me push my new bride around in a wheelbarrow after our wedding ceremony, a sincere helping of Americana that brought smiles to the Texans awaiting the reception.

Nebraska was cold that night, in the low thirties according to the pregame show. It looked cold on television anyway. Once again I found myself watching not a live football game, but one delayed, this time by a party at my brother-in-law's house in Dallas. The circumstances had improved greatly from the midnight viewing on my tiny bedroom set. Erin's brother Kirk had a huge screen, a den full of serious football fans, and free beer. Even better, he was an early adopter of a new technology called TiVo, a digital recording system that allows you to start a recorded game at the beginning even when the game hasn't ended yet. If you skipped through the huddles and commercials, you would eventually catch up with the game in real time. This race to reality was black magic, a grotesque twisting of the space-time continuum that made me very nervous. You violated the fan's code by not watching your team live. Reproducing their efforts for your convenience was no different than taking photographs of native peoples who feared that part of their soul would disappear when the image was taken from them. For fear of being branded a loon by my new family, I avoided this philosophical discourse and hoped for the best. Perhaps if Texas could hold on through the recorded game and deliver me to the live broadcast, then the bonds of superstition would be loosed. It was best not to dwell too much on the metaphysics of it all.

Both teams started slow and the first half was a boring field-goal-kicking contest that Texas won 6–3. Neither team got untracked until the second half, a battle royal between Simms's left arm and Husker quarterback Jamaal Lord's legs. The classic Nebraska running quarterback, Lord made the Texas defense look like children to the tune of 234 yards rushing. Just when you thought you had him contained, he would drop back after play-action and beat you deep. The Longhorns bit twice for touchdowns, one on a perfectly timed 60-yard bomb to his tight end, Matt Herian. But Simms was nails. He equaled Lord with his arm and some major help from wideout Roy Williams.

Roy Williams, "The Legend." *(University of Texas Athletics)*

Williams was a man-child, a deceptively fast, six-four, 210-pound pass-catching machine. Pro scouts salivated at the sight of him. He was tagged with the nickname "The Legend" before playing a single down at Texas, which didn't particularly do him any favors during his career, as he was not a model of consistency. But when Williams was brilliant, which was often, he burned brighter than any Longhorn wide receiver who preceded him. Nebraska simply couldn't contain the Legend. Again and again Simms went to his side of the field. Respecting his speed, the Husker cornerbacks played well off of him, and Simms exploited this defensive weakness to pick up easy first downs throughout the game. This was how West Texas State should have used Reggie Spencer. Of course, dear old West Texas never had a blue-chip quarterback who could flame fastballs to the outside of the field all night without breaking a sweat. Williams helped his own cause with masterfully sneaky push-off moves that were never called. Watching the helpless Nebraska corners contend with Williams reminded me of my grandfather's advice to the young defensive back at Canyon High School. Perhaps Husker coach Frank Solich, too, was encouraging his guys to pull their collective thumb out of their ass and cover the sonofabitch. If so, such exhortations weren't helping as Simms connected with Williams thirteen times, including two for touchdowns, leading Texas to a 27–17 lead in the fourth.

The Nebraska Cornhuskers never quit, especially not in their own stadium when a twenty-six-game home winning streak hangs in the balance. Lord led a brilliant drive to bring Big Red to within 27–24 with about two and half minutes remaining. Then, in a moment of laughable home officiating, the refs flagged Williams for offensive pass interference on a first-down catch that would have iced the game. The Longhorn faithful swelled with righteous indignation that an official would tag Williams on one of the few plays all night when the Legend *hadn't* actually pushed off to get open. No matter, Texas would have to punt and what little faith the Horns had left disappeared chasing Nebraska punt-returner DeJuan Groce 44 yards down the sideline to set up Jamaal Lord at the Texas 16. The turn of events was complete. A sure Texas victory had become at best an overtime toss-up, assuming a chip-shot Nebraska field goal. Of course the Nebraska offense could win the game outright with a touchdown, which is just what Frank Solich had in mind.

Solich had forgotten a minor detail—Jamaal Lord really wasn't a

Nathan Vasher holding his prize aloft. *(University of Texas Athletics)*

particularly reliable thrower. The kid was hell on wheels in the open field, but asking him to throw a clutch pass to win a football game was not a particularly sound bet. With sixteen seconds remaining, Solich put his money down anyway. Nathan Vasher snatched it like a playground bully. Cutting in front of the projectile's path at the one-yard line, the gifted cornerback leaped high and wrapped both hands around the ball. Falling backward, he planted his left foot firmly in bounds and tumbled out of the end zone. He popped up and held the game-winning trophy aloft in his left hand. What Jamaal Lord giveth, Jamaal Lord hath taken away. The kid deserved better than to end the game on Nate Vasher's personal NFL audition tape.

Only twice in seventy-five home games had Nebraska lost. Major Applewhite chalked up the first one, and Chris Simms, the maligned Golden Boy, the poster child for Texas failure in the big games, was responsible for the second. What's more, Applewhite never beat Kansas State, and his left-handed successor had turned that trick under intense pressure. Was there any doubt that God's countenance shone down upon the Texas Longhorns?

10

LUBBOCK, TEXAS, IN MY REARVIEW MIRROR

Texas vs. Texas Tech University

CLIFFORD B. AND AUDREY JONES STADIUM, LUBBOCK, TEXAS, NOVEMBER 16, 2002

Grief provides an opportunity for everyone in the world to try and help you; most of the time you don't want their help. If you are gracious, you learn how to convey this without telling the would-be helper to go butt a stump. My father was gracious. Every time we asked what we could do for him in the fall of 2002, he instructed us to take care of our own business—not to *mind* our own business but to *take care* of it. In other words, the best thing we could do for him was to make sure he didn't need to take care of us. This would have been grounds for a sustainable peace were it not for the Texas Longhorns. Because of their success at Nebraska, the last major barrier to overcome in the magic season of 2002 sat only 119 miles south of Amarillo down I-27 to Jones Stadium in Lubbock, where the Texas Tech Red Raiders would host Texas just before the Thanksgiving holiday. There was no question that making this road trip was an essential part of my father's grieving process. This was all for him. Dad needed to get out of the house. He obviously needed our help. My brother Sam would go with us, along with Zach and my nephew Matt, a freshman at Texas. Matt's presence not only gave us an extra grandson to use as leverage with my father, but also a real live undergraduate member of the faithful. He was the human talisman.

Life delivers a great gift when someone accepts your help. Dad understood this concept. Actually, the old psychiatrist understood almost everything else about human behavior, but he hid it well. Otherwise, all of us would have felt like complete morons in his presence. His love of college football had never left him, and he loved his grandkids even more; it wasn't really hard to persuade him to make a day of it. There was a lot at stake on November 16. Texas had returned from Nebraska fifth in the new Bowl Championship Series rankings. The BCS was a complicated algorithm of human polls and computer rating systems that was created to ensure the best two teams in the nation played for the national title. No longer would the powers that ran the NCAA simply trust this job to the Associated Press voters. Instead we needed computers and strength-of-schedule ratings. The national title was still mythical in the sense that it wasn't decided on the field by a play-off format, but it did at least create one winner-take-all game at the conclusion of the season. The BCS preempted the vagaries of game-day performance, at least for everybody but the two teams that survived the crucible of its digitized beauty pageant. Texas was still in the mix. If the breaks fell their way, they could end up playing for all the marbles. I believed this would happen. I was going to be damned if, after watching two huge wins on tape delay, I was going to miss this game. Traveling to Manhattan or Lincoln was not in the cards, but if I didn't make the effort to get to Lubbock I would regret it.

Southwest Airlines delivered us back to the family home on Friday. I rose early the next day for coffee with Dad, which was one of the great pleasures of life. No one ever got up before my father. Not only was he already in the kitchen, he was always showered, shaved, and dressed. He was glad when someone stumbled into the kitchen and broke the morning silence. The next stage of the ritual was his recited litany of breakfast options. "Can I get you some toast? English muffin? Bacon? I thought I would make Zach pancakes . . ." The litany was a call and response, so it did not end until you acquiesced to Dad's yearning to be helpful.

"Coffee."

You never knew where the conversation would go from there. It was like picking out a Trivial Pursuit card: current events, arts and literature, sports, postmodern currents in Jungian therapy. The curriculum was even more varied than the kitchen sessions with Bulldog. Today we settled on nicknames. I noted that Nathan Vasher was nicknamed "ESPN3" after the ubiquitous sports channel, because of his uncanny knack to make the Saturday evening highlight reel. Dad laughed at that and countered with Weldon "Bird Dog" Trice, a great Buffalo defensive back who could track 'em down and sniff 'em out.

Bird Dog was one of the men who had served my family lunch at the fellowship hall at First Baptist in Canyon the day of my grandfather's funeral. This was a long-standing tradition among the Baptists—in serving and comforting the bereaved, you honored the deceased. I didn't hear anything that week other than what a fine upstanding man my grandfather was, which was well appreciated, if widely known. I lost interest in these plaudits after a while and relied on the rote responses of the grieving to get me through the conversations. Then I talked to Mr. Trice.

Bird Dog was on the WT track team when Grandad accompanied them on a road trip. They were driving through rural New Mexico and stopped for gas. The service station had no indoor plumbing, only an outhouse. Not uncommon for the place and time, but this particular facility had an interesting added feature. The proprietor of the service station, a shameless practical joker, had wired a speaker just underneath the outhouse seat. He gathered Grandad's boys around the cash register and pulled out the microphone as Dean Jones went out back to do his business. Practical jokes are all in the timing. This one was perfect. The proprietor picked just the right moment to shout into the microphone:

Hey, buddy, I'm trying to paint down here!

My grandfather probably failed to see the humor in this as he burst out of the outhouse. Trice was doubled over in laughter on the floor of the gas station. He never let Grandad forget that one, and Bulldog and Bird Dog became fast friends. As our traveling crew slowly made their way into the kitchen, I wondered what Weldon Trice was up to these days. Perhaps he would want to go to the game with us.

From Amarillo to Lubbock, driving north to south, you pass by several hallowed playing fields. As you round a turn and hit the straightaway on Interstate 27, you pass Kimbrough, the old Buffalo Bowl. Not only do the WT Buffaloes still play there, but so do the Canyon Eagles, making it one of the biggest high school stadiums in the state. You then pass by one of the smallest, the Cowboy Corral, where the Happy— "Happy" is actually the name of the town, not the general disposition of the football team—Cowboys play six-man football, a fast-paced version of the game created for schools with tiny enrollments. From Happy, in roughly fifteen-mile increments, you pass by the homes of the Tulia Hornets, Kress Kangaroos, Plainview Bulldogs, Hale Center Owls, Abernathy Antelopes, and New Deal Lions. My father knew these grounds well and had played high school football on many of them. He was part of the lineage of small-town football players that wove together the culture of twentieth-century Texas. Except for an occasional Plainview Bulldog, few of these kids had any illusions of playing the big-time game. Being heroes to the community for three hours every Friday evening in the fall was reward enough.

Dad was a tremendous high school football player, but not necessarily a community hero—he hadn't played for Canyon High School. Instead, Dad attended West Texas High School, which was a "demonstration school" attached to the college, serving as a training ground for the WT Education Department. Because of this status, the WT High football team was not subject to regulation by the University Interscholastic League, the state regulatory body for high school sports. They were a renegade program, enrolling anyone they could get through the door. In

My father, a stalwart of the West Texas High School renegade football squad. *(University of Texas Athletics)*

Dad's time this meant a number of soldiers returning from World War II in need of a high school diploma. These Panhandle boys—now men— had brought down Hitler and were some pretty tough hombres, but Dad held his own. Unlike my grandfather, Dad had some serious size. This was, of course, part of Bulldog's master plan when he married Audrey Watson, the country girl with the huge hands. Dad was 6'2" in high school and a great tackle on both offense and defense. His devastating run blocking earned him the respect of his bearded nineteen- and twenty-year-old war-veteran teammates. This was smash-mouth football, played without face masks. Dad once finished a game with a badly broken nose, courtesy of a Dumas Demon stomping on it in the middle of a scrum.

Their coach, Hatcher Brown, was a colorful character who would have made a great salesman. He spent hours each week calling around trying to find a game. WT High wasn't part of anyone's district schedule, so Hatcher tried to convince his colleagues to use an open date to "keep their teams sharp." I found it hard to believe this worked. Playing a renegade school having Tom Airhart, a blazing fast halfback, running behind a bunch of veterans and Bulldog and Audrey Jones's oversized kid was no way to keep your team sharp. WT High was so tough I don't even think they had a nickname.

"Why did anyone schedule you?"

"They didn't know any better."

"Did you ever get beat?"

My father just smiled, probably conjuring up a memory of bowling over some poor Tulia Hornet while Airhart glided into the end zone behind him. I smiled along with him as the traffic began to thicken and we rolled over the last few miles of I-27 looking for the Jones Stadium exit. We slogged through the caravan and found a parking spot. I took one last inventory. I had my son, my brother, my UT undergrad nephew, and the old renegade tackle for WT High. No way the Longhorns lose with this group in attendance.

Lubbock completely comes alive when the Texas Longhorns are in town. The Red Raider fans arrive in full force and full voice. They have a well-deserved reputation for drunken and rowdy behavior but, as opposed to my feelings toward the Sooners, I tended to embrace the Tech crowd. I never found them mean-spirited or rude. It helped to be from the Panhandle, where dozens of your friends went to Tech and the Texas–Texas Tech games felt like homecoming, even if you were in the other guy's stadium. The Tech students threw great parties, like Calf Fry, which brought fairly well known country stars to play the Lubbock Municipal Auditorium. Calf Fry is named for the signature dish served to the crowd, and the beer is so cold and the famous Tech co-eds are so showstoppingly hot that most folks forget that they are dining on batter-fried bovine testicles all night, which actually make for pretty good eating. I wondered where my "I Had a Ball at Calf Fry" T-shirt had disappeared to and made a mental note to go through the drawers of my old bedroom when I got back to Amarillo that night.

It occurred to me that Texas didn't get such great results when I traveled to Lubbock. This started when my friend Greg Stafford used to invite me down to the games. Greg's father, Bob, was a former Tech player and he loved his Red Raiders, especially in 1980, when I sat very silent next to him and watched his beloved guys whip No. 12 Texas 24–20 in a major upset. This game came flooding back to me along with the two Tech games I attended in college, both losses, in 1986 and 1988. The 1986 game was doubly distressing. The Tech win helped raise the profile of Red Raiders coach David McWilliams, leading Texas to hire McWilliams the next year and seal a tight lid of mediocrity on the Texas program for the rest of the decade. Bad things happened to the Longhorns in Lubbock.

For that matter, bad things even happened when Texas wasn't playing in Lubbock. The Staffords took me to watch Texas Tech play Southern Money in 1982. I relished the chance to get a personal look at SMU's remarkable Eric Dickerson and the best team money could buy. Little did I know that the afternoon would transform me into an unabashed Texas Tech fan as the mediocre Raiders took it to the second-ranked Mustangs. I was rooting out of self-interest of course; an SMU loss would get Texas back in the race for the conference championship. My breaking of the fan code and becoming a Red Raider partisan no doubt fueled one of the most remarkable endings in Southwest Conference history, as SMU defensive back Blane Smith fielded a Tech kickoff with seventeen seconds remaining and lateraled the ball to Bobby Leach who, of course, brought the ball back 91 yards for the winning touchdown. It wasn't for nothing that the Tech students derisively called their own team the Red Faders.

Too bad they never faded against Texas; the Raiders always seemed to bring their A game. Today, however, would be different I thought as we wedged ourselves into the ridiculously narrow end-zone bleachers for the kickoff. Zach promptly stretched out and went to sleep in my lap, no doubt tired from a fried chicken lunch and his grandfather's stories. I had to move him and created a pallet on the metal bleachers out of our discarded coats so that he could lie down and I could stand up. A Longhorn ass-kicking was about to commence and I was not going to miss it. On the first play from scrimmage, right on cue and directly in front of us, Texas defensive end Brian Pickryl got loose and crushed Tech's quarterback, Kliff Kingsbury. Kingsbury coughed it up and Nathan Vasher dived on the leather-wrapped egg and cradled it like a baby. Texas took over, Simms drilled a pass to fullback Ivan Williams to the Tech 2-yard line, and Cedric Benson scored an easy touchdown. Game. Set. Match. The Longhorn Band was seated right next to us and as they exploded into "Texas Fight" I dialed Erin on my cell phone. She didn't pick up. I raised the phone above my head so she could hear the fight song when she checked her messages. True to her spirit, she had escaped to the back bedroom at a boring couples shower and was with the men glued to the television set.

The Texas defense stoned Tech again and the teams traded possessions. As the first quarter wound down, Texas put together a 90-yard drive helped along by a successful fake punt. Golden Boy delivered a perfect strike to the Legend, who was greeted by our end-zone contingent celebrating what was now a 14–0 lead for our fourth-ranked Horns. Mom would have loved this and I wondered if she was watching as I lifted my eyes up to the South Plains skies.

"Of course I am."

"Really?"

"Yes, I can see the whole field, and I am a little worried about the Texas pass defense."

"Kingsbury can't do anything about that when he is flat on his back."

"You better keep him that way. I really wish I could be sitting next to Zach; you need to explain these things to him."

The Texas defense forced another Tech punt. The Longhorn return squad was flagged for illegal participation on the punt, which Tech had downed at the Texas three. The penalty wasn't enough to give Tech a first down and I assumed they would decline it, having pinned Texas down 97 yards from the end zone. But I had forgotten a fundamental rule of the college football universe: there is nothing more dangerous than an opponent with nothing to lose. This rule was particularly applicable to Tech's head coach, a wild-eyed gambler named Mike Leach. Any reputable mental health professional who observed Leach vigorously chewing through fountain pens on the sidelines like a nervous badger might suggest institutionalization, or at least an aggressive regimen of psychopharmacology. True to his nature, Leach accepted the penalty and went for it on fourth and five. Dumb decision. Kingsbury overthrew a deep ball and I breathed a sigh of relief. I stopped breathing when I saw the yellow flag on the field. The Horns were offside; their illegal breach of the line of scrimmage unraveled the weave of impenetrability of the Texas defense. This was the transforming moment. Day begin to turn into night, the weather turned cold, and Kliff Kingsbury turned glowing hot like a red-and-black vision from hell. He drilled a touchdown to Wes Welker and the game was joined.

The next Texas possession ended with Simms being sacked. Kingsbury got the ball back and drove it straight down the throat of the Texas defense to tie the score at fourteen. Kingsbury didn't have the pedigree or national reputation of Simms, but when he was hot—and right now his right arm had smoke coming off of it—he was a damn fine college quarterback. Simms didn't seem fazed. Texas got up off the mat and drove the ball back down the field. Simms went to Roy Williams for the

Legend's second touchdown. The Texas D held the Red Raiders in check the next two possessions and after a Texas punt pinned the Raiders at their own 14-yard line with a minute remaining in the half, the Longhorn faithful would have been very pleased with a 21–14 lead going into the locker room. Kingsbury victimized the Texas prevent defense with a 24-yard strike to Welker, but his next pass fell incomplete and he was running out of time. With thirty seconds remaining, he settled for a short slant to Nehemiah Glover. The Texas defensive backfield, doing a perfect reenactment of a Keystone Cops movie, missed the diminuitive Glover no fewer than seven times. Sixty-two yards later, the game was tied again. Welker and Glover were tiny, albeit fast, gamers, the likes of which Texas didn't bother to recruit, but who dependably burned the Longhorn's blue-chippers. This underscored every game between the two schools: underrated tough kids from tiny rural high schools versus the superstars lured by the glory of the state's flagship university. Nobody cheered for Goliath on days like this.

Kingsbury completed his first eight passes of the second half and Tech took a 28–21 lead on a Welker touchdown. Tech fans celebrated their first lead of the ballgame and I quietly decided that I would ask forgiveness later for hating Wes Welker. Compounding my emotional fragility was a rash of injuries to the Texas defense, most notably to Derrick Johnson, the All-American linebacker who usually kept everything together for the Horns. On top of it all, I had befriended the young couple next to me, perfectly nice Tech fans who were family friends of Longhorn freshman tight end David Thomas. Not good to cavort with the enemy I thought—it robbed a fan of needed focus. This was a clear violation of the fan's code that could get me drummed right out of the Cult of 1969.

Meanwhile Simms looked like a kid in a candy store, sharply dicing through the Raider defense down the field on a drive that ended with Roy's third touchdown catch, tying it at twenty-eight. Texas stopped Tech and kicked a field goal to take a 31–28 lead going into the fourth quarter. My shaking subsided as I remembered that God was clearly on my side.

Tech went up 35–31 on a perfect strike to Glover, whom I began to dislike as much as Welker. My ethical dilemma was short-lived. While I pondered the Christian thought that perhaps Welker and Glover were perfectly nice young men away from the football field, the Texas Tech defense completely forget that B. J. Johnson was blazing unimpeded down the left sideline. Simms lofted a perfect 84-yard strike to make it 38–35. Kingsbury, believing that Simms was simply showing off, drove methodically down the field to make it 42–38. The last team to possess the ball would certainly win this game. The other certainty was that Texas was moving too fast. If I could have slowed down time, I would have. Chris Simms was at the reins of a runaway stagecoach, and at some sharp turn it would tumble over a cliff.

Games like this gave me a queasy feeling. I had grown up watching Texas grind out games and break the will of their opponents with defense. There was something reassuring, comforting even, about Texas staking a lead and knowing that the only way a team could come back was to defeat a whole host of All-American players on the defensive side of the ball. Some teams could do it, Oklahoma chief among them, which is one reason the Cotton Bowl contests were such emotional wringers. But most of the time Texas fans were secure in their knowledge of victory early in the second half. As the college game got more wide open, especially when the Big 12 became the province of mad geniuses like Bob Stoops and Mike Leach, the playing field between haves and have-nots leveled somewhat. A wide-open passing attack could put pressure on a topflight defense: One mistake and David, in the form of the Wes Welkers of the world, was celebrating in your end zone. The Texas Tech spread offense drove me to distraction, and if they had the ball last on this chilly November evening, the dream season of 2002 could simply collapse in a blown coverage and a Kliff Kingsbury rocket.

As the clock ticked down, however, Texas had the ball and an opportunity to score the game winner while draining away almost every last tick. With Kliff Kingsbury relegated to the sidelines, my confidence began to return. That's when I realized that dreams die in all sorts of ways.

Deep in Tech territory, Simms threw a strike to a soft spot in the Tech zone where B. J. Johnson wasn't. My dream died in the arms of a Tech defender named Ryan Aycock. David had beaten Goliath. The fatal smooth stone struck Texas as I sat in almost the exact spot in the stadium where I had watched Quentin Jammer be convicted of pass interference in the 2001 Oklahoma game and in the same spot where Tony Many-weather smiled at me in Memorial Stadium in 1989. In celebration of Aycock's pick, the Tech students actually dismantled the section bleachers at the far end of the stadium and held them unsteadily aloft like a sway-ing aluminum victory totem. I vowed never to sit in the end zone again.

The drive back from Lubbock was cold and black as pitch, which didn't matter to me—I could negotiate the interstate from Lubbock to Amarillo blindfolded, instinctively feeling the fast straightaways and the sweeping curve past Kimbrough that would deliver my family to the fa-miliar Bell Street exit. Still believing God owed me one, I thought per-haps I had misunderstood the terms and conditions. Maybe cheering for Goliath forged a spiritual and ancestral disconnect after being raised by parents who taught me to cheer for David. The car fell silent and I picked up KGNC on the radio while passing by the home of the Tulia Hornets. Top 40 radio had died years ago, and KGNC was now just all talk; Ruby "Lady Soul" Lewis had no station left to spin records for the people of the Panhandle.

Dad broke the silence and we begin to recount the game's highlights and lowlights. He kept repeating, "That Kinsgbury is one whale of a quarterback." My father had more than a little bit of Mom in him; it was evident from our conversation that what he had enjoyed most about the day was that he had just watched one of the great college football games Lubbock had ever seen. More importantly, he had made the journey with the boys he loved the most. He was in the moment.

I thought back on many of the winter nights as a child driving back from West Texas basketball games with Dad, nights just as black and cold as this one. When I was seven, a young basketball player had arrived on campus from Chicago. He would change my life as a sports fan. His name was Maurice Cheeks, and though I didn't know it at the time, he would be the greatest player in Buffalo history. Dad and I saw nearly every home game of his brilliant career. At the apex of his years at WT, Cheeks led the Buffs to a real live AP ranking: they were nineteenth in the nation during a wonderful week in 1974 after an upset of Louisville. If only briefly, Cheeks and his teammates had cracked the big time. When he left WT, most thought he would have his cup of coffee in the NBA and move on. After all, he was a second-round draft pick from Podunk U. But he didn't go quietly. He became the starting point guard for the powerful Philadelphia 76ers. Cheeks made all-star teams, he helped Philly to the 1983 NBA title and then retired as professional basketball's all-time steals leader. Cheeks was my first sports hero, even preceding Earl Campbell. I thought about all the times Dad and I had dissected his performances coming home on nights just like this. On special mornings, Dad would take me to Dunkin' Donuts on Western Street on the way to school and we would listen to the regulars talk Buffalo basketball. He would then drop me off at school. All those years, I thought that Maurice Cheeks was my hero. It was evident to me on this night that I was wrong. My hero was in the passenger seat. His grandkids were asleep in the seats behind him.

My father was the best guy I knew. I wondered as I drove through the Panhandle night if I had taken this for granted for the last thirty-five years. Of all of the events of life that separate fathers from sons, the dysfunction, the distance, the lack of communication or even abandonment, of the litany of disappointments that men eventually find a way to forgive and forget about their dads, I didn't have a damn thing to forgive my father, not a whit of bitterness or recrimination. Could I have been more fortunate than to have been raised in this man's household?

Though the Longhorns lost, for one more night my father and I had shared the passion of college football. I silently hoped that there would be many more. How incongruous it was to venture north to help heal my father but for myself to be healed instead. But it made perfect sense: I needed to help someone. Dad was kind enough to accept my help.

The family at DKR (from left: Erin's mother, Pat Florence, Erin, Dad, my brother Sam, and Zach). *(Jones Family)*

Dad joined us in Austin for Thanksgiving two weeks later and I scored tickets to the Texas A&M game. Simms started our holiday season by shredding the Aggies' pass defense in a 50–20 blowout in the last game of the season, which proved my presence was not the kiss of death for Texas fortunes. Simms left the field to a rousing standing ovation as the Texas faithful bid farewell to perhaps the most celebrated and maligned, the most anticipated and regretted, the most enigmatic, complicated, conflicted character in the drama that is Texas football. All Chris Simms ever did was to accept the challenge of being the quarterback of the Texas Longhorns. Such acceptance requires courage and the integrity to live in the public eye and all of the pressure and consequences it brings. This was the dark side of fandom, the adulation that turns quickly to disdain. Simms seemed to understand this as he left the field to thunderous cheers. I stood applauding and said a prayer for the kid's future success.

Nobody deserved the shit he had put up with during his four years in Austin.

"Your prayer for Simms is noted. That is a noble and selfless thought from you. Nice to know you are capable."

"Where have you been? This was supposed to be my year—"

God interrupted. God always interrupted. "This was your mother's year. You have many years left."

"What about the national title?"

"That's not really what you want, is it?"

I thought about this. "Yes, actually it is."

Texas accepted another invitation to the Cotton Bowl, which was no longer a top-tier postseason destination. Ever since 1996 when the South-west Conference and Big Eight merged to form the Big 12, the Cotton Bowl no longer had a conference champion to host and slowly slid down the postseason pecking order. The old stadium was still a jewel, and it maintained that magical quality of being played on New Year's Day, but it was a long way from Tempe, Arizona, where the Fiesta Bowl would host undefeated Miami and undefeated Ohio State in the game I desperately wished the Longhorns could play in just once. Just once.

Texas destroyed Louisiana State that day. Roy Williams turned the Cotton Bowl into his personal playground by scoring on a 51-yard touchdown from Simms and setting up another Texas touchdown on a brilliant 75-yard catch and run. For an encore, the Legend ran 39 yards for a touchdown on a wide receiver reverse. Simms was brilliant as well, right up until the end. With 2:22 remaining in the game, he threw the last pass of his tumultuous career. It was intercepted.

The Texas Longhorns finished the 2002 season a respectable fifth. Fifth is nice, but it ain't first. Mom might have reminded me that life is an adventure, but there are no guarantees that your team will always win the game. Not an easy lesson to remember, especially when Mom wasn't around anymore.

Barely any traces of Mom's generation remained. In the spring, the last Killian sibling, Mom's sister Bobbie Silcott, passed away. Southwest Airlines faithfully delivered me home for the funeral. My brother Sam picked me up at the airport and we rode together in the morning cool through the broad flatlands northeast of Amarillo, driving alongside the railroad tracks toward the Canadian River breaks on our way to Pampa, the industrial oil patch outpost that raised the Killian clan. We drove past Pantex, the nuclear weapons assembly plant that loomed over Amarillo like apocalyptic doom as our good citizens did their part to win the cold war. The feds must have figured that the Russians would have trouble locating Carson County, Texas, much less infiltrating it. We drove through White Deer, and Highway 60 deposited us fifteen miles later in Pampa, where the First Baptist Church had arranged the traditional lunch before the burial.

The Killians were always full of laughter and good spirits, and I drank in this scene before we all assembled our convoy in the parking lot and drove back toward Amarillo to the Carson County Cemetery, where Bobbie would be laid to rest. Amid the Panhandle wind and dust there would, of course, be singing. The night before Mom's funeral the Killians sang "Amazing Grace" like angels around my father's table. My uncle Dee had first steadied himself on his walker and offered grace as only a Southern Baptist deacon could, invoking in a gravelly but confident tone "Our most omnipotent and gracious heavenly Father." This left the Killians primed to lift every voice. Aunt Bobbie was always the best of the bunch. Now the remaining Killians owed it to Bobbie to return to her all of the sweet sounds she had shared with us over the last seventy years. And so it was that three generations of Panhandle family breathed in deep and battled the forty-mile-per-hour gusts with a rendition of "I'll Fly Away." The notes were clear, cutting through the high plains wind just as they had the previous summer at my mother's graveside. A few words were said. Then the immediate Silcott family left the rest of us behind by joining hands in a tight circle and singing goodbye to the John E. and Eulah Killian family who lived in the house on Starkweather Street.

The Lord is good to me . . . Mom's sister Tessie had died in the same long summer of 2001, not two months after Mom . . . *and so I thank the Lord* . . . Her kid brother Jimbo had a heart attack in the fall; he was way too young for that . . . *for giving me* . . . Sister Norma had died years before . . . *the things I need* . . . And now Bobbie listened one last time to her family's dinnertime prayer . . . *the sun and the rain and the apple seed* . . . David, Molly, Sam, and I joined in and sang Bobbie home with the last familiar words . . . *the Lord* . . . *is* . . . *good* . . . *to* . . . *me.*

The crowd slowly shared their last hugs and laughs before going their separate ways. Bobbie's Chihuahua, Skippy, sniffed around the head-stones and weeds wondering where his momma had gone. For some reason, these people—my people—were happy, not sad. The Lord was good to them. The Lord was good to me.

I remembered the old-time call and response of churches all over the south:

God is good.

All the time.

And all the time.

God is good.

Then the people say amen.

Part 3

REDEMPTION

11

THE BIRTH OF THE COOL

Texas vs. the University of North Carolina

DARRELL K. ROYAL–TEXAS MEMORIAL STADIUM, AUSTIN, TEXAS, SEPTEMBER 8, 2001

Zach aged out of having Harry Potter read to him by about the fifth book in the series. He could read it himself by then, and I noted this passing with some regret. Through the first four books, I read every word to him aloud. Through the last couple of installments, we marked our progress with the same family relic. A ticket stub, a permanent record of a perfect day: September 8, 2001, the day the Jones crew went to Darrell K. Royal–Texas Memorial Stadium and watched our Longhorn heroes dismantle the University of North Carolina Tar Heels. The stub from the game is for me the last tangible proof of a simpler world. Three days later, that world would never exist again.

Reading to Zach made me nervous. I would catch him out of the corner of my eye absentmindedly playing with my sacred artifact. He would rub it in his hand or curve it with his thumb or, God forbid, fold it in half.

Somewhere in my subconscious I was convinced that the thin piece of cardboard with the free taco coupon on the back had talismanic power. Tear the fabric of that ticket and something would be, somehow, lost.

"Give me that."

Zach rolled his eyes. This was part of the ritual. I would start reading. He would start playing with the bookmark. I would get edgy and lose concentration and demand the bookmark, which I would slide into a spot farther along in the text as if I were putting Mickey Mantle's rookie card back into its plastic sleeve and dropping it in a safety-deposit box. This was a neurosis that Zach tolerated, even if he did not fully under-

Through the generations: Dean Jones reads to his sons. My father is standing; seated is his brother, Marshall. *(Jones Family)*

stand its depths. Then again, he will mature having no real memories of life when the World Trade Center still stood.

Lots of little boys live in a world where their dads don't read to them. Many of them live in places where their dads don't live. Long before Zach found Harry Potter, there lived a boy just like that in Houston, Texas. He lived in a neighborhood called Brentwood inside a larger community called Hiram Clark. This was industrial south Houston, a great place to put an auto salvage yard or a concrete and aggregate plant. Hiram Clark was ringed with large manufacturing and distribution sites that changed hands regularly, open for business one day, space for lease the next, sitting vacant while an unknown tenant pondered how to use the space to achieve the next American dream. Houston is a city of dreamers, a giant economic engine fueled by a huge ship channel and zoning regulations that, if you had the means, allowed you to do just about whatever you wanted to do with whatever land you owned. The Hiram Clark community lived with this reality: It is cut clean in half right along its main thoroughfare by a Centerpoint Energy regeneration plant. Huge transmission towers stretched from the plant in both directions, separating the neighborhood with industrial steel reaching seventy-five feet high with three or four long crossbars holding dozens of cables. In some places these towers ran four or five across, providing the energy to feed the economic beast. You could raise a family under these towers, and thousands did it, but "not in my backyard" as a political statement did not apply to this community. Corporate powers don't lobby for working-class neighborhoods; that job is up to the people. And the people don't always win. This was a neighborhood where kids didn't learn to swim, even in a city full of bayous and lowlands. This was a neighborhood where sometimes people got shot, and most kids knew someone who met this fate. Orem Street, which runs the length of the neighborhood and intersects Hiram Clark Boulevard at the center, provides a battleground between package stores and churches. Folks switch sides between the two depending on the day of the week. The Hiram Clark community provides home for people of faith and family trying to make it all work. Mostly black, but increasingly brown, they would grow to love and embrace this little boy in South Houston—far enough south that if you pick up a laminated tourist map of this huge city, Hiram Clark drops right off the bottom of it. This little boy lived in the part of the city that people didn't bother to see.

The little boy was enjoying being a kid when something terrible happened. The articles that would be written after he became famous never fail to mention that he was trying to get a girl's attention. He probably never even saw the car that hit him and his dirt bike and sent him sprawling. The injury ripped through his intestines and left him dying. Another light would be extinguished in a place where the larger world wouldn't bother to notice.

But he didn't die. God was looking out for this kid. He spent months and months in the hospital slowly building the strength to walk and run and play. He had heart. He was a survivor. A winner. God saw that right away.

I have no idea what I did on September 10, 2001, the last day the world seemed OK. I doubt that many people do. I certainly don't remember September 9, but September 8 might as well be yesterday to me. Game day on a perfect fall afternoon—when college football season starts, it's fall, no matter what the calendar says—found Erin and Zach and me on our way to DKR to commune with our people and watch our guys. Time for celebration, this was a great Longhorn team facing a pretty fair North Carolina squad.

As with all great church services, this one started with reverence. A Longhorn named Cole Pittman had died the previous spring. He was on his way back to Austin from Shreveport when he crashed his truck into a creek bed. His teammates got the news the day before spring practice. He was twenty-one. Today the Longhorns would come out of the tunnel with "CP" on the back of their helmets, but without their teammate.

Pittman's parents were on the field, and their son's number was painted in the south end zone. This game was for him.

The Longhorns whipped Carolina up and down the field. Star defensive end Cory Redding took an early interception back for a touchdown and front-flipped over a Tar Heel and into the end zone for dramatic effect. Roy Williams outraced the entire Tar Heel defense on a wide receiver reverse. The Longhorns made every play. When a touchdown pushed the lead to 44–14 with little time left, they inexplicably sent in the regular offense to go for the two-point conversion. What was this? Major Applewhite took the snap—and knelt down. Then Applewhite flipped the ball to the referee and pointed to the scoreboard. The crowd murmured their way to understanding of this singularly poignant gesture. By foregoing the extra point, the Longhorns ensured the left side of the scoreboard would read "Texas 44," which is exactly what had been printed on the front of Cole Pittman's jersey. I cried at this realization. God blessed me with this memory, the last I still carry from the time before 9/11.

"Applewhite's kneel-down was a nice touch, didn't you think?"

"I didn't really watch."

"What do you mean, you didn't really watch?"

"What, you think I care who wins a football game?"

"Well, yes."

"I don't."

"You're just jerking my chain."

"No, don't you understand by now that I don't do that? Oh, and tell the players that it is not necessary to thank their Lord and Savior Jesus Christ when they win."

"So you do watch the games?"

"You really want to believe I do."

Yes. I really wanted to.

I was listening to sports talk when the first plane hit the World Trade Center. Sounded like a small plane got off course, with terrible results.

I wished they'd get back to the postgame analysis on North Carolina; since the Longhorns had an open week, Erin and I were taking a vacation to Costa Rica that Friday, which meant I probably wouldn't even have access to a decent sports page.

Costa Rica never happened. No way were we getting on an international flight. We pointed the car west and just started driving, filling the car with newspapers and reading articles to each other in a desperate attempt to try and make sense of it all. We comforted each other reading aloud through the long barren stretches of the West Texas desert—one of the last vestiges of America where "last water and gas for fifty miles" are not advertisements, but legitimate warnings. In this age of on-demand news, we were itinerant Luddites gathering scraps of paper for new information.

We went through Fort Stockton, Fort Davis, and the Davis Mountains. Occasionally we would see an American flag draped over a farmhouse fence or catch an AM radio station encouraging neighbors to share their feelings in between sad country songs. Heading south through Marfa, the home of displaced artists and the mysterious horizon lights many attribute to the spirit world, we stopped for coffee and more newspapers to last us through our drive down the Mexican border road through Presidio, a cinder-block and metal roof-constructed, unpaved vision of poor America that really does exist beyond the viewfinders of public television documentarians. We slept in Lajitas, the strange resort oasis with both a beer-drinking goat and a private airstrip to accommodate fantasy golf trips. Driving through our first border patrol checkpoint on our way to Big Bend National Park, the agents decided we weren't Arabs and waved us through. Scarcely a soul was in sight, and we liked it that way. Our return to reality came in Marathon, home of the famous Gage Hotel, which is not so remote as to be without CNN in the lobby. It really wasn't a dream.

The last day of our escape a late-afternoon thunderstorm rolled through. The desert smelled like rain, and the sunset was magnificent. It took me back to the Panhandle with its uninterrupted vistas giving a view of the sun slowly falling through the breaks in the squall line. You never knew what colors it would create; this scene haunted Georgia O'Keeffe and dozens of lesser artists in search of a muse. Erin and I walked across the street to a pockmarked parking lot paved for a purpose long forgotten. The uneven blacktop filled with random pools of water, and those pools changed colors as the sun's angles grew more acute, playing hide-and-seek between the thin clouds blocking their path. The whole world could end tomorrow and I wouldn't care. My last memory would be with this girl, watching the colors of the desert sun play reflecting games on the watery asphalt marsh.

The world didn't end. It couldn't, not before I married this woman and welcomed two more sons to the world and, yes, said goodbye to a mother. All of this before the Longhorns could win another lousy national title. In the seven hundred miles back to Austin, we continued to read to each other, perhaps trying to hold some comforting memory of those who read to us when we were children. Erin indulged me with the sports page around Del Rio. There was a small piece on the quarterback from Madison High School in Houston. He was the best player in the country, truly a once-in-a-lifetime talent. Thank God it was my lifetime. I would never meet him, but he would have a grand impact on my world.

Greater Houston produces an endless stream of fantastic high school football players. College recruiters know every freeway exit and high school campus. If recruiting is the lifeblood of college sports, then Houston is one of the major arteries. Cut it and Texas, Texas A&M, Oklahoma, LSU and a dozen others would suffer. If you can't recruit southeast Texas you cannot be a big-time winner. This part of the country has seen it all. And yet never had the people of Harris County seen anything like this little boy from Hiram Clark.

The boy from Hiram Clark had become a man by now and he played football the way Miles Davis played jazz. His own brand of cool was born on the fields of Madison High School, and it was an astonishing new creation. Six feet five, 200 pounds and swift like a gazelle—this was not a sports cliché; he really did run like a gazelle with his long almost leaping stride and ability to change vectors unerringly, instinctively, and with such rapidity and fluid motion that it left the cheetahs of the defensive backfield grasping at air and heading to the sidelines for more ankle tape.

He was a twenty-point scorer on the basketball court, a gifted baseball player, and, needless to say, a star sprinter. One day, while waiting to play in a summer league basketball game, he noticed a quarterback competition was under way. He went to his car, put on his cleats, walked to the adjacent field, and won the competition going away. Ah, what he could do with a football. As a senior quarterback at Madison, he threw thirty-seven touchdowns and only four interceptions. Even then, one of the interceptions proved a defining moment: He chased down the defensive back, made the tackle, forced a fumble, recovered the fumble, and threw a touchdown on the next play from scrimmage. The kid created his own mulligans. When faced with a choice between legend and fact, it didn't matter which you chose to print, for they were the same. This was not a fantasy; it was his life and you could read about it for the price of a Saturday *Houston Chronicle*.

An enormous television console dominated my grandfather's family room. During the holidays, back when life was at its most innocent, his grandchildren would congregate around it, spread on the floor. Audrey would bring us sticky homemade popcorn balls and peanut brittle while we watched college football. Grandad usually kept to himself, but one day, when I was thirteen, our excitement became too much for him to bear. He drifted in to watch a Georgia Bulldog freshman tailback named Herschel Walker run roughshod over Georgia Tech. His assessment was quickly formulated and confident.

"That Walker is a fine player. He may be as good as Sam Baugh."

Most of my cousins did not notice this, but I did. Bulldog Jones had just proclaimed that Sammy Baugh might have an equal. Baugh was the greatest quarterback in the history of our state and would have easily won the 1936 Heisman Trophy had anyone east of the Mississippi bothered to see him play, or had anyone outside the impenetrable conclave of East Coast sportswriters been given a vote. He was called "Sammy" or, better yet, "Slingin' Sammy" by most everyone but my grandfather, who had met Baugh and insisted on "Sam" out of respect. Not only was he the best quarterback of his day, both in college and later for the Washington Redskins, but he was also the best punter and the best defensive back. His greatness, like that of perhaps Red Grange and few others, overstepped the limits of amateur historians engaged in the classic parlor game of comparing eras. Mr. Sam Baugh defined greatness on the football field for my grandfather, and while the young Georgia tailback, Walker, would go on to win the Heisman Trophy, lead Georgia to the national title, and go down in college football history as one of the greats ever to play the game, I am not sure he ever surpassed Baugh in Bulldog Jones's estimation, and certainly not in his heart.

Grandad died content in the knowledge that never would a quarterback in the Lone Star State shine as brightly as Slingin' Sammy Baugh.

The Devil cares not for stories of God's people rising above the meanness of the world and bringing hope and joy where there is only despair and sorrow. He could have easily derailed the boy from Hiram Clark. By the time he was in middle school the police knew this kid who survived the car wreck; they knew him as a physically imposing bully who ran with the wrong crowd. No one really cared about his life story or that his dad was in prison—this was a part of town people would rather not see. Mount Horeb Missionary Baptist Church could save only so many souls, and his may not have been in the cards. The little boy might just fall through the cracks.

Jesus entrusted the Apostle Paul with relaying a number of instructions to God's people. Paul, in turn, entrusted many of these ancient lessons to his young friend Timothy. The Bible tells us exactly why Paul chose Timothy; he saw in him the strength of two generations of women. A grandmother and mother grounded Timothy in the faith and raised him up with love. So it was that a grandmother and mother anchored the boy from Hiram Clark in the well of a tiny church on Gray Street. They did this precisely at the most dangerous time in the young man's life, the time when bad decisions lead to consequences that cannot be fixed.

The boy needed this. He needed love and faith and sanctuary. He also needed a ball in his hands. By the time he was fourteen, no one doubted that he possessed remarkable gifts. He was already the man of the house, but he was also a man among boys. Always the best player on field, court, or track, he set out to prove that he could also lead. He started at quarterback as a sophomore at Madison and never looked back. Football transformed him, and he would transform football. Football heals.

God granted him the spiritual gift of presence. The boy had it in the form of an engaging smile, a relaxed manner, and an ability to shoulder the burdens and dreams of his grandmothers and mother and sisters, his neighborhood and community and school, and he did it all with effortless grace. He wasn't just a football player; he was a phenomenal child of God. He had already walked once through the valley of the shadow of death and emerged in the light unscathed.

In the terrible weeks and months after the planes hit the World Trade Center, he added the burdens of the city of Houston to his shoulders, bringing joy to the masses by playing his game. And on one afternoon, on the famous turf of the Houston Astrodome, he made an entire city smile.

This memory made God smile, as well.

"You like this kid, don't you?"

"I do," God replied. "I like Vincent Young."

12

DOWN FROM
MOUNT HOREB

*Houston Madison vs. Galena Park North Shore Texas
High School Class 5A Regional Semifinals*

THE ASTRODOME,
HOUSTON, TEXAS, NOVEMBER 30, 2001

Mount Horeb Missionary Baptist Churchs sits on a nondescript street corner of Gray Street in Houston's Fourth Ward. The building has a narrow front and goes straight back to the end of the lot. There's no front lawn and the walls press right up against the surrounding sidewalks, as if the builders knew that the neighborhood needed all the church that could be crammed into the space. The steeple spire stretches up toward heaven and keeps vigil over the neighborhood. From the front door of Mount Horeb, it's a short hop over to Main Street, and if you take Main southeast about three miles, you come to the Harris County Domed Stadium, which most people just call the Astrodome.

The Astrodome has seen better days. The old building is no longer the Eighth Wonder of the World; there's not much wonder left in the massive and dilapidated inverted bowl of concrete in the middle of

Houston. It resembles a giant discarded hubcap, its shiny top graying slowly from exposure to the elements. The mass doesn't even impress anybody anymore; it's dwarfed by Reliant Stadium. The home of the NFL Houston Texans, Reliant is a temple of shining corporate perfection and luxury boxes that sits mockingly close to the gloomy Astrodome. Wringing any remaining magic out of the grand old stadium is a Herculean task.

Eighteen-year-old Vincent Young was up to it. On November 30, 2001, the Madison Marlins and their prodigy quarterback came to the Astrodome to face the North Shore Mustangs from the Galena Park school district. Longhorn fans knew North Shore very well as the home of their own defensive star, Cory Redding. The Mustangs were on a steep rise, and the 2001 squad was a scoring machine. A few weeks earlier they had overwhelmed state power Baytown Lee 77–34 in a pyrotechnic offensive show that solidified the Mustangs as the state's No. 1 team in 5A, the largest high school athletics classification. *USA Today* proclaimed North Shore the fifth-best team in the entire country. A typical North Shore team would have perhaps a dozen players who would eventually play college football, sometimes more. Madison's dreams, in all likelihood, would end in the Astrodome on the last day of November.

But the dreams didn't just belong to Madison; the entire city had embraced these south-side kids and their brilliant quarterback. It had been years since the people of Houston proper could cheer a team of their own with this much promise. The schools of Houston Independent School District don't typically compete at the highest levels of high school football, and they hadn't won a state championship since Yates High School seized the brass ring in 1985. The district is a far-flung mess of over 200,000 students with two dozen high schools campuses. The athletic facilities are lacking, the coaching is often subpar, and many of the neighborhoods over time are places families move away from, not toward. The balance of power in high school sports long ago shifted from the inner city into the suburbs and exurbs. Around the Houston metropolitan area, the high school football powers were teams far from the city's core in more attractive neighborhoods and facilities. This was not always the result of white flight—although major powers like the Woodlands and Katy benefited from that phenomenon—some of it had to do with mega high schools erupting in emerging neighborhoods. Alief school district was an ethnically diverse community on Houston's west side with two high schools of over 4,000 students, twice as many as Madison. Districts like Humble and Galena Park had large industrial tax bases and an ever-increasing number of players to pick from every year. Madison High School had none of these advantages. They did have a tenured and respected coach named Ray Seals, a number of kids from Hiram Clark who aspired to greatness on the football field, and the hopes of an entire city behind them. But that was probably insufficient to take down North Shore. This wasn't David versus Goliath, but it was close.

The City of Houston—a Goliath if there ever was one—found itself in David's corner. They came out in throngs to the Astrodome. Security was tight with 9/11 still a fresh memory; there were few points of entry into the stadium, and the lines stretched well into the parking lot at kickoff. Many of the fans didn't get into their seats until halftime. Houstonians to this day remember the stadium as packed to the rafters, but the truth is, about 25,000 were in the stands, still a huge high school crowd, but some 35,000 short of capacity. Not enough to give Madison a dominant home-field advantage, and every other advantage seemed to favor the North Shore Mustangs. North Shore did have one small problem. Playing the role of David was not a small shepherd's son with a slingshot, but rather an indestructible man-child possessing the acceleration of a Porsche and a howitzer permanently affixed to his right shoulder.

The indestructible part was evident early in the game. North Shore's defense welcomed Young to the contest in the first quarter with a clean shot on the sideline. The Astrodome stands come right down to field's edge, making the environment dangerous for players. The tattered and spotty artificial turf stretched thin over the concrete floor was bad enough, but heaven help a player if he was knocked from the relative safety of the playing field. Hit hard, Vince went sprawling into the concrete and metal spectator stands just beyond the lines. Anxiety hung over the Madison crowd as it watched their favorite son's violent collision with the ungiving embankment. When Young hopped up, shimmied, and did his familiar trot back to the huddle, the anxiety quickly shifted to the North Shore side.

"We're in serious trouble." The thought raced through the North Shore partisans.

They were correct.

Vincent Young then went otherworldly. Racing through the North Shore defense with effortless grace, he racked up 192 yards rushing, mostly on plays where four or five or sometimes all eleven defenders seemed to have a shot at him. His 61-yard touchdown run was a simply ridiculous weave through Mustang defenders who seemed to freeze at just the moment Vince changed direction. Once he found a small opening, he exploded through it, and the defenders had nothing to do but return to the sideline, shake their heads, and come out for another snap to try again later. At times the contest looked like a game of tag with the Mustang defense on one side of the playground and on the other Vince and his childhood friend Courtney Lewis, Madison's splendid tailback, who would go on to play for Texas A&M. Other times Vince would launch the ball, usually after a deft play-action fake, and the rainbow would elicit wide eyes and thoughts of "who the hell is he throwing to?" just as a Madison receiver magically appeared and the ball settled gently into his hands.

Of course, North Shore was no one's patsy, and they rolled out plenty of their own weapons, namely a tailback named Kevin Lewis who gashed the Marlin defense for 291 yards. Madison did manage one final defensive stand, and when the sixty minutes of football were over, even the gloom of the Astrodome was lifted; it shook all the way up to its famous roof at the exploits of Hiram Clark's favorite sons. Great things could still happen here. Young had scored three touchdowns by land and three by air in one of the most memorable games in the long and rich mythology of Texas high school football. Madison 61, North Shore 58.

Madison didn't quite close the deal. The Marlins fell to another major state power, Austin's Westlake High School, 48–42, in the state semifinals. The Westlake Chaparrals slowed the Madison running game, which required Vince to calmly throw five touchdowns, but it wasn't enough. Westlake, for its part, lost the state championship game to Lufkin, led by another phenom quarterback, Reggie McNeal. In any other year, Vince Young would clearly have been the finest player in the state, a quarterback with an inestimable upside. But in 2001, there was a legitimate argument that McNeal, the more polished player, was the better major college football quarterback prospect. This argument was not confined to Texas. These two signal callers were perhaps the best in the nation. McNeal, Young. Young, McNeal. You could analyze the outcome to death, which is precisely what the masses on Internet message boards and dozens of largely self-proclaimed recruiting gurus did. This puzzle, however, posed zero problems for the master recruiter and Longhorn evangelist, the Right Reverend Mack Brown.

Brown knew exactly who he wanted. Getting him to come to Texas would require him to understand where Vincent Young had come from.

The massive buildings of downtown Houston cast imposing shadows. When the sun is behind them, their darkness seems to spill over the freeway to Mount Horeb's front door on Gray Street. But just as the darkness does not overcome the light, so it is that Houston cannot overcome Mount Horeb Missionary Baptist Church. Not that the city hasn't tried. The church sits in the middle of Freedmen's Town, the first settlement of freed slaves in Houston. Ironically, the historical marker welcoming a modern traveler to Freedmen's Town now serves as an entrance to a canyon of beautiful high-rise condominiums with stylish retail, food, and drink purveyors on the ground floors. In the sidewalk cafés, well-dressed Houstonians line the red-brick sidewalks sipping wine by the ten-dollar glass. The Missionary Baptist church on the corner sits quietly in the way of progress, gently defiant and tax exempt.

After a fire destroyed Mount Horeb in 1984, the congregation toiled to rebuild it. This was not what the city fathers had in mind, nor the city lenders, who didn't give the church access to a single dime. Despite being poorer than Job's turkey, the people of Mount Horeb rebuilt without anyone's help, simply with the money they had painstakingly raised and on the faith of one of God's servants, the Reverend Samuel Smith. Telling God's people what they cannot accomplish is a dangerous game the Devil sometimes plays. Pastor Smith plays these games to win.

This sanctuary was Vincent Young's spiritual home, this pastor his spiritual guide. Samuel Smith is a small man, but not a slight one. He's thin through the shoulders and hips but has a barrel chest that proclaims the Word by giving breath to a voice that in his younger days could lead a mass choir into heavenly resonance. He walks spine straight, shoulders back, with closely cropped silver-edged black hair and a neatly trimmed mustache. The straight jawline and penetrating eyes suggest the visage of a soldier, which he once was. He's seventy-six, but has the vitality of a man thirty years younger. When you give Pastor Smith your full attention, your eyes find the distinctive mole above his right cheekbone and then move over to eyes that seem to dissolve into gentleness and peace. These eyes remind you of Jesus. Pastor Smith would never say such a thing, of course. He has no use for approbation or titles. Reverend, Doctor, Pastor are all unnecessary. His parishioners simply call him "Papa."

Papa speaks gently of those who fall through the cracks, but he does not accept such failures of the spirit very graciously. The "missionary" in Missionary Baptist requires its adherents to take to the streets and live out Christ's Great Commission. If you fall through the cracks, Papa Smith might watch you fall, but he is also likely to go after you and bring you back. Papa worried about Vincent falling through the cracks; the young man had been in trouble before, and south Houston can be a dangerous place to be an adolescent. God had already saved him once, when

The Reverend Samuel "Papa" Smith. *(Adam Jones)*

he was seven. Who knew whether such divine intervention would come the next time?

God told Papa that Vincent was special. This was probably unnecessary; Pastor Smith is old, but he is not blind. When Vincent was fifteen, Papa thought that he, with his long frame and huge hands, might become a Jordanesque player on the basketball court. Later, when Papa finally saw him on the gridiron, he understood what the young man could do with a football.

When high school football players are evaluated, there are a few each recruiting season who defy easy description and positional classification. While a lineman is a lineman, a skill position player—a cornerback or safety on defense, receivers and backs on offense—with enough speed and instincts can play multiple positions for a college team. In recruiting parlance, these players are not labeled quarterbacks or running backs or defensive backs, but simply "athletes." Kids described this way are usually talented, extremely fast, and somewhat unknown quantities. A small-town quarterback might play quarterback only because he is the best athlete on the team. On a college team, these physical gifts might put him in the defensive backfield or at wide receiver. There is still some tinge of prejudice here—most "athletes" are black—especially high school quarterbacks.

Vince Young was the ultimate athlete. As a wide receiver, he would be almost impossible to cover. If you put Young in a college backfield, then he would be very difficult to tackle and could even throw the ball on occasion. At quarterback, however, Young's unorthodox mechanics would lead to trouble against well-coached college defenses, and his decision making could lead to disaster as well. He would no longer be a man among boys, but rather a man among men. Taking a raw talent and teaching him the finer points of quarterbacking a major college football team would take time. The learning curve was steep. Surely the immediate gratification of scoring touchdowns from a wide variety of positions would better appeal to a talented young athlete.

Papa Smith was one of the few who understood that Young was not defined by his athletic ability as a football player, but by his powers as a leader. His mind and spirit were his greatest gifts. He had heart and courage; he lifted others up and inspired them to be better. At the end of his final high school game, when Madison's dream ended, he held his head up and went around the locker room telling his despondent teammates "good game" and wanting them to hold their own heads up and be proud of what they had accomplished. He was the perfect "gamer." He had moxie and guile and all of those other intangibles that Longhorn fans sought; he also just happened to be built like Adonis, only faster. Oh, and he was a quarterback, not an "athlete." When he was approached by recruiters he made it clear that he either played quarterback for your school, or he would go somewhere else. On this point, there was no negotiation.

Mack Brown understood. He certainly would not let Vince leave his home state to become a Miami Hurricane over a trifling issue like heart or courage or leadership. Like the rest of his colleagues, Brown was seduced by Young's multiple talents; what he could do running with the football, or split out wide as a receiver, could transform the

Texas offense. But unlike most of his colleagues, Brown was willing to wait.

Unlike most star high school athletes, Vince was also willing to wait. He wanted to be the starting quarterback for the Texas Longhorns, and he was willing to take a redshirt year—a season away from the action that allowed a player to adjust without being penalized a season of eligibility—to learn and acclimate. This agreement required patience. And Mack Brown was a patient man. He and the young man from Hiram Clark had that much in common.

A large fading painted mural of the River Jordan provides the backdrop to the altar in the modest Mount Horeb sanctuary. If God were to bring it to life, it would flow right down on the choir and drench them in holy water. There is an old spiritual that proclaims God's people will have peace like a river. Vincent Young had this peace. The walls of Mount Horeb had instilled it within him. Papa Smith had blessed him and prayed over him and sent him out into the world.

On Sunday, January 13, 2002, Vincent Young told the world that he would be a Texas Longhorn. The next great savior of Texas football waited in the wings, preparing to do battle with the ugly spirits that tormented the Cult of 1969.

Would the Longhorn faithful be willing to put their hopes in the hands of an eighteen-year-old kid? Could he change our lives?

We were certainly willing to give it a shot.

13

WAITING FOR VINCE

Texas vs. Oklahoma

THE COTTON BOWL, DALLAS, TEXAS, OCTOBER 11, 2003

My mother believed that life was an adventure. This was her constant trope: no matter what your circumstance if you were up against something you had not experienced before, then it was, by Mom's definition, an "adventure." This ability to see the essence of life was amazing—in a culture desperate for self-help books that purported to provide the blueprint for a better life, she had unlocked the secret using nothing but her own instincts. She wasn't a bystander during a single moment of the seventy years the earth was lucky enough to have her.

Once the Jones family Chevy Suburban threw a rod and stranded us late at night on a desolate New Mexico highway coming back from a family trip. We were desperate for home at the end of a long weekend of skiing, and inside the disabled car we fell silent as a morgue. Mom broke the hush.

"This is an adventure."

No, Mom, this is desperate and sad, not to mention dangerous. Her attempt at morale building would have been a complete failure had it not been for her sincerity. The evening progressed from grumbles and depression to Mom leading us in harmony to her selected favorites from the Baptist hymnal. Thus lifted up, God delivered us home eventually. I don't recall the details, just the adventure. We were in the moment.

College football fans do not live in the moment. It is simply not part of who we are. Texas fans, as a subset, are particularly impatient. Even though the wait for the next national championship had now stretched past thirty years, it did not imbue patience in us. It simply fueled our desires to an increasingly unsustainable pitch. The Cult of 1969 was not an easy club to be a member of and someone desperately needed to relieve us of our shared burden. I, for one, was still convinced that somewhere God must have owed me this, despite living in the moment back in 2002 when Ryan Aycock, with God as his witness, had intercepted Chris Simms right in front of Zach and me and thousands of delirious Texas Tech students. Beyond that disappointment, I was not privy to any of the divine agreements other members of the Cult of 1969 may have struck with the Almighty, but there must have been a number of obligations floating around upstairs in some great cosmic game of accounts payable to the rabid and all too pious legions of college football fans. But the Texas invoice was never honored. We would instead return to our off-season hibernation period intently following the decisions of talented teenagers, hoping that the best of them would choose Texas, which, with Mack Brown minding the store, most of them did. The tricky part was that these kids would then have to perform at an exceptional level under immense pressures.

The faithful had put great expectations on Chris Simms, the national High School Player of the Year. His ride at Texas offered a lesson in many subjects, first among them a lesson in how easily college football fans discard their saviors. A new one always comes along and we were very grateful that Vincent Young was willing to be the next one to give it a shot. Simms out, Young in.

Of course, it wasn't that simple. While the faithful continued to read the press clippings of the savior from Madison High School, Mack Brown had a football team to run. In his judgment, Vince Young wasn't ready. He was, instead, second team, stuck behind a talented player named Chance Mock. Mock had been a Top-10 quarterback himself coming out of high school. His own father had been a linebacker in the NFL and the son possessed his father's spirit and aggression, but transplanted into a quarterback's body. It was child's play for Mack Brown to convince Mock the younger to leave behind Texas Tech, his father's alma mater, and come instead to suit up for Goliath.

Texas started the 2003 season with Mock under center, which wasn't a bad situation. Chance Mock could fire the ball with velocity and confidence almost equal to Simms and Texas had one year remaining in the brilliant careers of Roy Williams and his partners in speed, Sloan Thomas and B. J. Johnson. Mock knew what to do with this bounty of talent. In the opener against New Mexico State, he only threw fifteen passes, but among them was a beautiful 53-yard bomb to the Legend. The Texas offense didn't see the field much that evening because the Longhorns scored every way you could score—kickoff return, punt return, twice on interceptions—overwhelming the visitors with superior speed and strength all over the field. The only thing missing was an appearance by the Chosen One.

Mack Brown was always biased toward experience, not exactly uncommon for coaches; Bulldog Jones had the same philosophy. Texas fans were often frustrated that dynamic young talent waited in the wings while Mack's trusted journeymen held down the starting spots. Mack was partially a victim of his own success; when you recruit five-star athletes, the faithful tend to have unrealistic expectations that they will dominate from the moment they arrive on campus. At quarterback, everything is magnified a hundredfold. With a comfortable lead over New Mexico State, the 80,000 in DKR were ready for the debut of the Longhorns' new star.

Brown uncorked the genie from the bottle at the 14:45 mark of the fourth quarter. The crowd, bored at a pay-to-play affair that had long gotten out of hand, exploded into a standing ovation as number 10 took his trot onto the field, a confident skip well known to fans of the Madison Marlins. At that point, the bottle could never be recorked. No one knew exactly what would build up in the heart of Vincent Young during the long months where the passion of meaningful competition had been denied and bridled up within him. The passion quickly spilled onto the field and carried away the New Mexico State defenders in its wide deluge.

Vince ran like a man possessed. On his first college snap, he kept the ball and went for nine yards around the left side. Two plays later he ran his first quarterback draw for another seven yards. The Longhorns were flagged on the play and the gain erased. Facing second and 18, Young calmly ran over the right side for 23. Disappointed that he was tackled on his first quarterback draw, he ran his second one 16 yards for a touchdown.

I looked over at Zach. He grinned at me and let out a measured "Ohhhhh . . . kaaaay . . ." Our positions in the fan hierarchy were changing. Vince Young would be the first great Longhorn star of Zach's generation. Zach did not understand as a two-year-old why I had bundled him up against the cold and rain and taken him to see what we all thought would be Ricky Williams's final game in Austin. Nor did he fully appreciate his father's disappointment the night the Red Wolfpack beat the Longhorns by blocking three punts. He also did not fully comprehend the road trip to Lubbock when he was seven and the Red Raiders broke our hearts. But this, this grand show that Vince Young was previewing tonight in DKR, this he got. And so did thousands of other eight-year-old boys, just as I had discerned that Earl Campbell would hold a special place in my heart back in 1975 when I watched him from the top of the west-side upper deck. The year 2003 was a great time for a young boy to find a hero in Austin. We would relish this moment forever. Zach's gaze returned to the action, but my eyes stayed focused on my partner in crime and wondered who he would become.

Mack let Vince throw the ball on the team's next possession. He let loose a Madison High School rainbow special that arched sixty yards down the field. The sure-handed Sloan Thomas made an adjustment to the ball and hauled it in and the crowd exploded again. The ball was actually underthrown, but the faithful would forgive all sins to watch this kid perform, especially when he scored on a six-yard run on the very next play. Young had now carried the ball five times for 61 yards in his college career and not a single defender had gotten anything resembling a clean shot at him.

New Mexico State was one thing, but Arkansas was quite another. The Razorbacks, as the next visitors to DKR, would not be overwhelmed by the dizzying array of talent and speed Mack Brown had assembled. Arkansas and Texas had ended regular hostilities when the Razorbacks left the Southwest Conference for the Southeastern Conference back in 1990. The last time we had seen Arkansas was in a 22–6 loss in the 2001 Cotton Bowl, where the Hogs took out the only good knee Major Applewhite had left and added fuel to the Simms-Applewhite quarterback controversy that nearly sent the good ship Orangeblood right over the side of the world. Yeah, it would be just great seeing them again.

Except I wouldn't see them. God calls you to do some funny things in life, and in September 2003 he called me to go on a spiritual retreat called Walk to Emmaus. The name comes from the story of Jesus returning to Earth and walking along the roadside with two travelers who slowly comprehend that they are in the company of the Messiah. I did not at all mind re-creating this walk with the Lord and nurturing my spirit with my fellow pilgrims, but did I have to do this on the weekend of a Longhorn home game?

"Yes."

"Why?"

I knew better than to ask, and God deigned not answer this question. He may have spoken through Erin. And I may have failed to mention that there was a newborn baby in our house. Ben Jones was born in July and brought great blessings and comfort to our household, especially to my father, whose heart was full again after saying goodbye to the great woman in his life, the grandmother Ben would never meet. Ben also brought with him a nasty case of intestinal reflux and an unpredictable sleeping pattern that rendered his mother entirely unsympathetic to my terrible plight of missing a Longhorn football game over a three-day period when I would engage in adult conversation, be assured eight uninterrupted hours of sleep each night, and, being in the company of sober Christians, was unlikely to have to clean up any vomit.

"It's just awful when your two religions conflict, isn't it?" She said this in a warm and sympathetic tone, the way Audrey Jones might have said it. That was my first clue that I should leave well enough alone.

Much to my astonishment, the retreat participants were not issued radios upon arrival and there was not a television. Our full Saturday afternoon agenda did not include tailgating. One retreat leader took pity on us and brought out a small radio with an earpiece during one of the breaks and several of us huddled around him. He anticipated our question.

"Arkansas, 28–14."

Huh? Arkansas was a battle-tested SEC squad, but they weren't among the top rank and they sure as hell weren't two touchdowns better than Texas. Just the opposite, the Horns were favored by thirteen. We didn't have time to get into the details, but someone did ask the pertinent question.

"Has Vince been in the game?"

Our only access to the outside world pursed his lips and slowly shook his head. We returned to praise and discernment. None of us would understand the details of a 38–28 Arkansas upset until our return to Austin on Sunday afternoon. Number 10 did not take a single snap for the Longhorns. Arkansas, on the other hand, had a brilliant athletic quarterback of their own, and he tortured the Horns through the air and on the ground. Matt Jones, a 6'6" freak of nature with remarkable speed, rushed for over a hundred yards against the Longhorn defense and made all of the big plays the faithful had expected from our own precocious freshman, who was consigned to the bench to watch Chance Mock. Mock actually played well; he threw the ball accurately, and the Razorbacks often had no answer for Roy Williams and B. J. Johnson, but the Longhorns had bigger problems. Arkansas physically whipped them. The Hogs ran the ball at will and completely shut down the Texas running game. Texas got punched in the mouth and didn't hit back. This brilliant collection of athletes lacked toughness. And they lacked the heart of a great leader. Many of us believed that great heart was beating slowly beneath the unsoiled home jersey of number 10 as he walked back to the locker room past the Razorbacks and their obnoxious coach, the aptly named Houston Nutt, who had paused for an impromptu photo session in the Texas end zone.

One of Mack Brown's greatest strengths is the ability to rally the troops after disappointment. Texas rarely lost back-to-back games during his tenure. He exhorted his charges to never let "a single loss beat you twice." It was easy to let negative emotions hang around the next Saturday, and with terrible results. This never happened to Texas, although, to be fair, the Longhorns played no one of any consequence after the Arkansas game. They ripped through Rice and Tulane, and Young played very well. The brilliance really came into focus against the sixteenth-ranked Kansas State Wildcats. Mock started and led the team to a 17–3 lead by hitting Sloan Thomas with a 51-yard pass just before intermission. But when the Texas offense stalled and the Wildcats worked their way back to a 20–17 lead in the fourth, Mack turned to Vince, just as he had not done against Arkansas. Tony Jeffery pulled in a 52-yard bomb from Young at the K-State 13 and the Horns were in business. The Wildcat defense stiffened, and it took six plays before Vince powered into the end zone from the one-yard line on fourth down. The 24–20 lead held to the end and Texas brimmed with confidence facing the annual trip to Dallas to face the No. 1-ranked Oklahoma Sooners.

Again, a big Longhorn game brought with it marital conflict. Erin noted that we had been invited to a game-watching party and relayed this to me with great enthusiasm when I arrived home from work.

"I'm not going." This was the wrong thing to say; it was tactless, arrogant, and unkind. It had the added benefit of being backed by uncompromising conviction.

"What do you mean you are not going?"

"They are not good enough football fans." I figured I would go for broke and add judgmental; women love judgmental. Now the cat was out of the bag. We were going to have this fight at some point in our marriage, we might as well have it early. But my feelings were true; the Texas-Oklahoma game is not a social event. Even if I was not going to actually be in the Cotton Bowl, the contest still required both my complete concentration and my unassailable right to the television remote. Being surrounded by lighthearted chatter would not do at all. Anyone joining me in this blessed sanctum had to know at a minimum the starting twenty-two players on both sides of the ball, Longhorns and Sooners, possess a general knowledge of how the rivalry fits into the context of college football history, and hate the Oklahoma squad with an equal passion Americans reserve for terrorists. Erin's invitation came from a group of people whose company I very much enjoyed, but not only did they not fit any of my criteria of fandom, there were also a number of New England baseball fans in their midst who would no doubt spend valuable television time following their beloved Red Sox march through the playoffs. And so it was that I was left alone in my big blue chair connected only by phone to my friend Birke's house in Amarillo, a huge bachelor-pad gambler's paradise with no less than seven televisions and a full crowd of well-lubricated Panhandle Orangebloods who held the same warped fascination with this contest that I did.

Chance Mock started for the Longhorns, which must have delighted Bob Stoops, but few others. Mack's close-to-the-vest approach of playing not to lose against Oklahoma had raised its ugly head again. Having the opportunity to throw at the Sooners a dynamic force that they would be ill prepared to face, Texas chose the reliable and experienced. The die was cast; we would live or die with Mock on this day.

On the first series, Mock hit B. J. Johnson on an out pattern and was clearly robbed by the clueless officiating crew of a first down, as the pass was ruled out-of-bounds. As I was drafting a letter in my head to the Big 12 office concerning the offense, Mock threw a beautiful interception right into the hands of Sooner All-American Derrick Strait, an Austin native who returned it to the 6-yard line. "Jeeeeee-suz," I proclaimed to the empty room absent any religious context. The Sooners cashed it in for a quick 7–0 lead with almost zero resistance from the Texas defense, which showed all of the resolve of Neville Chamberlain as the Germans poured into Poland. Down a touchdown, Mock returned to the field. He promptly led Texas to a three and out, missing Roy Williams on a slant and then throwing to Sloan Thomas for no gain on third and nine. Of all the things Texas fans were certain of in this life, none was a surer bet than Texas offensive coordinator Greg Davis calling for a wide-receiver screen on third and nine. It was as predictable as the swallows returning to Capistrano.

Fortune finally smiled on Texas when OU return man Antonio Perkins fumbled the ensuing punt and the Horns recovered at the Oklahoma 44. This was a huge break and maybe the only one Texas would get all day. Mack Brown was left with no choice. Two possessions too late, he unleashed the hounds of war. Vince Young took the sacred Cotton Bowl gridiron with his signature Madison Marlin trot. Against him was a formidable Oklahoma squad. Their defense, as usual, was the nation's best, featuring players who would all soon be on NFL rosters like Strait, defensive linemen Tommie Harris and Dan Cody, and linebacker Teddy Lehman. Surveying this stout opposition, Young collected his thoughts and decided that he did not give a tinker's damn about their collective résumé. Mack ran the ball with Cedric Benson on first and second down, but he went nowhere. He had to let Vince play. On third down, Young moved from the pocket and threw a perfect strike on a crossing route to Roy Williams, who was off to the races and finally brought down at the OU 11-yard line. Three plays later, Benson barreled over right tackle to tie the game.

Oklahoma's offense, led by the eventual Heisman Trophy winner, quarterback Jason White, stumbled out of the gate. A Texas sack led to a punt, and the Longhorns set up shop at their own 33. But Young made an awful decision on a sideline pass and Sooner safety Brodney Pool picked it cleanly. With second life, Jason White made Texas pay, directing a quick touchdown drive to make it 14–7. I buried my head in my hands and called Birke. My friend Owen Bybee picked up and I skipped the opening pleasantries.

"If Mack puts Mock back in the game I am going to throw this bottle straight through the damn television set."

"Nice to talk to you, Adam."

I set the phone aside and watched number 10 trot back onto the field. Pretending the last play had never happened, Vince took the snap on first down, started left, and then cut back right all the way across the field, flying 59 yards through the collection of Oklahoma All-Americans, setting up blocks, veering, weaving, evading, and breaking four different tackles all the way down to the Sooner 21 before Lehman finally tripped him up. I jumped off the blue chair and begin to pump my fist in the living room screaming "How do like us *now*, Oklahoma? How do you like us *now*?"

Turned out the Oklahoma Sooners liked us just fine. Three plays later, Vince took the ball from the seven and stretched out at the two to try and cash in the touchdown. Brodney Pool struck again, popping the ball free and into the waiting arms of Strait. I collapsed in a heap.

OU drove the ball the other way for a field goal, forced Texas to punt on the ensuing possession after a blitz caught Vince unaware and led to a sack, then drove for another field goal. With OU leading 20–7, the wheels came completely off. Dropping back to pass from his own 30, Young was hit and the ball flew skyward. Sooner defensive end Jonathan Jackson honored his alma mater, Galena Park North Shore High School, by accepting the former Madison Marlin's bad fortune in his hands and returning it 21 yards for the decisive score. I do not know if Jackson shouted out "Remember the Astrodome" on his way to the end zone, but that is what he would have done in a perfect world. Football karma is a strange and mysterious force.

Vince did lead one more nifty touchdown drive, but by then the Texas defense was completely back on its heels, and the Sooners were in a zone. Bob Stoops dissolved into maniacal satanic laughter on the sidelines. Then he shouted across the field in his confident, clipped tones.

Mack Brown, you dare bring me this boy you say will save you? He is no match for my legions of destruction. Come, I will show you the full power of the dark side.

Well. That's how I remember it anyway.

The game ended 65–13. Oklahoma retained their No. 1 ranking and Texas went back to the drawing board like Wile E. Coyote after another defeat at the hands of the evil Road Runner.

"The Longhorns just quit on me. What is this? This is some sick joke. We have the one guy in the whole world that Oklahoma can't contain and the Horns just quit. The hell with it."

God thought, then answered.

"Be still and know that I am God."

"What?"

"Be still. And know that I am God."

"That's Psalms."

"Is it? Good, I'm glad someone wrote it down."

"Great. Well, it's very helpful."

God accepted my anger and answered it with Grace.

"Why must you always assume that the story has ended?"

"Because I enjoy being mired in hopelessness."

God spoke slowly.

"Be still."

"You said that."

"Yes, but you didn't hear it."

One rule in my life should be never to talk to God after a Texas-OU game. But I could never comply with this. Pondering the Forty-sixth Psalm, I watched the remainder of the Longhorn season wondering what might have been. Texas worked their way back to the Top 10 with a series of wins, but Vince struggled through interceptions and dumb mistakes. When a polished passing attack was needed, he was often relegated to the sidelines as Chance Mock took the field. Mack Brown saw him as the more dependable arm. Mock actually saved the Longhorns against Texas Tech, further torturing his father's alma mater with a brilliant two-minute drill that ended in a 43–40 Longhorn win as his final pass sailed into the outstretched arms of B. J. Johnson for the game-winning touchdown. Vince had his own moments of brilliance in the passing game, including a perfect 67-yard strike to Roy Williams in a 55–16 rout of Oklahoma State.

These brief glimpses were just enough of a tease to make us all wonder how anyone could possibly stop this machine that Mack had created. But Young was a model of inconsistency, and it grated on the star Texas receiving corps that he would often run as they streaked wide open downfield. The quarterback shuffle continued, and though Texas kept winning, the air in Austin held the stench of dissatisfaction. Vince Young, he of the six touchdown passes and seven interceptions (Mock's own ratio was 16/2), was not trusted to win football games for the Texas Longhorns. Maybe he wasn't a quarterback. We all began to wonder where this story would end.

The wonder continued through the Holiday Bowl, the second-tier invitation to San Diego with which, thanks to the Oklahoma Sooners, Texas had grown depressingly familiar. The two quarterbacks rotated through an uninspired offensive game plan that left the passionless Longhorns on the short end of a 28–20 upset loss to Washington State. Vince had completed six of fourteen passes for a paltry fifteen yards. A little over one yard per pass attempt wasn't exactly Messianic. I shut off the game in disgust sitting in my mom's chair in the den of my family's Amarillo home. Once again, I passed by the molten wax of the Advent candles on my way to bed. I wasn't in much of a mood for spiritual reflection this season. The Advent season might promise new birth to God's people, but the rebirth of the Longhorns as a real national title contender would have to wait another year. If Vince Young didn't learn to throw the football, then the wait would be much longer.

One day at Mount Horeb, a three-year-old boy had climbed onto Pastor Smith's lectern and pretended to preach. The parishioners were not amused and told the child to get down. Papa stopped them. Let him stay, he said. "You don't know who that boy will become." He always had patience. Patience came with faith. Papa Smith could live in the moment.

The end of 2003 was not Vince Young's moment and I wondered who Vince Young would become. As I drifted off to sleep that night, I remembered holidays from my childhood when my father would be on call for psychiatric emergencies. Sometimes it would be his turn on Christmas Eve. One year I asked him if it was the worst day of the year to be on call. His answer surprised me.

"Not at all. Christmas Eve is quiet. Everyone still has hope on Christmas Eve. No matter how depressed they are, folks believe that they will wake up the next morning and everything will be better. Christmas Day? That's another story."

Sometimes in life you need to be reminded of your blessings. With or without national titles, the good life moves ever forward.

Our return to Amarillo for the holidays this season had brought with us a new grandson. Ben had my mother's big brown eyes and my father recognized this brilliance right away. On the first night, we laid Ben in the crib that my father had pulled down from the attic, cleaned up, and assembled the day before. It had been a long time since an infant had slept in my father's house. He slept in the crib purchased twenty years before while awaiting the arrival of the first grandchild, surrounded by the bumpers that Mom had lovingly sewn herself out of blue gingham fabric suitable for either boys or girls. Ben didn't know whose roof he slept beneath. He didn't know that he brought joy to a house that had said goodbye to a mother two Christmases before. He didn't even know

Reba really would have loved this one. *(Jones Family)*

that the Longhorns would put on a miserable display in the Holiday Bowl. He was safe, content. Still.

Dad looked in on him.

"I'm sorry Reba isn't here. She would have really loved this one."

A single tear moved slowly down his right cheek as he gazed at Ben. We sat in silence and wondered who he would become.

14

LUBBOCK, REVISITED

Texas vs. Texas Tech

CLIFFORD B. AND AUDREY JONES STADIUM, LUBBOCK, TEXAS, OCTOBER 23, 2004

Mom instinctively covered my eyes. Not to hide me from some corrupting cultural influence, although we were in an art museum: She wasn't protecting me from some voluptuous Titian nude, but rather my own ignorance. I was an insolent adolescent and had been subjected to one modern painting too many during one of my mother's many insistent outings designed to make me a better citizen. My brother Sam used to refer to the experience as a "forced cultural march." We were the prisoners living on overpriced and undersized sandwiches in an endless series of museum cafés where the tables were always too small by half. Looking at the work before us, I couldn't help but goad my poor mother.

"Anyone could paint that."

This was the wrong thing to say. She responded by covering my eyes.

Unfazed by the stares of the patrons around us, the interrogation began. She started in on some funny questions about the painting I could no longer see. Can you picture the colors? Can you remember the points at which one color blends into another? Can you remember where they are in the frame? Do you remember where the artist "cut" the painting by using sharp straight lines?

Now that she issued the challenge, I rose to it. I began to answer these questions and concentrate on the unseen.

She raised the stakes. Can you *feel* the painting?

"Yes"—and I could.

Then she uncovered my eyes.

"Then not 'anyone' could have painted it."

Point made. Not "anyone" can paint. With the best painters, you can see the work, but you can also feel it, long after the image fades. Vision didn't depend on the eyes. Whether an artist had it or not was a line so thin it could dissolve in a single drop of paint.

Vince Young might not have it. He no longer had a feel for the game. The remarkable prodigy from Madison High School was lost on a bigger stage, confused by the complexity and speed and bad intentions of the opposition. This terrified the faithful. We were infuriated that Chance Mock had finished the ugly Holiday Bowl loss to Washington State to end the 2003 Longhorn season.

The loss was bad enough, but the damage it did to Vince's confidence must have lingered into 2004. The season started fine with the Longhorns gutting out a 22–20 payback win at Arkansas—although Vince played inconsistently and victory was not assured until Arkansas's own prodigy Matt Jones did us a tremendous favor by fumbling away the last chance for a Razorback win deep in Texas territory.

Texas went on to destroy the teams on the pay-to-play circuit, but then the real season began, as always, three hours north, in Dallas. Texas emerged from the Cotton Bowl tunnel again full of confidence and, again, the Sooners found new and inventive ways to torture and discourage the Longhorns. This time Texas went into the game owning the

NCAA's longest scoring streak—it had been over two hundred games since anyone had shut out the Longhorn offense. But by the end of the day, the Sooner defense had accomplished the impossible. Oklahoma 12, Texas 0, read the scoreboard—the Sooners' fifth-straight win over Mack Brown's Longhorns. Young and his offensive teammates didn't score a single point. In some ways, this was far more discouraging than the 65–13 loss the year before. It made me wonder what Bob Stoops could possibly do for an encore. Perhaps next season he could defeat Texas by fielding only ten players on defense. Or maybe he could simply stay in the locker room and watch the proceeding on television while his players coached themselves to victory over their hapless Texas cousins.

Worse, the hero that day for the No. 1-ranked Sooners was a freshman tailback named Adrian Peterson from Palestine, in East Texas. He had been billed as the next Earl Campbell, until the young superstar turned down the pleas of the Texas coaching staff and signed instead with Oklahoma. He told the press that Oklahoma gave him the opportunity to win national championships and that players simply didn't "develop" at Texas. Peterson proved his point by gashing the Longhorns for 225 yards in the Cotton Bowl while his defensive teammates held the great Vince Young scoreless. If this moment did not represent rock bottom for Texas in the history of the rivalry, then I couldn't fathom what did.

Texas followed up the miserable performance with a lackluster home win over Missouri. The Tigers, ranked twenty-fifth in the AP poll, were an average team led by a single great player, quarterback Brad Smith, to whom Young was often compared. Smith outplayed his young counterpart that day, but the Texas defense held him in check enough times to survive with a 28–20 win. Young's day ended in the first half when he threw interceptions on back-to-back possessions. He then gave way to Chance Mock and did not return to the action because of suspiciously "bruised ribs." Consulting a well-worn copy of *Gray's Anatomy*, the UT training staff quickly upgraded the injury to the dreaded "bruised sternum." No one bought this. Mack was notorious for underplaying and obfuscating the physical health of his players, which sometimes, of course, served his own strategic purposes. An injury to a young quarterback after he throws his second pick of the day was dubious at best.

Despite Vince's lousy afternoon, two remarkable first-quarter plays in the Missouri game reminded us of the player that he was and might be again. The first tease began from the Texas 34 as Vince handed the ball to Cedric Benson moving left, who flipped it to a talented freshman named Ramonce Taylor on a reverse back to the right. Taylor faked the run and then drifted back and launched a pass down field. Young had slipped into a deep route down the right sideline. Blanketed by a Missouri cornerback who never bothered to look back at the ball in flight, Vince turned completely around and, backpedaling, found the ball. The Mizzou defender slammed straight into him. As an official threw a yellow flag for pass interference, Young leaped up and stretched his long arms around the Tiger draped onto him. He grabbed the ball as it descended, securing it as he and the parasitic defender crashed to the ground. Half the Texas fans were mesmerized by the athletic ability of their young quarterback; the other half—the cynical half—immediately wondered why he was wasting his time playing quarterback when it was obvious that he was a potential superstar wide receiver in the NFL.

The very next play, drifting in the pocket to his right from the Missouri 23, he ran flush into the teeth of the Missouri pass rush and a Tiger defensive end delivered a crushing blow to his unprotected right side, the force of which knocked Vince straight backward. The blow should have laid him cleanly on the ground and brought the training staff onto the field, but somehow, defying all of the rules of physics, he remained upright. Taking two very uncertain stumbling steps backward, he righted himself, pivoted, and then calmly froze the Tiger defense with a pump fake. Then he was off to the races in the open field to his left. He outraced one would-be tackler to the sideline and turned on the jets aiming for the pylon. Cut off by the Missouri safety, Vince went airborne at the 5-yard line. His huge right hand had a death grip on the pigskin as if it were the last apple in the hands of a starving man. Completely parallel with the ground beneath him, Young absorbed a hard shot from the Tiger defender, stretched the ball across the plane of the goal line, and hit the ground. He then leapt to his feet with both arms hopefully pointed to the sky. The field judge agreed. Touchdown, Texas.

These two great plays somehow gave way to an otherwise uninspiring performance. The second interception of the day left the faithful wondering whether Vince would ever get it back. "Bruised sternum, my ass. Mack Brown doesn't trust him to win the damn football game . . ." The ugly second half drew to a close, and it did not feel like a Longhorn victory. Instead, it resembled a funeral procession and the casket contained the last dead hopes of Longhorn Nation that yet another savior quarterback would lead us to the promised land. The wait for the Messiah would continue as we pondered what it meant that Vince had completed 11 out of 32 passes for a measly 105 yards with two interceptions and three sacks in his last two outings.

This was the state of Longhorn football when Erin and I boarded a plane to Chicago for a needed fall vacation. Chicago is the great American city, a cultural crossroads of all the best our nation has to offer dropped right into the middle of the lower 48. Exploring its streets presents pleasures at every turn. Our expedition was necessarily interrupted on Saturday night, of course. Regardless of how dispirited I was by Longhorn football, not watching my guys was unthinkable. Tonight's opponent was Texas Tech, and the game was distressingly played on their own familiar turf at Jones Stadium. Because of the Longhorns' shaky start, Tech was actually favored. Small as it was, the one-point spread upset the natural order of Texas college football. Nevertheless, the twenty-fourth-ranked Red Raiders were rolling along behind a quarterback named Sonny Cumbie—really it didn't seem to matter who played quarterback for Tech, the result was that they scored lots of points very fast. Unlike most Raider squads, this version actually played something resembling defense. The spread would have been more but for the benefit of the doubt the gambling public tended to give Texas simply by virtue of being Texas. All of these factors were insignificant when held up to the one single overwhelming immortal truth: Bad things happen to the Longhorns in Lubbock. This night could end in disaster and I could lose an entire night of vacation depressed about the outcome. Erin understood this and steeled herself for the inevitable. We would not abandon Texas in their time of need. We were wayward fans in search of comfort far from home.

Luckily for us, Chicago is the greatest home for wayward fans ever created. Every team, no matter how far-flung, has its own bar. For Michigan fans it's Duffy's Tavern; Ohio State fans silently hate the Michigan fans from the comfort of the Gaslight on Racine. Notre Dame fans congregate at O'Donovans, and just about everywhere else with beer on tap. Tennessee fans sing "Rocky Top" to confused Chicagoans at the Goose Island-Clybourn Brew Pub, and the Oklahoma Sooners, along with half of the SEC, go downtown to Joe's, presumably to enjoy the indoor plumbing. If you are a homesick Longhorn, you have several options, but we bypassed them in favor of the Tin Lizzie, which was technically Michigan State territory, but the Spartans had already played earlier in the day. We were the first customers of the night, and the amiable bartender honored this status by dedicating a television to our cause. He even gave us the remote. The game from Lubbock was a national telecast on Ted Turner's station, and any bar worth its salt could conjure it up by the magic of digital cable with a couple of flicks of the thumb. The screen provided us a close-up view of the screaming red and black Tech student section. The waitress brought close into reach two Bass Ales. We were under way. I silently repeated the mantra, playing the karmic reverse-hex card: Bad things happen to the Longhorns in Lubbock.

Over the next three hours we watched Vincent Young, the kid from Hiram Clark, become Vince Young, the Man Who Would Be King of the College Football World. Two events had happened during our week in Chicago to which we were not privy. The results of these momentous happenings in the life of Vincent Young would be revealed in time to the two lonely patrons far from home in a Chicago bar. The Sunday after the Missouri game, he had returned to Mount Horeb, taking his friend Selvin Young, the Longhorn tailback and kick returner, with him. The two teammates worshipped and prayed. Papa Smith took them in and blessed them, reminding Vince of his spiritual home, the one with the defiant exterior and the peaceful heart. Could it be that he had forgotten?

Upon his return to Austin, Mack Brown the Evangelist went to work.

The Sanctuary at Mount Horeb, Vince Young's spiritual home. *(Adam Jones)*

The young quarterback was treated to a film festival celebrating his own greatness. The missed reads, the confusion of defensive shifts, the careless ball handling, the interceptions were all edited out. Instead, Vince was reminded that his remarkable talent knew no bounds. The unerring cuts with the football, the powerful arm, the ability to move and fire on the run like only the rarest of quarterbacks, the leadership required to raise up an entire team, this is who he was. All Vince needed to do was to be who he was.

We all need to be reminded of who we are. It was time for Vince Young to remember who he was and from where he had come. God did not bless him with these gifts to live a life of discouragement or, for that matter, to play wide receiver. Mack didn't wait to be asked about his starting quarterback in the Monday press conference.

"Vince will start."

He did not return to the topic. Six days later Vince Young's game flowed like a river. The dam of discouragement didn't burst right away. The Longhorns wasted their first possession, and Texas Tech quickly brought back bad memories as my old friend Nehemiah Glover took a Cumbie pass 58 yards to set up a Red Raider touchdown. But with the score 7–0, the frustrations of my life as a Texas fan began to be lifted piece by miserable piece. The first piece Vince cleared away was the overriding fear the faithful had that he could not throw the football. With Tech primed to stop the run, Vince calmly tossed back-to-back thirteen-yard completions to get a drive going. Then he simply ran the ball. To the left, to the right, up the middle—it didn't seem to matter. With everyone on the Tech defense trying to stop him, number 10 progressed down the field until the Raiders had no turf left to defend and the score was 7–7. After a Tech turnover, he did it again and the score was 14–7. Tech tied the game, but this only served to irritate Vince. He went bombs away to Tony Jeffery for forty-four yards to start a drive that ended with him throwing his first touchdown pass of the night to Lubbock's favorite son, the fine Longhorn tight end David Thomas.

Tech was not going to keep up. It got to the point, as Texas scored on nine out of their last ten possessions, that Erin and I started to laugh uncontrollably. The entire scene was surreal. We hadn't noticed that the Tin Lizzie was now full of baseball fans; it was the first game of the World Series after all. Why this throng was glued to the Fall Classic between St. Louis and Boston when they could be watching greatness in the making live from Lubbock puzzled me. At regular intervals, someone in a Halloween costume would push his way through the baseball fans making their way to a party in the back room. As the clock struck zero in Lubbock and we waited to pay our exorbitant bar tab, I stood in line for the men's room right between an old man in a Red Sox cap and Count Dracula, who was maintaining his spot in the queue while trying to talk Madonna into some late-night liaison back at the castle. Dracula struck out, but the Red Sox eventually won the World Series, breaking the Curse of the Bambino, which dated to 1918. This was a good omen. The cool Chicago breeze felt good on my face as we exited the Tin Lizzie onto Clark Street. The world was full of possibility.

Grandad Jones got conned once, in 1918. The U.S. Navy welterweight boxing champion was touring the Texas Panhandle and needed opponents in each of the small towns along the route. My grandfather was a seventeen-year-old country schoolteacher in Ochiltree County. This was a year before he would enroll at West Texas; you only needed a high school degree to teach in the public schools at the time. Ochiltree County was apparently devoid of topflight boxers so the organizers were dispatched to visit the young teacher. He was a football player, they had heard, and folks around town noticed that he was always up early running along the dusty farm roads to stay in shape. When the day of the exhibition came, Grandad laced up the gloves and, at the sound of the bell, rushed to his opponent's corner and, with perfect form for an offensive guard, knocked him straight backward onto the mat by striking him in the chest with his two gloved palms. The champ got up—either amused or angry, my grandfather wasn't sure which—and, never showing the human decency to simply knock him out, proceeded to punish Bulldog Jones in cruel and innovative ways for the remainder of the three rounds.

The 2004 Texas offense became innovative and cruel. If you didn't knock it out quickly, then you were doomed. It depended on a strategy called the "zone-read." The Longhorn version put our fleet quarterback in the shotgun formation with a single tailback offset to his right or left. After securing the snap, the quarterback moves toward the tailback with the football; some coaches call this the "reach and ride." Reaching the ball toward the tailback's belly, the quarterback makes a decision. If the opposing defensive end, who is intentionally unblocked, maintains his responsibility for the quarterback, then the tailback gets the ball and runs to the hole in front of him. If the defensive end "crashes" down to tackle the tailback, then the quarterback runs the ball to the spot the defensive end vacated. When the quarterback is Vince Young, this means serious trouble for the opposition. The defenders were always in a "damned if you do, damned if you don't" posture, for the Longhorn tailback was a 225-pound dreadlocked wrecking ball of a man named Cedric Benson. Benson had been a Texas high school football legend prior to Vince Young raising the stakes on legend status in a state that churns through high school football legends like hot coffee in a diner. Of course, Benson was no overrated local hero; he was the real deal. As part of Zach's spiritual formation during our postdivorce year in the condo, we had taken the short walk down to DKR to watch Benson score five touchdowns for Midland's Lee High School in the 2000 5A state championship game; this was Lee's third state championship in a row, and Benson had scored fifteen touchdowns in the three title games. Like I said, he was the real deal. Benson went on to a great first three seasons at Texas, but never had he had a partner like Vince Young. A linebacker watching Benson and Young run the zone read was like a fish watching bald eagles hunting in pairs: swift, ferocious and decisive. You never knew which one was going to swoop down and take you.

A defense could stop the zone read by "selling out" to it—committing an extra linebacker to the same side as the unblocked defensive end, which reversed the "damned if you did" calculus and put the onus on the quarterback to make a bad decision. Texas countered this by adding wrinkles in which Vince would run an outside option play, or simply a quarterback draw. Or, oddly enough, sometimes the Texas quarterback would actually throw the ball. While Vince's critics fretted over his unorthodox throwing motion and his decisions with the football, Young quietly became a very accurate and confident quarterback. Do not tell God's people what they cannot do. They will respond by rebuilding tiny churches in tough neighborhoods or launching 44-yard bombs to Tony Jeffery.

Despite these feelings of invincibility—or In-Vince-ability in the parlance of the day in Austin—God decided to frustrate me anyway. He did this as I returned to the upper deck at DKR to watch the sixth-ranked Horns rip through nineteenth-ranked Oklahoma State. As usual, Oklahoma State appeared like the Ghost of Christmas Past at a crucial moment in my personal football history. What made it worse was that I was seated in almost exactly the same seat where Zach and I watched Kansas State mercilessly beat and bewilder poor Major Applewhite back in 1999. None of this occurred to me on a pleasant night kickoff. I fully expected Texas to roll. After the teams politely traded touchdowns—Texas always started slow—I was fully prepared for the ass-kicking to commence, which it did. Oklahoma State commenced to kick our ass. They got the ball after sacking Vince to force a punt. A quick touchdown made it 14–7 Oklahoma State. Then Vince threw a pick right at the Cowboy goal line. Then he threw another on a crossing pattern.

"What is this, a Chris Simms retrospective?"

God wasn't listening.

With the score an unbelievable Oklahoma State 35, Texas 7, Erin and I were convinced by our game companions to violate the Reba Jones rule of fandom and head down the ramps to the alumni center to get a drink. It wasn't quite the International Food Pavilion at the state fairgrounds, but it was close. I would have to do without the beef Wellington and rely on the nutritional content of Shiner Bock. This is when I learned an essential football truth. Never turn your back on Vince Young. Halfway down the ramps, the crowd roared. A middle-aged man was chasing a small child up the ramp just opposite of us, his telltale earpiece stretched to a radio on his hip.

"What happened?"

He managed a quick "Vince! . . . Bo Scaife . . . ," and his voice trailed off behind him as he chased the ascending five-year-old. We got the translation upon seeing the replay in the alumni center. Vince had driven the Longhorns to the Oklahoma State five and hit Bo Scaife in the left flat. Two Cowboys converged immediately and rode him out of bounds, but not before the big tight end from Colorado had stretched the ball out over the plane of the goal line. The official signaled touchdown with four seconds left on the clock. To this day Oklahoma State fans are not convinced that Scaife scored. God may have simply moved the pylon.

Trailing 35–14, Texas, remarkably, had some momentum going into the half. Knowing that his guys would start with the ball in the second half, Mack Brown did some quick locker room math and informed his players that they would win the game 42–35. Damned if they didn't believe him. Vince quickly drove the team eighty yards to make it 35–21. The defense forced a three and out, and by the time my friend Robert Scott had returned to our corner of the alumni center with four more beers, Cedric Benson was flying through the defense untouched on a 23-yard touchdown run to make it 35–28. Our friend Holly Jacques insisted we return to the stadium, which I found strange. Holly, a Lake Charles Cajun and a dyed-in-the-wool LSU fan, was suggesting we give up access to cold beer to watch her adopted team finish a game. This didn't compute, but I would have none of it anyway. Having already violated the fundamental rule of fandom by leaving our team behind, we could not now return in fair weather. It wasn't right. God wouldn't approve of this even if he was paying attention, which, at this point in the evening, he must have been.

"You're kidding." Why did Erin always think I was kidding?

"Nope, I'm staying right here. I don't deserve to see this one in person."

And I didn't. I had no right to watch Vince line up in the zone-read formation, move right on an option play to Benson, and then casually flip the ball to Ramonce Taylor on a reverse. The blazingly fast freshman took the ball 48 yards the other way and the lid on the alumni center, boiling over from hundreds of penitent fans in close quarters seeking forgiveness, completely blew apart in a cascade of noise, sweat, and beer. 35–35. Oklahoma State was done. Texas didn't stop at 42–35; they pushed it to 49–35 and then, with one last spectacular 42-yard touchdown run, Vince made it 56–35. Texas had just won a game by three touchdowns in which it had been down by four touchdowns. If you asked me, "Was I there?" I would simply smile and shake my head.

Texas might as well have had the week off the next weekend against the conference doormat Kansas Jayhawks. This game was not going to be close, so I did not mind in the least watching the Horns in an early morning start with a toddler in my lap. Ben enjoyed this as much as I did, and it was the first time just the two of us had watched a game together. This brought back memories of Zach and me being bachelor roommates; had Ben been just a little older I might have taken him to the Posse East. Of course, we couldn't play on the floor at the Posse. With Texas being twenty-two point favorites, I could play with Ben and keep just one eye on the game. I wouldn't miss much before putting Ben down for his nap and watching the Longhorn subs finish running the poor Jayhawks out of their own stadium. Once again, I expected the Good Father Award for this and, once again, God disappointed me. Texas started by missing a field goal, then Vince threw a pick, then another one. Texas missed another field goal, then shanked a punt for 21 yards, followed by the Texas secondary blowing a coverage on a 73-yard pass play that led to a Kansas touchdown. Things went so bad for the Longhorns that Kansas fans, upon hearing about the proceedings, actually left a basketball exhibition and drifted over to the stadium for the second half. In hoops-crazed Lawrence, Kansas, this would be roughly equivalent to a group of Benedictine monks leaving evening prayers to watch a badminton match. Kansas led 23–13 with about seven minutes to go in the game when Vince finally drove Texas down the field to make it 23–20. Texas got the ball back with plenty of time, but my hope dissipated on the final drive when Vince was sacked for an eight-yard loss and then couldn't find an open receiver with a map, sailing two incompletions in a row to bring up fourth and eighteen with just over a minute to go.

The dream ended here, I thought as I looked at Ben, who simply wanted to play cars. I had no use for cars or toddlers. I thought instead of a lie his dying grandmother had probably told me to protect me from my own worst instincts.

I never did learn to live in the moment, not the way you did.

You're wrong. You do just fine in the moment.

Not in this moment. Had Mom been here she would have continued to play with cars and the game would have ended however it was going to end. Final scores never defined her. Tender moments with her grandsons did.

"Mom, we're going to lose to Kansas."

The outcome in my mind was already decided. But that thought didn't capture my true feelings.

"We're going to piss this whole season away by losing to the worst team in the Big 12."

That didn't cover it either.

"We're going to fucking lose to Kansas."

That did it. I wondered for a moment if I had said it aloud. Unfazed by the pending doom, Ben continued to play.

So did number 10. Vince Young doesn't share my lack of faith. He does not panic. He does not fret. And he does not lose to Kansas. Living completely in the moment, he took the snap and drifted back to pass on fourth and eighteen. A cold chill shuddered through me as he left the safety of the pocket. He was running.

"Eighteen yards . . . He has to get eighteen yards . . ."

He went for an open lane to his right, but it closed quickly. Kansas linebacker Kevin Kane, who had already intercepted Vince earlier in the day, closed the path upfield to the left, forcing Vince into the arms of linebacker Nick Reid. Reid was one of the few legitimate NFL prospects on the Kansas roster. He set up for the tackle with technical perfection, his eyes centered on the big burnt-orange 10 coming toward him. Vince Young was still six yards from grace when he headed straight at Reid.

The traditional Texas road uniform includes white socks pulled all the way up the knee giving way to unadorned white pants and simple white jerseys with burnt orange numbers. The "tight whites" make the players look even faster than they actually are. In Vince Young's case, with his long, bounding stride and his six-five frame, there are times when he is simply a blur to the television cameras. Only on the slowest playback could one see the precise moment at which Vince changed vectors to his right, away from Nick Reid. Like the fine linebacker he was, Reid had properly accounted for this in his pursuit angle. What he hadn't allowed for was Young taking three remarkably quick half steps as Reid tried to wrap him up. The poor Jayhawk might as well have been trying to catch Casper the Friendly Ghost as the white streak floated through his grasp and landed safely out of bounds six steps later—a full four yards beyond the first-down marker.

Four plays later, with eleven ticks on the clock, Vince took the snap, drifted left, and fired the most anticlimactic game-winning touchdown in college football history 21 yards to Tony Jeffery.

I looked down at Ben, who offered me a car. His grandmother's familiar deep brown eyes looked intently through me, perhaps wondering who this strange man was who had been screaming at the television set.

"That Vince Young can paint, son."

He can paint.

I've got peace like a river,
I've got love like an ocean,
I've got joy like a fountain in my soul.

15

ROSE BOWL DREAMS

Texas vs. the University of Michigan

THE ROSE BOWL,
PASADENA, CALIFORNIA, JANUARY 1, 2005

The game is never close. Chris Simms ends it by simply kneeling on the football. The clock runs out and he holds the ball above his head briefly before flipping it to the ref. I'm not even sure who Texas has just defeated, but they are definitely the national champs. I am crammed into the Rose Bowl—definitely the Rose Bowl, I can see the mountains in the background—with thousands of delirious fans. Except I am apart from the joyous throng. Standing like a bystander in an impenetrable bubble, I don't hear the cheers and am not touched by the hugs and high fives. This must be what a ghost feels like. I look around to see if anyone else looks like a ghost as the scene fades from view and the stadium lights go out. Now I am alone as I trudge down the steps to the tunnel and walk past some guys in coveralls cleaning up in the dark. Emerging in an empty parking lot, I don't know where my car is.

This is when the dream evaporates. My own subconscious cannot conjure this moment, and I wake up and vaguely remember that Chris Simms didn't lead the Longhorns to the national championship. Reality intrudes. In 2001, the national champ was crowned in the Rose Bowl, but Texas didn't play in that game. They blew it in the Big 12 Championship in Dallas. My dream season didn't come true, and now Simms plays quarterback for the Tampa Bay Buccaneers in the National Football League. Here it is in the fall of 2004 and I am still dreaming of a game that never took place. The fate of Texas now rests in the hands of a new cast of characters. When reality becomes apparent, I shake off this dream of a national championship not won and the fog of sleep slowly lifts. I check the clock and walk down the hall to watch Ben sleep. Mom and Bulldog enjoy this scene.

"That one's going to be trouble." Bulldog said this not with concern but pride.

"Yes, I'm sorry I won't get a chance to meet him. There's another grandson on the way. I left them too soon, didn't I?"

"We all leave too soon."

Mom paused to ponder Bulldog's philosophy. Deciding she didn't buy it, she continued.

"You didn't. You were ready to go."

"I guess so, but I would have enjoyed this. Of course, I would be 105 right now, so it probably wasn't in the cards."

"Maybe not for you, but I got robbed. Do you think he worries about the Longhorns too much?"

Grandad laughed. "Yes. But it's mostly our fault. I'm glad he kept the Sun Bowl watch."

"I've been meaning to ask you, do you think Vince Young might be better than Sammy Baugh?"

There are, in all sports, fans. And then there are FANS. As the new millennium progressed, I started veering into the small f fan group. I was not, for example, a "committed traveling fan." I no more had to go to every game home and away to know I loved the Longhorns than I had to go to the Holy Land with Billy Graham Ministries to know I loved Jesus. If tickets to DKR were in my hand, I was there, and, after the Oklahoma State drama, I would never leave early again. But if the home tickets were atmospherically high-priced or the Horns were away, I didn't go to any great lengths to see them in person. My maniacal screaming from the comfort of my living room sufficed. Maybe the two-year hiatus at Duke helped teach me to survive without the endless endorphinal rush of live Longhorn athletics. More likely, it was just life. You get to a point where you settle in and contentment comes. You are no longer the "bright young" anything, not at work and certainly not on the court for the Tarrytown Methodist basketball squad, where my thirty-seven-year-old legs made steps without any spring in them. Playing for the Methodists was a problem anyway. Traditional liturgical churches aren't exactly havens for young college graduate athletes eager to fill out recreational basketball league rosters. My teammates and I continued to get older and to face a never-ending stream of up-and-coming talent from the Baptists, Charismatics, and the huge nondenominational five-thousand-member Bible churches like Shoreline Christian Center in North Austin, which must have employed talent scouts. The Episcopalians and Presbyterians never fielded teams, which was a shame, because my Methodist boys and I would have whipped the everlasting crap out of our Christian brothers from those neighborhoods. Instead we led the league in "number of children at home" while finishing a gentlemen's sixth in the Hyde Park Baptist Tuesday Night League and looking bad doing it. Of course, we all went home to wives and kids who loved us, and that made it all worthwhile. My passions had turned from sports to kids. I missed the 2003 Texas-Nebraska game, even though I had tickets in hand, in order to watch Zach play flag football in the YMCA league. It was Zach's decision, and I told him I wouldn't be disappointed either way. I was proud of him for picking his teammates and participating in a real football game, instead of just watching one. But, of course, that did mean I missed

Texas—unveiling the zone read for the first time—killing the Cornhusk-ers that day, 31–7, among the scores a jaw-dropping 65-yard run by number 10. Zach's team also won that day, and he even got to take a turn at quarterback, although without any jaw-dropping 65-yard touch-down runs. I hoped again to receive some godly approbation for being a good dad.

We still made a few games a year as a family, even with Ben securely fastened to his father in a Baby Bjorn, the Norwegians' version of a re-verse papoose, the uncoolest way ever invented for a man to watch a football game. This is especially true if the kid is crying, which Ben did for about thirty minutes straight one afternoon after I—forgetting I had an infant strapped to my chest—jumped out of my seat screaming when Vince hit Roy Williams on a deep post. His mother was mortified. With me, not with Roy Williams.

The rhythms of our lives settled into a gentle cadence. We were the happy and functional American family, the kind that television and the movies don't believe exists, not since *Cosby* hung up the cleats anyway. As 2004 came to a close, Erin was pregnant with the next great Texas football fan, another son, whom we would name Charlie, but I'll get to him later. In the face of all of this peace and contentment, the search for the national title began to fade and Longhorn football became less of a driving force in my life. Would I trade one of Ben's morning smiles for a Longhorn national championship? Or trade a session of one-on-one bas-ketball with Zach for a national title? Of course I would—but the margin was getting closer. Perhaps I was learning to live in the moment.

Vince Young, to his credit, dismantled this entire gestalt in the fall of 2004. Just as I had settled in to my zone of domestic bliss, Vince re-minded me of the importance of college football. A balanced life would have to wait; Texas was going to do great things.

After the Houdini-act victory at Kansas, only one hurdle remained in the path of Texas greatness in 2004. Our land-grant cousins from Texas

A&M would come to Austin the day after Thanksgiving. The Aggies always caused a great spectacle, congregating for a huge rally on the steps of the state capitol. On the morning of the game, the 2,000-member Aggie Corps of Cadets would parade down Congress Avenue in full regalia. The Corps dated to the beginning of Texas A&M, long before women were admitted to the university. The military traditions of the school were most evident in the Texas Aggie Band, pardon me, the "Fightin' Texas Aggie Band," one of the few true military bands in college football outside of West Point and Annapolis. They put on exactly the same complicated precision-marching show at halftime for the last hundred years and I bought it every time. I don't know why—many of the Longhorn faithful treated A&M tradition with derision, like any good fan would—I must have had a soft spot in my heart for the Aggies. Maybe it came from my mother, who loved to sing the "Aggie War Hymn" around the house, probably just because she liked the sound of it; the fact that it annoyed her three Longhorn children was merely a side benefit.

One morning after Thanksgiving, I remember reading the newspaper at the Posse when an Aggie freshman cadet came up to me in a fright because his uniform was incomplete. He asked me if I had an extra black tie and I got the sense that he was facing serious consequences if he couldn't procure one before the Congress Avenue parade started. I dug around in my car looking for a strip of black cloth that might suffice, but couldn't come up with one. He appreciated the gesture anyway. I guess I could have been accused of aiding and abetting the enemy, since most Texas Aggies hate the University of Texas with a passion, but largely I was ambivalent and reserved this kind of hatred only for the Oklahoma Sooners. There was, of course, a practical reason for my good nature: Mack Brown owned Texas A&M.

This was completely out of character for Mack. He was considered one of the good guys in college football, and, if anything, Longhorn fans sometimes were irritated that he seemed to lack the "step on the throat, humiliate your opponent" mentality we secretly admired in Bob Stoops. Mack was almost too classy. But ever since the famous Bonfire Game in

1999 when Texas players were awakened at all hours of the night before the game by Aggie fans who had somehow secured their room numbers, which was followed by the hotel not serving the team breakfast in violation of their contract, Mack seemed to delight in destroying the hopes and dreams of Aggieland under the wheels of the Longhorn juggernaut he was slowly building. Chris Simms might have hated the Aggies even more than Mack did. Of all of the people who took Major Applewhite's side in the great quarterback controversy, the Aggies were the most annoying. For starters, it was not even their controversy, and they should have minded their own damn business. But they loved to fuel the fire that painted Mack as a snake-oil salesman who had shoved aside the moxie gamer Applewhite for the fair-haired silver-spoon-fed Simms. The whole melodrama fueled the classic land-grant inferiority complex against Big State U. Simms represented everything the Aggies hated about Texas—arrogance, elitism, smugness. Simms responded by humiliating the Aggie pass defense in a series of ugly one-sided games. Texas didn't ever let up against the Aggies; the last four contests had been decided by 26, 14, 30, and 31 points. In 2003, Vince picked up where Simms had left off, leading a rushing attack with Cedric Benson that steamrolled the Aggies on their home turf for 393 rushing yards.

With Texas in firm control of the rivalry—a blessed state of affairs—it didn't even register with me to leave Erin's family in Dallas, where we had celebrated Thanksgiving, to make a three-hour drive back to Austin for the 2004 game. Texas was going to kill them, and I preferred to stretch out in the living room, perhaps even drifting off for a fourth-quarter nap if Vince and the boys put the game out of reach. When Erin's brother Kirk called from Waco with an offer of a pair of tickets from his wife Liz's family, I politely declined, not wanting to deal with the logistics. I was spoiled.

Erin's brother Craig, our weekend host, called me on it. Craig had not gone to Texas, opting instead for a small liberal arts college. He then followed in the steps of his father and mother to Baylor Law. None of this stopped him from being a devoted Longhorn fan. College football fans sometimes embrace an ugly hierarchy that puts alums at the top; those who attended the school take on an air of authenticity that others don't enjoy. Really, we don't own our teams and we are no better fans—and sometimes worse ones—than those who come to love the Longhorns out of feelings not rooted in academic affiliation. State pride, the bonds of community, tradition, the cool helmets, a fascination with Vince Young, it made little difference why you loved the Longhorns.

"Call him back . . . We're going to the game." Craig said this with the intensity of one who had seen only a handful of Longhorn games up close, as opposed to the dozens I had enjoyed the great fortune of attending.

I calculated the amount of time I had spent as a Thanksgiving traveler during the week. Six more hours in the car to watch a Longhorn blowout held no appeal for me, especially since I would then turn around and make the same drive back to Austin the day after the game. My mother, no doubt, would have been very disappointed in my lack of "adventure." Then Craig threw a curve.

"Who said we're driving?"

Before I could contemplate what that meant, he came even stronger.

"I'll pay for your airline ticket."

What to do about this? By the time his second sentence had come out, Erin had already slunk behind the computer and brought up the Southwest Airlines schedule. It was as if my wife actually wanted to kick me out of the house. Shocking.

In the space of two hours, I had evolved from couch potato in Dallas to superfan, standing on the sun-splashed porch of the Texas Alumni Center drinking a cold Shiner Bock and anticipating a Longhorn victory. Craig and I quickly found Kirk, and we made our way across the street to DKR. Kirk was traveling with his six-year-old son, Will. My godson by marriage, Will reminded me of another little boy whose hand I had held countless times moving up these stadium ramps. Zach was with his mom this Thanksgiving; so go the holidays of a divorced dad. I paused at the mezzanine of the massive west-side upper deck and looked out over my beloved Austin. Zach was out there somewhere. I wasn't resentful. He was safe. He was loved. But he wasn't with me, about to watch the Longhorns do battle in DKR, and that caused my heart to cry silently as I broke the threshold of the tunnel and took in the familiar sights and sounds of the great rivalry. The stadium cheer was a full-throated roar.

TEXAS!

I reached back to 1975 when I first heard this thunderous boom.

FIGHT!

It had hit me right in the gut back then, even though I was not much older than Will, who sat to my left soaking in the same magic that I remembered from long ago.

TEXAS!

The feeling never left. I felt the same shiver of excitement course through my body as a student trying to coax victory out of a team with limited talent.

FIGHT!

The feeling was there when I carried Zach on my shoulders to DKR four years before and we watched Simms torch the Aggies in a 43–17 runaway, exchanging high fives throughout a second half when the Horns could do no wrong.

TEXAS!

I remembered the days before 9/11 when the Longhorns left a 44 on the scoreboard for Cole Pittman. I was with the next great woman in my life, and all seemed right in the world.

FIGHT!

The night against New Mexico State when the young prodigy from Hiram Clark first teased us, shining with a brilliance we had never seen before.

TEXAS!

This was it. I wanted to explode into the mass of sound and become one with it as the rumbling noise lifted up into the heavens.

Game time.

Texas started slow, as had become their norm, and the two teams traded punts. On the second Longhorn possession, the Aggies found themselves mauled by a nasty Texas rushing attack. Fourteen straight times the Longhorns ran the ball, and the crowd exploded as Vince strode into the end zone on a three-yard option run. A missed extra point left it at 6–0.

From the time he had been the star quarterback for state champion Lufkin back in 2001, the Aggies' Reggie McNeal had spent his entire career compared to Vince Young. Today he played with the intensity of a man tired of comparisons. With strong arm and quick feet he directed a crisp Aggie drive that ended with a frozen rope of a pass to DeQwan Mobley for a 33-yard touchdown to tie the game. Thankfully, the imposing form of Texas All-American linebacker Derrick Johnson obliterated the extra-point attempt and left the game at 6–6.

The teams traded ugly possessions and the Aggies were kind enough to miss a very makeable field goal. With about seven minutes to go, Vince set up shop at his own 11-yard line with fire in his eyes. Vince mastered the Aggie defense, getting everyone involved: Bo Scaife here, Tony Jeffery there, alternating runs with the Texas battering rams Cedric Benson and fullback Will "Headache" Matthews. The Aggies were back on their heels. Texas drove all the way to the Aggie one-yard line when, once again, my internal space-time continuum was broken and God decided to intervene to make sure I was paying attention.

As Vince stretched his six-five frame toward the goal line for what should have been a sure touchdown, the Aggies knocked the ball loose and 80,000 aghast Longhorn fans endured the sight of Aggie cornerback Jonte Buhl sprinting 98 yards for an incredibly unlikely 13–6 A&M halftime lead. The Longhorn balloon deflated, and you could hear pins dropping throughout the upper deck. Kirk finally broke the silence.

"I wish he'd stop doing that."

I'll say this: Vince Young sure as hell had a flair for the dramatic. Half the time I figured he must have thrown picks and fumbled the ball away on purpose just to add to the excitement. He reminded me of my brother David, the best game player in the family, who would occasionally throw a Monopoly game simply so his siblings would continue to play with him. When Zach and I would play catch, he would often pretend to be Vince. Usually he demonstrated this by launching a long pass to me or by making some wicked cut around the crape myrtle. But the one thing he would do that perfectly captured the essence of his quarterback hero was proclaim: "Look, Dad, I'm Vince Young," then proceed to drop back and, instead of firing a pass to his old man, pretend to check his watch and hold the ball to his side, as if bored with the whole affair. Zach would then let out a yawn and check his watch again before shouting out in mock surprise, "Hey, there's David Thomas," pretending that I was the sure-handed Longhorn tight end. Zach would nonchalantly fire a touchdown pass to me and I always managed to get one foot inbounds on the driveway. Then we would both laugh hysterically. My young son had figured out the essence of Vince Young: unflappable, frustratingly calm, icy, and fearless. The faithful had never seen anyone play football quite like this. But on this day after Thanksgiving as I pondered the ugly turn of events while waiting in line for a watered-down Coke, I wondered how he was going to get us out of this one. Jonte Buhl had managed to suck the life out of DKR in a way that I had never before experienced.

The stadium lights were on and the late afternoon had grown overcast and chilly as we took our seats for the second half. It took Texas exactly 87 seconds to exorcise the demon of Jonte Buhl. Vince had nothing to do with it. After holding Texas A&M to a three and out to start the second half, Longhorn safety Michael Griffin crashed through the Aggie line and blocked a punt. Bobby Tatum scooped it up, and the Longhorns were ready to tie the game. Just to keep things interesting, the Aggies blocked our extra-point attempt—someone had apparently forgotten to feed the extra-point gods on Thanksgiving. But the ball didn't cross the goal line and the Aggies tried to advance it, since a blocked extra point returned by the other team is worth two points. The Aggies, however, fumbled the ball back into the Texas end zone, where Aggie safety Jaxson Appel covered it and was tackled by a host of Longhorns. Still with me? The referees conferred in what resembled the

Council of Trent and decided, according to NCAA rule 8-3-2, that the Longhorns had scored a "one-point safety." Game tied 13–13. The only thing that remained was the enjoyment we all got out of Kirk, a UT Law graduate, trying to explain this to a six-year-old.

A&M was finished. The Aggie offense completely broke down after that as Texas tacked on a pair of field goals and a short Benson touchdown run. With the score 26–13, Craig checked his watch and we faced the tough decision whether to stay to the final gun and miss our flight or preserve peace within our marriages. We headed down the ramps into the dark November night. We missed Reggie McNeal's last four plays in Austin. The Aggie quarterback was sacked three times before throwing a desperation interception. The interception loosed the Gregorian chant that followed every Longhorn win over our in-state rival.

Pooooooooooooooor Agg-eeeeez . . .

Trappist monks couldn't have done it better—and Trappist monks rarely gather in groups of 80,000. The sound of the long rolling "O" hung in the November night and echoed in sweet victory out of the stadium as Craig and I raced up San Jacinto Street in search of a taxi. Within the safe confines of Yellow Cab, Craig checked his watch. We were going to make it.

Our seats on the plane were across from an LSU fan, which was always a happy thing. The LSU fans were the SEC's version of Nebraska fans: passionate and knowledgable, but also friendly and hospitable. You were their friend if you loved college football; the Tiger faithful welcomed you with beer and whatever Louisiana delicacies were on the grill. They differed with the Cornhuskers only in rowdiness and alcohol consumption, which was not simply Cajun mythology. Win or lose, the LSU fans would happily drink you under the table, and you would enjoy the trip. We talked about the season over canned Budweiser. The short flight was turbulent. When the bumps got so rough they made the lights flicker, I even took some solace in the knowledge that I would be going down with committed college football fans. But this would be a lousy time for a plane crash; the Longhorns were ranked fifth in the Bowl

Championship Series and the wall separating us from the elite powers of the game was slowly showing signs of wear. Surely I would live to see it collapse.

Mack Brown the Evangelist had some work to do. His boys should have been in line to play in one of the major bowls. We had been denied this shot in cruel ways throughout Mack's tenure. This season, the Sooners, as usual, had blocked our path to the national title game. Oklahoma would play undefeated USC in the Orange Bowl, since it was the city of Miami's turn to host the championship. The Rose Bowl, which traditionally paired the Big Ten champ with the Pac Ten champ, wanted Texas to face Michigan, creating a matchup of legendary powers. The Rose was free to make this deal since the Pac Ten champ, USC, would bypass the Rose Bowl for the Orange Bowl. There was one problem. Ranked fourth in the BCS, one spot ahead of Texas, were the California Golden Bears, another Pac Ten squad. Tradition and fairness suggested Cal deserved the Rose Bowl's invitation to Pasadena. Tradition, of course, to Texas fans died when the Southwest Conference broke apart in 1991, sinking the once proud legacy of the Cotton Bowl in its wake. Fairness was then replaced with cash in the college football world. The Rose Bowl committee owed tradition nothing. Their play was to maximize revenue to their sponsors and network television. Texas fans traveled big and spent big, and their Longhorns commanded the viewing attention of millions of homes. They also boasted the most exciting player in college football. Cal was a fine team, but represented a campus more famous for civil disobedience and marijuana than for Heisman Trophy tailbacks and the thick ooze of oil money. For the Rose Bowl it all came down to simple economics, summarized by that quintessential Texas saying: Money talks, bullshit walks.

Texas would play Michigan. For the first time ever, these two eminent powers would settle things on the gridiron. Michigan had won more games in the history of the sport than any other team. Texas was tied for third with Nebraska. The matchup was historic, and when the Texas fans woke up on New Year's Day and reached for the ibuprofen, they had no idea what Vince Young had up his sleeve.

Our family was extended a New Year's Day bowl-watching invitation shortly after Christmas. After subjecting Erin to a scrupulous interrogation, I concluded that her friends the Johnsons were, indeed, acceptable football fans and I would be willing to join them. As we arrived, the smell of black-eyed peas and cornbread filling their house was a good sign. It took me straight back to the family home in Canyon and the giant L-shaped table shoehorned into the kitchen. Audrey had always insisted her grandchildren eat black-eyed peas on New Year's Day, an Old South good-luck tradition. She served them alongside cornbread and whatever god-awful piece of meat she had cooked to the point of unconditional surrender. Courtney Johnson proved a much finer cook than my own grandmother, which admittedly was not a high bar to clear, and her own dishes came alongside cold beer, a liquid that never graced the refrigerator of the famous teetotaler Bulldog Jones.

I had watched a lot of Rose Bowls on Bulldog's giant television console. As a child this was always a pure Big Ten–Pac Ten game: the brawn of the corn-fed boys of the Midwest versus the finesse and sophistication of the Left Coast. No teams brought more brawn than the Ohio State and Michigan squads of the 1970s and they were usually matched up with the flashiest team in the nation, the Southern California Trojans. This was cultural anthropology on the football field, pure red state–blue state long before anyone had ever put a name to it. Now that the BCS had set aside tradition, anything went for the Rose Bowl, the most famous playing field in college football and a game that had been contested since 1902. How strange it was to spend a lifetime watching the Texas Longhorns start the New Year on chilly Dallas mornings in the Cotton Bowl and now to see them emerge for the first time from the tunnel in tranquil Pasadena.

The familiar Georgia drawl of Keith Jackson, Mr. College Football, would be today's sound track. Longhorn fans long suspected Jackson as a Pac Ten homer, which he was, and also as anti-Texas, which I never quite bought. And I didn't care. Despite his advanced years and his occasional stumble over the down and distance or player identification, his was the most famous voice in the history of the game. Texas deserved to have him on the play-by-play, just as he had been for dozens of classic Texas-Oklahoma games.

Today's challenge was formidable. Michigan was 9-2 and ranked thirteenth, but many thought they had underachieved and were better than their record. The Wolverines had four of twenty-two starters on the consensus All-American team, including Braylon Edwards, the nation's best wide receiver. In addition, their young quarterback, Chad Henne, had a strong arm and a talented young tailback behind him named Mike Hart. Finally, the Michigan speed demon Steve Breaston, who had struggled with injuries all season, was finally healthy. He proved it by torching the Texas kickoff coverage team for 44 yards—and damn near a touchdown—on the game's opening play. The Texas defense settled in and both teams played a boring first quarter marked by numerous misplays and penalties. Finally, as the quarter came to a close, Vince exploded up the middle on a quarterback draw for a 20-yard touchdown. I leapt to my feet and encouraged all my fellow southerners to keep eating black-eyed peas for luck. Michigan answered with a Henne rainbow to Edwards, who made a beautiful grab, just planting a foot in the end zone. Vince then engineered a long drive that ended with a dartlike flip to David Thomas to make it 14–7. After forcing a three and out, Texas had Michigan in the crosshairs, with plenty of time to make it 21–7. Unfortunately, my capacity for not living in the moment showed itself as Ramonce Taylor muffed the Michigan punt. The Wolverines recovered and cashed it in for a 14–14 halftime tie.

The Longhorns always did things like this to frustrate me. Would it kill them to blow somebody out once in a while? I sent these thoughts out to no one in particular. God would not acknowledge them. Mom would no doubt instruct me to enjoy the second half, since what more could any fan want than a tie game? Total annihilation of an opponent was never her style; it wasn't sporting. If my grandfather were here, he would still be disappointed in Ramonce Taylor for not keeping his eye on the ball while catching a punt on the run and would have replaced him with a more experienced player, which, as a matter of fact, is precisely what Mack Brown did in the second half.

While Texas fans were mired in first-half what-might-have-beens, Vince shook us out of it and reminded us all of the genius before us. Keith Jackson watched with the rest of us as Vince dropped back from the Texas 40 in the third quarter and then left the pocket to his right.

"Young loose . . ."

He turned on the jets and Jackson added: "I mean *really* loose . . ."

Yes, he was, sixty yards loose, right down the sideline for a 21–14 Texas lead. But it wasn't just what Vince did on the play. Looking back, the impact he had on his teammates was crystal clear. As Vince left the pocket, David Thomas, covered by Michigan All-American safety Ernest Shazor, reversed field, stumbled, and spread his arms as if blocking out for a basketball rebound, shielding Shazor from a clear shot at Young. Shazor escaped the block-out, but Thomas kept after him, chipping him on the left shoulder and then diving at his ankles until Vince was long gone and Shazor was out of the play. As Vince found a running lane, he escaped the grasp of Michigan's tremendous cornerback Marlin Jackson and then, out of nowhere, Longhorn receiver Nate Jones crushed Ryan Mundy, the Michigan safety. Vince raced up the sideline and Michigan cornerback Leon Hall had a pursuit angle. Tony Jeffery, trailing the play, accelerated into the picture and took away the threat of Hall, shielding him from Young with his left forearm.

From that moment on, I never doubted that his teammates would do anything for Vincent Young. Vince would never let them down. Papa Smith knew this long ago. The patient are rewarded and those who waited for Vince Young the athlete to become Vince Young the quarterback and leader of men were reaping a great reward on the playing fields of Pasadena. Texas would not be denied.

"He's getting ahead of himself again. Can't he just enjoy the moment?" Mom knew better than to call a college football game in the third quarter.

Bulldog agreed. "The whole Texas sideline needs to settle down. Wallace Wade would never stand for such exuberant behavior."

Forgetting for the moment just how fast Steve Breaston was, the Texas coverage unit allowed him 43 yards on the ensuing kickoff. Not to be outdone, the Texas defense gave up 50 more yards to Breaston on a bomb from Henne, and the score was tied again. The black-eyed peas were all gone, which probably explained why Vince couldn't hit the broad side of a barn on the next Texas possession and Michigan quickly drove the ball downfield to take a 28–21 lead on a nine-yard pass to Edwards.

Vince then lofted a pass right into the arms of Michigan linebacker Prescott Burgess, which Burgess returned 23 yards, setting up an eventual field goal. Texas had now gone from unbeatable to ten points down. I had gone from Father-of-the-Year candidate happily exchanging high fives with Zach to Stark Raving Maniac About to Chew Through the Couch Cushions. As the fourth quarter started, I began to ponder next fall's Texas schedule and recruiting class.

What I didn't know was that Texas football was about to change forever. I had been fooled by moments like this before, immediately extrapolating isolated events into future greatness. But over the next fifteen minutes of game time, the Longhorns would be fundamentally changed. Down ten in the fourth, Vince Young flipped the amazing switch and the legend born on the playing fields and parks of industrial south Houston was confirmed in front of me, Erin, Zach, the Johnsons, Keith Jackson, the 93,000 spectators in the Rose Bowl and a national television audience, not to mention God and all the company of heaven. Ben regrettably won't remember this; he was painting.

Under relentless Michigan pressure, Young's passes somehow grew increasingly more accurate. He worked Texas down the field, and with the drive stalled at third and goal from the Michigan ten, he simply did the impossible. Vince dropped back to pass and a Michigan lineman named Pat Massey—a 6'8", 280-pounder who even dwarfed Young—broke through the gap and wrapped number 10 completely around the waist, then spun him like a corkscrew in one full rotation and to the ground. But Vince didn't go down. Any small, quick quarterback would have collapsed under Massey's weight, and any larger, more physical quarterback would not have had the balance to remain upright. Vince went with Massey counterclockwise and rocketed out of his grasp like a javelin launched from an atlatl past the shocked Michigan defenders and into the end zone. Dan Fouts, Jackson's color man in the booth, simply exclaimed "No . . . NO . . . ," as if he were a mathematics professor staring down a proof that didn't add up. Texas was within three.

Michigan didn't have the decency to quit and drove the field again. The Longhorn defense made just enough plays to hold them to a field goal and the Wolverines were back up by six. Irritated, Vince went the distance the other way in three plays: two clutch passes covered about 40 yards and then, from the Michigan 23, Vince bootlegged left, pointed out the one block he needed, and raced into the end zone for a 35–34 Texas lead.

The Texas defense held Michigan to another field goal and Young took the field with three minutes to go, down 37–35. He then methodically drained every second of the clock and the hopes and dreams of Michigan fans everywhere. Vince carried the Longhorns down the field to the Michigan 20, and from there, an unlikely hero took the field. Dusty Mangum, a walk-on kicker, never in a million years would have thought that he would take center stage as an encore to a player like Vince Young. Yet there he was, 37 yards away from Longhorn history. As he headed out to the field, Mack Brown called Mangum back to slap him playfully on the helmet and tell him that he was the luckiest guy on the planet, for he was about to win the Rose Bowl. After an interminable dance of Michigan time-outs, Mangum approached the ball and struck it. We all watched its arc for an eternity as it descended just barely over the crossbar and inside the right post. I am convinced my mother must have helped it over.

"You might as well play the fight song," as Keith Jackson was fond of saying. The Texas Longhorns were Rose Bowl champs. For once, I left a season behind content with its outcome.

Vince Young was not content. He had just put on a performance for the ages with 180 passing yards and 192 on the ground, accounting for five touchdowns. He did it not against the pay-to-play scrubs of New Mexico State. These were the Michigan Wolverines, whose every defensive starter was a legitimate NFL prospect. Young accepted his accolades gracefully, but he only said one thing that was in any way relevant:

"We'll be back."

Next year, the Rose Bowl would host the national championship game. The one, I hoped, that God owed me. I suggested that scenario in evening prayer.

"He certainly works in mysterious ways, doesn't he?"

"Vince? No, just spectacular ones. There's no real mystery to your mortal world, other than love. And you're surrounded with it if you would only bother to pay attention."

Sound advice, but I was still focused on Vince. There was no reason for me not to believe everything Vince Young said. For if you pricked him, his blood would not run red, nor would it be tinted orange like that of the Longhorn faithful. Vince Young's blood would flow clear and cold, for this man had ice water in his veins.

16

THE LONE STAR DRINKING CLUB

Texas vs. the Ohio State University

OHIO STADIUM, COLUMBUS, OHIO, SEPTEMBER 10, 2005

Charles Killian Jones joined our family just in time for the Texas Longhorns to beat the living boudin out of Louisiana-Lafayette in the 2005 season opener at DKR. We felt somewhat bad about this since Hurricane Katrina had mauled our visitor's home state a few days before. Charlie was born on August 17 and was only twelve days old when Katrina made landfall. Since my new son wasn't much for sleeping, we watched the storm together late into the night. Strange to hold an infant in a safe, warm place and watch disaster unfold a few hundred miles to the southeast. CNN flickered in blue light in the otherwise dark family room bringing terrible—and sublime—images of wind and rain battering the Gulf Coast. I was transfixed as Charlie fell asleep on my chest; I could have put him back to bed and gone to sleep myself, but I couldn't take my eyes off the television. CNN kept returning to shots from earlier in the day of gridlocked highways as people gathered up their belongings and fled their homes. Those without means filed into the Louisiana Superdome for refuge. Most of them likely couldn't afford to come to this building for the joyful purpose of watching their hometown Saints or the annual Sugar Bowl. I started counting blessings and thinking of how little I actually appreciated my gifts, how most of these people I kept vigil over in the early hours of August 29 would trade places with me in the bat of an eye. I prayed for them and was comforted when the talking heads noted that the storm didn't hit New Orleans directly and that the worst predictions would not come true, that the levees would hold. But, as it turned out, the levees wouldn't hold. Over the next few days the Big Easy would be reduced to a desolate landscape of pain and violence.

Our entire nation watched this awful show and, unlike in the days following 9/11, sometimes it felt like nobody gave a damn. This was a complete disconnect for me; I had everything in life. A perfect little seven-pound college football fan breathed slowly in and out in rhythm with my own lungs, on top of which he slept. We were both prone on a couch in the family room in the house that I believed I would never leave. Erin and I had bought the big house on Highland Hills Drive the previous spring and had decided upon crossing the threshold that this was a special place. We would bring our new baby home to this house and watch our rambunctious boys grow up here. We would celebrate birthdays and anniversaries and light Advent candles and open Christmas gifts here. If I listened very intently to these walls I could hear my mother's laughter surrounding them. I was thirty-seven, exactly the same age as my father when he bought the big family house on Henning Street.

Dad and Mom had moved our family back to the Panhandle in 1969. He was a young doctor on the go and the split-level paean to 1970s architecture halfway up the Henning Street hill was the perfect place for the Jones family. It had five bedrooms, just enough for me and my three siblings. The concrete slab in the backyard was too short for tennis, but it accommodated countless neighborhood basketball games and throws and catches of baseballs and footballs. When we didn't want to be confined by the yard, then we strolled down the hill a half block to Olsen Park, our own private football stadium where the games we played were limited only by what my childhood imagination could conjure. I always issued the invitation to play, and Dad always accepted, with the caveat that he needed some time to "let his supper settle." He retreated to his chair, read part of the evening paper, and then, with a remarkable sense of when my patience was on the verge of turning me into a fidgeting mess, popped up, and said: "Let's go." I gathered whatever sporting equipment was appropriate for the season and we bolted out the door. This simple social contract between father and son was executed thousands of times during my life. Now that I owned my own family house with a spacious front yard, the evenings and Saturday afternoons of my childhood would be repaid to his grandsons. The wide expanse of grass that fronted Highland Hills Drive was a great place for a kid to pretend he was Vince Young.

The real Vince Young had some concerns as the 2005 season commenced. For starters, finding someone to throw the ball to was a problem. His burly tight end Bo Scaife had graduated, although the dependable David Thomas remained. Wide receiver Tony Jeffery, though not a star, made several clutch catches throughout the previous season, and he, too, would be gone from the fold. The Longhorn receiving corps would have to depend on journeyman senior Brian Carter, the talented sophomore Limas Sweed, a tall and fast Roy Williams clone, but with little of the Legend's playmaking ability, Billy Pittman, a converted high school quarterback with next-to-no experience, and Quan Cosby, a twenty-two-year-old freshman just returning to the football field after trying his hand at minor-league baseball. Other than Thomas, this was not exactly a group that would strike fear into the hearts of opposing secondaries. But the biggest problem for Vince was that, when he looked to his left or right while awaiting the shotgun snap, the imposing figure of Cedric Benson would no longer be there ready to punish opposing linebackers. Vince would instead be flanked by Selvin Young. Selvin was a fine player, and he was also Vince Young's best friend. He was not, however, an All-American tailback. Also missing for Texas was linebacker Derrick Johnson, a first-round draft choice of the Kansas City Chiefs the previous spring. This year would certainly prove Mack Brown's recruiting prowess.

Despite all of the personnel losses, the AP ranked Texas number two. I suspected this was a trick, a cruel artifice to crush my hopes once again under the unbearable weight of dreams deferred. The Texas baseball team was part of the conspiracy. They had once again won the College World Series, which I took as an omen that God was continuing the old bait-and-switch ploy he had used so effectively in 2002. He always interrupted my best efforts at discerning his divine will.

"Did it ever occur to you that maybe Texas just has a great baseball team?"

"Stay out of this. I wasn't talking to you."

"Nor were you listening. We've been over this before. Think about the blessings you have and better still the ones the people of New Orleans don't have. The blessings yet to appear are beyond your control."

God was instructing me to live in the moment, which was impossible given the circumstances of Longhorn football. Even though Texas had many questions to answer in the opener against Lafayette, the faithful could only focus on one thing: Ohio State.

The second week of the season our heroes would have to travel to Columbus to face the fourth-ranked Buckeyes. For the first hundred years of Texas football, the Longhorns had avoided playing either of the Big Ten's flagship programs, but in the span of nine months in 2005, the Horns would play both of them: Michigan in the previous Rose Bowl and Ohio State in the biggest game of the 2005 college football season. A win in Columbus would put the Longhorns on the inside track to play (finally, and in my lifetime) for the national championship. A loss would simply be another big game disappointment for Mack Brown, to which I had grown accustomed. Of course, when we last left Vince Young in Pasadena, he had made very clear to the world that he had no intention of ever losing a college football game again. During the off-season, he made it clear to his teammates. He left a message in the locker room that simply said: *If you want to beat Ohio State, meet me here every night at 7 p.m.* As the players drifted in for summer conditioning, they had to have known who wrote this. It wasn't a coach; coaches wrote things like: *Please concentrate on learning your assignments and focus on the season opener. Take them one game at a time (and for the love of God don't say anything that will piss anybody off).* No, the message on the locker-room board was written by their leader, the genius from Houston who discerned that his winning on the football field was God's divine will.

Vince's teammates came out in droves for the evening sessions—no coaches allowed. The agenda consisted of seven-on-seven passing drills to improve timing among the receivers and coverage assignments among the defensive players. These drills irritated the linemen, however, who felt disenfranchised. You don't want the big guys to feel left out; they are the backbone of any top-flight football team. But I am not quite sure that they came just to enjoy seven-on-seven passing drills, making them eleven-on-eleven passing drills. There was something deeper.

Those who covered the Longhorns always talked about the family atmosphere at Texas; indeed, "family" was within the first few words of any Longhorn player when interviewed about why he came to Texas. Lip service? Some, perhaps, but if you watch teams long enough you notice the divisions within them: The separation between black players and white players can be stark; divisiveness can occur between offensive and defensive players, especially if one unit is clearly superior to the other and is always "bailing the defense out," or vice versa. In Texas, there is also a huge difference between the experience of players from rural Texas adjusting to the wonderland of Austin and players from Dallas and Houston making the same adjustment. But these divisions were absent on this Texas squad.

Vince Young was the neighborhood kid who organized all the games and invited everybody to his house afterward, except he wasn't doing this just up the hill from Olsen Park on Henning Street, he was playing this role for a championship-caliber college football team with over a dozen players on the roster who would eventually play professional football.

The kids from Vince Young's neighborhood had a ball. Opening night demonstrated that Vince had a few friends to play with, even without Cedric Benson to help carry the load. Ramonce Taylor, for one thing, was no less exciting as a sophomore than he had been as a freshman. After watching Taylor scoot 30 yards for the Longhorn's fourth touchdown of the day against Louisiana-Lafayette, Zach turned to me and noted: "Dad, I think Ramonce Taylor is faster than you are." Damn, I was a good father. Not only was I instilling a deep love for college football in my eldest son, but also creating a foundational ear for smart-ass commentary. I wished his grandmother could be here.

The Longhorns also discovered a brilliant eighteen-year-old freshman tailback had somehow made the roster. Jamaal Charles was yet another Texas high school legend, not as legendary as Cedric Benson, but faster. As a senior at Port Arthur's Memorial High School, Charles had completed the 110-meter hurdles in a remarkable 13.69 seconds, the fastest time in the nation. For an encore, Charles ran the 300-meter hurdles—one of the most difficult races in track—in 36.03, also the fastest in the nation. This double was about as easy to accomplish as performing heart surgery in the morning and brain surgery in the afternoon, but the résumé got better. When Charles signed with Texas, he noted that he would make the Cult of 1969 "forget all about Adrian Peterson," the Oklahoma star who spurned, and then tortured, the Longhorns in 2004. But most remarkable of all, Mack Brown actually put Charles on the field against Louisiana-Lafayette. The ever-conservative Brown was loath to play freshmen running backs, and this drove the faithful crazy. Brown was always worried about silly things like blocking assignments and ball security, while the faithful worried more about the next high school legend kicking ass up and down the field in our team's colors. Not even Benson saw any meaningful time in his freshman season until after (another) loss to Oklahoma, when Texas desperately needed his help and was held to 27 net rushing yards in a 14–3 disappointment. But Charles played early and often in the 2005 opener, rushing for 135 yards on only fourteen carries.

The defense was inspired as well. They were led by a soft-spoken senior named Michael Huff, who was the best safety in the country. A starter in the secondary since his freshman year, he delighted the crowds with a penchant for big plays, returning four interceptions for touchdowns. Oddly enough, his athletic brilliance—he was a track star nearly the equal of Jamaal Charles—overshadowed a brain that fired effortlessly on all synapses. He may have been the most cerebral football player the Texas defense had ever seen—Major Applewhite with 4.3 speed. Like the deaf and dumb and blind kid from *Tommy*, Huff could play football by "sense of smell" if he had to. He played strong safety, ostensibly the position in the defensive backfield that requires the most strength and least speed. The strong safety hits the line of scrimmage hard in run support and, in pass coverage, typically covers the third- or fourth-best receiver—a tight end or perhaps a fullback out of the backfield. The speedy receivers on the edge were the province of cornerbacks, helped deep by the free safety. A strong safety needed to be a physical hitter, which Huff was. However, Huff turned conventional wisdom on its head. He had a tightly coiled 6'1", 205-pound frame—light for his position, but he was a sure tackler and could cover the fastest receivers any team placed across from him. In addition to handling multiple defensive assignments, Huff made all the coverage calls in the secondary, sometimes switching responsibilities entirely with another player if it played to the Longhorns' advantage. And my God, was he fast. Zach and I used to play a long-cherished father-and-son game on the way to school, categorizing the Longhorns with boyhood questions about who was the hardest hitter, who was the best blocker, et cetera. When we discussed the fastest Longhorns, the conversation went straight to the flashy ball handlers like Ramonce, Jamaal, and Billy Pittman. From there, we would always remember that Aaron Ross, the cornerback and punt returner, belonged in the conversation. We were usually halfway to school before one of us would note that we had forgotten Michael Huff, which might have been the right answer all along. Huff held it all together for the Horns when Vince wasn't on the field; his combination of speed and brains were the equivalent of having a twelfth player on defense. Deep within me, I suspected Huff might be the vital missing piece to the puzzle that hadn't been completed since 1969.

Texas had a fine day against the dispirited and exhausted visitors from Lafayette; twenty of them hailed from devastated New Orleans and couldn't possibly have been focused on a football game. But none of that mattered; Texas would have beaten this group even on a bad day. The real season started next week. I knew that Vince Young was not alone as we basked in the glow of an easy 60–3 opening-day victory. These were my 2005 Longhorns, and their prospects looked limitless. What I did not know was that they would desperately need my help against Ohio State.

There comes a time in everyone's life when you simply have to win one for your team. You must be prepared when this time comes, just as Jesus tells his followers to be ever watchful and vigilant. I didn't know how important my vigilance would be to the Longhorns when I woke up on September 10. Ohio State was a night game, and I spent the entire day imagining my lifetime home on Highland Hills Drive becoming the next great college football gathering spot. Just like in my grandfather's den, or the basement of my parents' house on Henning, or at the Posse, great things could happen in the new family room. Except, unlike at Bulldog and Audrey's house, we didn't have any family around; Erin and I had to invent our own. We set about assembling our new college football family with the care and precision a casting director would use to fill out an infantry squad in a World War II movie. We started with Erin's boarding school classmates; Terry Lynch and Juan Shepperd were practically brothers to Erin as adolescents. Juan was Ben's godfather and Terry was Zach's favorite friend, who could be counted on to bring good beer and endless comic relief. Both of them, needless to say, knew football inside and out—a criterion on which I refused to give ground. We had to have Holly Jacques, the Cajun LSU fan who had adopted Texas as her hometown team. Figuring that Charlie needed a little Louisiana in him, we asked Holly to be his godmother; that Holly was actually Catholic added a level of legitimacy to the assignment. Courtney Johnson, our hostess for the previous season's Rose Bowl, was an enthusiastic Texas partisan with beautiful burnt-orange hair to match both her personality and the Longhorn uniforms. She and Erin had been cheerleaders together at St. Stephen's Episcopal School, and both believed in the value of complete and passionate personal immersion in the fortunes of your team. Texas needed all of us on September 10.

Juan and his fiancée, Ann Erickson—a Nebraska fan, but she would be forgiven that, for Cornhuskers met all of my criteria of good fandom—brought with them a very special gift that evening, a six-pack of Lone Star beer. I hadn't drunk Lone Star since college, when it was available for a dollar a can at Eric's Billiards on Airport, our favorite Tuesday-night hangout in the days when free pool proved much more attractive than the rigorous study required to make ourselves better citizens. Lone Star was pure Texana. Its 1970s heyday fueled the rise of the outlaw country music movement in Austin and also produced one of the great ad campaign taglines: "Lone Star, no place but Texas." The distinctive longneck bottle with the white label and red lettering became a necessary prop in the iconic photographs of the Austin music scene and spawned a series of bumper stickers: LONGHORNS AND LONGNECKS, NO PLACE BUT TEXAS one might read on the back of a pickup in Austin. Or, in College Station, the sticker would be changed to read AGGIES AND LONG-NECKS. There were dozens of variations. My favorite was displayed on the back of my high school car, a 1972 Chevy Carryall, which was the precursor to the giant Suburban. I found the sticker in San Antonio when my parents had taken me to see the NBA Spurs play and their slick shooting guard George Gervin was leading the league in scoring. Gervin had one of the great nicknames in sports, and it graced the back of my vehicle in the Tascosa High School parking lot: LONGNECKS AND THE ICE-MAN, NO PLACE BUT TEXAS. Brushing off the nostalgia, I carted the Lone Star back to the garage refrigerator, where it would go undrunk. Lone Star tasted like hell, which didn't matter much to the hippies and red-necks of thirty years ago, but we fancied ourselves a more sophisticated lot. It was yet another great example of Texas hubris that would get us into trouble.

The evening's seating arrangement was incredibly important. The family room had a circle of two comfortable chairs and a sofa. Terry staked out the big leather chair, which handled his large frame easily and lent an air of class to his quaffing of expensive Czech brews. Erin took the other big chair, while Holly, Courtney, and Ann piled onto the couch, leaving it at times to play with the younger boys. When he was with us—and he was regrettably not on September 10—Zach squeezed in wherever there was room. Juan always preferred a cane-backed side chair away from the action. He was a cerebral fan of great concentration. I was in Juan's camp, but I added the burden of physical discomfort. I was the penitent fan and, as such, staked out the edge of the brick hearth closest to the television. I had no need for comfort, for my team needed me.

As the game began, it didn't look like they needed me much. The Texas defense forced a three and out on Ohio State's first possession. The Longhorns took over and, operating from his own 30, Vince knifed through the vaunted Buckeye defense for 32 yards. Ohio State could no more contain him than had Michigan. Vince was probably irritated that one of the Buckeye linebackers, Bobby Carpenter, had said that Young would leave Ohio no longer a Heisman Trophy candidate. Carpenter did not know the rule about telling God's people what they could not do, and Vince made a mockery of him, racing unfettered through the Ohio State defense. The Texas drive ended with a field goal.

On the second possession, State loaded up against the run and Vince calmly tossed the ball 33 yards to Billy Pittman, who hauled it in at mid-field. Many Longhorn fans had to look up Pittman in the media guide at this point. He was a largely unknown quantity, a small-school option quarterback from Cameron Yoe High School, recruited, of course, as an "athlete." Unknown to most was the connection formed between Pittman and Young during those nightly seven-on-seven drills during the summer. The faithful had no idea how important Billy Pittman would become. The drive ended with another Young strike to Pittman on a slant right into the Buckeye end zone. Pittman kneeled in the back of the end zone in prayer, and I joined him. When I lifted my head, the Long-horns had a 10–0 lead. Cakewalk. This is a cakewalk. They can't contain Vince Young.

Again, my stupidity knew no bounds. The Ohio State defenders caught their breath and remembered who they were. Then they set about making Vince Young miserable. Containing Vince required great line-backers, and the Buckeyes happened to have three of them. Carpenter may have had a big mouth, but he also had first-round NFL talent as an outside linebacker. Another pro prospect, Anthony Schlegel, held down the middle. On the other side, the Buckeyes had the best defensive player in college football, a wrecking machine named A. J. Hawk. Never before had I seen a football game come down to a contest of wills between sin-gle offensive and defensive players. Football, unlike basketball, wasn't made for such individual combat, since offense and defense lived in separate worlds, and twenty-two different players determined any given contest. Was Hawk the premier player? Or Young? Hawk began to make his case in the second quarter with the help of the nearly 106,000 Buck-eye fans crammed into their "Horseshoe," perhaps the most hostile sta-dium in the country. Ohio State had never lost a night game here, and they were not about to start now. After a Buckeye field goal made it 10–3, Hawk and his mates went to work. Texas managed only 13 yards on their next possession when Vince was sacked for the first time of the night. Ohio State quickly scored to make it 10–10.

The next possession, Hawk intercepted Vince and returned the ball all the way to the Texas 18 before the quick-thinking freshman Charles raced across the field, hurdled a Buckeye, and laid Hawk out. Texas held Ohio State to a field goal and the offense took the field again. This time, the Buckeyes forced Selvin Young to cough up the football. Hawk came up with it at the Texas 30. Again the Texas defense held Ohio State to three points, and the Buckeyes led 16–10.

The entire second quarter was a terrible fifteen minutes for Texas, saved only by the guts shown by the Longhorn defense and a remarkable 36-yard catch and run by Charles to set up a field goal, cutting the Buckeye lead to 16–13. If Vince Young was Superman, then A. J. Hawk had brought the Kryptonite. The misery continued after intermission, when Vince started the second half with a pick, again in Texas territory, and again the Texas defense held Ohio State to three points. Ohio State made a crucial mistake on the next series and somehow let Billy Pittman free for a 62-yard Young-to-Pittman connection. I thought the nightmare was over, but it wasn't. Texas couldn't score a touchdown from the Ohio State four. Young was wrestled down for a four-yard loss by his good friend Bobby Carpenter, and the Buckeyes clung to a 19–16 lead.

God gives you signs in life that you often miss. Usually you are too absorbed in your own affairs to notice the wonder around you, or sometimes you are just not paying attention. With about five minutes to go in the third, Ohio State quarterback Justin Zwick hit his tight end Ryan Hamby for a sure touchdown. Hamby juggled the ball, but then pulled it in as he crossed the goal line. Just before Hamby gained control, Texas cornerback Cedric Griffin appeared in the picture like a fast-moving phantom and delivered a vicious shot to Hamby, separating him from the ball. Griffin's moment was a gift of grace, a tiny moment of redemption.

Back in November of 2002, my mother's life was a searing memory from dawn to dusk as I plodded through my days believing the Longhorns would put an end to my mourning. Eventually, those feelings faded and I moved forward. That same November, Cedric Griffin was a talented freshman thrown into the fire too soon against an overwhelming Texas Tech passing attack. The Longhorns' dreams of greatness ended that night, and I endured the long drive home. There was a picture of Griffin in the next day's paper; with tears streaming, he was the epitome of the man in the arena who had given all he had to give on a day when his best simply wasn't good enough. Leaping from the hearth as Griffin made contact with Hamby, I didn't remember this picture. I wonder if Griffin did. I wonder if he went to sleep that night in November emotionally devastated, never imagining that three years later he would make the biggest defensive play in the biggest game of the biggest season in Longhorn history. In that brief half second when he had drilled Ryan Hamby, separating ball from man, did Cedric Griffin feel the peace of redemption?

After Griffin's redemptive strike on Hamby, the Buckeyes settled for another three. The Texas defense, under incredible pressure, had now held Ohio State to an amazing five field goals in a row. Had any of those drives ended in a touchdown, Texas would have been finished. Somehow, the Horns survived. Unfortunately, the third quarter drew to a close with A. J. Hawk still in complete command of his universe, stuffing drive after Texas drive. Vince showed a flash of promise with a 27-yard strike to Pittman, but a botched reverse by Charles and then a sack—by Hawk, who else?—stymied momentum again.

Texas was running very low on chances when Juan silently got up from his side chair and went to the garage. Ohio State was in the middle of a brutal clock-killing, faith-killing drive—a punishing series of first downs draining all the spirit out of their tired opponent and leaving no time to respond. A field goal would give them a nine-point lead, basically putting the game out of reach. Ohio State had a first down at the Texas 29 when Juan returned from the garage. He distributed two ice-cold longnecks to Terry and me and kept the third for himself. Lone Star beer was our only hope.

I really parted company with my mother on this one. She didn't buy into superstition, which was a shame. She never knew the thrill of wearing a lucky hat to the game or of making sure she was seated in the right spot in the den. Opening a particular beer with friends hundreds of miles from the stadium as if it were a magic potion capable of changing the fortunes of twenty-year-old kids would have never occurred to her.

Being a woman of sincere faith, she hadn't raised me this way; instead, I came by my appreciation of black sports magic the old-fashioned way: by watching the Longhorns blow chance after chance at greatness and knowing that somewhere there must be a missing piece of mojo that a single fan could find that just might put our guys over the top. At desperate times like these, it occurred to me that maybe my mother had her own limitations as a fan. College football needed superstition; it is tradition's first cousin. I'm sure God didn't approve, but I at least hoped he was amused. Superstition was one subject on which we did not converse.

And so it was this small band of brothers, joined no doubt by thousands of others that night in Austin with their own potions and amulets, stood standing inches from a television screen looking for any harbinger of good fortune for our guys. The Buckeyes were held to no gain on first down by the Texas front. On second down the Buckeyes made a poor play call—a swing pass that Texas defensive tackle Rodrique Wright sniffed out and stuffed for a four-yard loss. We all drank to that as we watched an incomplete pass on third down. The fine Buckeye kicker, Josh Huston, would set up for a 50-yard field goal. If he made it, the game was probably over. If he missed, then Vince Young and A. J. Hawk would have to come back out on the field and settle things like men.

The power of Lone Star forced Huston's booming kick just to the left. We all looked at Juan as if he were a shaman. Vince Young then took his familiar Madison Marlin trot onto the coliseum floor to face down A. J. Hawk and his 106,000 screaming fanatics. The Texas offense finally showed some signs of life, working down the field with short runs and passes, eventually getting to the Ohio State 24. Our Lone Stars were nearly empty as Young set up in the shotgun. Carpenter cheated up to the line of scrimmage as if to attack Young and end the game with a devastating sack, but then he dropped back into coverage at the snap of the ball. Blitzing Young would only mean that he would leave the pocket and take off running, which is not what the Buckeyes wanted. They had seen the tape of the 2004 Rose Bowl just like everyone else. The message was clear: Vince had to beat Ohio State with his arm, and the Buckeyes didn't think he could do it. Likely none of them had ever been to Mount Horeb Missionary Baptist Church. Vince took the snap, surveyed the field and lofted the ball downfield to his left.

"He has Sweed," Juan noted, having paid attention to the alignment at the snap of the ball.

Juan was having one of the great nights in University of Texas fan history. Never in my life had I willed my team to victory, certainly not by strategic beer selection. Yet here I was, witnessing the indisputable fact that Juan's every movement controlled the ball in flight as it left Vince Young's right hand and arced down into the Ohio State end zone. He had Sweed all right, the rangy split end Limas Sweed. The Roy Williams look-alike haunted by his own unmet physical potential had beaten his man by a step and turned to find his potential placed right in front of his face in the form of a spiraling pigskin. He seized it, cradling the ball close as the Ohio State safety came too late from across the field to stop him. Sweed held on and crashed to the ground on the boundary line. The field judge paused. Please, God, please, God, please, God . . . Then the arms went up. Touchdown. The Buckeyes were finished. Texas had just won the biggest game of the Young season. The Lone Star Drinking Club was officially chartered.

At the end of the evening, after someone made a motion to adjourn and the three magic bottles were consigned to the blue recycling bin, Charlie and I were alone again. Erin had gone up to bed and deserved the rest; I would take the first shift with our tiny football fan who wouldn't sleep. The late game was LSU playing Arizona State from Tempe. The game should have been in Baton Rouge, a home game for the Tigers, but it had been moved to the desert since LSU's athletic complex was being used for Hurricane Katrina relief efforts. Charlie won't remember the ending—it will be one of those things I will have to explain to him on the way to school while he rolls his eyes and wonders why a ten-year-old football game has any relevance to his life in fourth grade. He might not appreciate that LSU quarterback JaMarcus Russell, trailing

Limas Sweed, "the catch." *(University of Texas Athletics)*

31–28, took the snap on fourth down late in the game and hurled the ball 39 yards downfield in desperation. Charlie will have no appreciation that Early Doucet, a receiver who looked for most of the night like he couldn't catch William Faulkner with free whiskey, was his target. Nor will Charlie remember that Doucet made a remarkable grab in heavy traffic with the burdens of an entire tired and beaten state on his shoulders. As Charlie grows older, he might not ever believe that college football has the power to heal and bring joy to the sorrowful. He won't remember watching late-night football with his dad. But I will. It was like another set of prayers were answered. Charles Jones looked at me, no doubt wondering who this strange man was and would become. His look reminded me of what my mother-in-law had said about my wife as an infant. Pat Florence swears that Erin, as a newborn, looked straight up to her, not in beatific, unconditional baby love, but instead with a look that said: "I'm not really sure I want you to be my mother." Perhaps I needed a little skepticism around for me, for tonight I thought the world couldn't possibly get any better.

No matter what Texas accomplished, however, they continued to look up in the rankings at the University of Southern California. USC hadn't lost a football game since the middle of the 2003 season, and the Trojans had been ranked No. 1 for twenty straight weeks, including the week in which they clobbered Oklahoma 55–19 in the Orange Bowl to secure the 2004 national title. Texas was stuck at number two, for the common wisdom held that USC would not be defeated.

In the aftermath of the Ohio State game, a part of my subconscious insisted on playing out terrible Texas loss scenarios. The Longhorns had always disappointed me before, and I tried to imagine how they would do it this time. But I just couldn't do it anymore. I didn't believe this team would lose—and they didn't either—not even to USC. There are only so many times you can watch Vince Young will a team to victory without falling irretrievably under his spell. His teammates believed, and so did I.

Bob Stoops probably didn't. If anybody could screw up my entire college football season, it was Bob Stoops. His Oklahoma Sooners would meet us in Dallas to try and extend their five-game mastery over Mack Brown. Texas was better at every position on the field than their Sooner counterparts—even at tailback, where my guys had a healthy Jamaal Charles and Oklahoma had Adrian Peterson, heroically, but ineffectively, trying to go on a sprained ankle. Not a team to lay down, the Sooners turned the first quarter into a 7–6 dogfight. Then Jamaal Charles decided to make us all forget Adrian Peterson. From the zone-read formation, the freshman took a simple handoff up the middle at the Texas 20. Charles took a quick step inside, just off the left shoulder of Texas guard

Kasey Studdard, the bald and bearded masher who looked like he had just stepped out of a *Lord of the Rings* movie. On the other side of Charles, Jonathan Scott, the massive left tackle, had completely obscured one side of the Sooner defense. Charles emerged from this tunnel of humanity quick enough to make two converging Sooners collide into each other like castle gates crashing too late to prevent our hero's escape. Charles ran flush into a Sooner linebacker but somehow shook him off, and then Zach and I were treated to a scene that happens all too rarely in a college football game: a ball carrier shifting gears and bursting into an open seam, an adrenaline rush not unlike being pushed back in your seat while a jet lifts off the ground. If this could make my heart quicken watching it, what must it feel like to Charles as he coasted into the end zone eighty yards later? He slowed as he crossed into the red-painted Oklahoma paydirt and dropped the ball harmlessly to the ground in front of the Sooner fans. He slowly lowered his head and headed up the field as if to say, "I have been here before, and I will be back."

The exorcism had begun. With seventeen seconds left in the half, Vince Young got out the final wooden stake and drove it deep.

Back in 2002—the first season God really owed me one—Mack Brown hadn't trusted Chris Simms to throw into the end zone from midfield at the end of the first half against Oklahoma. I resented Mack for this and assumed this character flaw of playing not to lose was essential to his being. He would have made a great Presbyterian, a member in good standing of the Frozen Chosen. But today, in the Cotton Bowl, Mack Brown defied all my expectations. Perhaps this was the voice of God and he was speaking to me through the parable of Vince Young. Or maybe Mack Brown was finally at that point of freedom and grace where a man has nothing to lose and nothing to fear. Whatever the explanation, what happened next made me finally believe that the darkness in the end could not overcome the light.

Vince gathered his teammates in the huddle in pretty sorry field position—their own 36—and called the play, a rollout pass to the left. The rest of the huddle, facing the Sooner defense, could hear the Oklahoma players warning each other about the exact play being called—OU had a knack for figuring out the Texas offense. Some thought Vince should call another play, or at least audible out to something less predictable when the Longhorns went to the line of scrimmage. Vince wasn't interested. He never did care what the Sooner defense thought, anymore than my mother cared for what fundamentalists tried to tell her about the nature of God. He took the snap and rolled to his left, where the Sooners were overloaded. Drifting back, he released a bomb that traveled fifty yards in the air and dropped into the outstretched fingers of Billy Pittman. Pittman had run a wheel route—a double move to the outside—and somehow had managed to get ten yards behind the nearest Sooner defensive back. He flew across the goal line and stopped off at the Dallas County Clerk's office to pick up the lien Bob Stoops had on Mack Brown, tearing it to shreds in front of the delirious Longhorn student section.

"Oklahoma is screwed," I said to Zach in terminology barely suited to a nine-year old. But what was I supposed to say?

My goodness gracious, Son, it appears as though perhaps the Texas Longhorn football team has finally overcome a repeated obstacle to their goals as a group of young student athletes aspiring to the highest levels of their chosen sport."

Parental discretion would have been summarily undone by the Texas fight song clearly playing in the background.

> *Texas fight, Texas fight,*
> *For it's Texas that we love best,*
> *Give 'em hell, give 'em hell*
> *OU SUCKS*
> *. . . And it's goodbye to all the rest*

Zach turned ten a few days after the Oklahoma win. I had now been a father for a decade. A good dad on most days, a poor one on some, and a lot of days in between I just did the best I could. We didn't go to the Posse much anymore, and I couldn't remember the last time we had shot pool together. Walking out the front door and down the street to DKR wasn't possible. Longhorn games now required infinitely more complicated logistics. While I missed the days of Zach and me against the world, it was really no way to live. I remembered mostly the good times, not the loneliness that struck me on half of the days of the week when I would wake up and my son would not be under my roof. Divorce really isn't about forgiving an aggrieved party. It's about forgiving yourself first. You tend to give up on the concept of love and walk around in a funk, pretending that every bad decision you make will be ruinous and terrible to those around you. But in the end that's just selfish and stupid. My father reminded me of this one morning on the back porch in Amarillo when he sensed that I no longer knew who I was.

"You know, there are kids of divorced parents who grow up and become wonderful people who do great things. There are also kids in loving families who grow up to be complete SOBs."

The parental pep talks I got were never sweetness and light. Neither Dad nor Mom ever just came out and told me that everything would be OK. Life wasn't that simple. What they did tell me was that today is all you have and tomorrow was life's great mystery. Dad didn't know a whit about tomorrow that morning when he tried to keep me from spinning out of control. He certainly didn't know that my mom only had two years to live and that he would have to rebuild his own life and spirit right about the time that his youngest son finally got it straight. Today is all you have.

Zach and I had traded the condo in Eastwoods Park for a new family and a huge front yard. He now had three little brothers—two at our house and one at his mother's. I could see his nurturing side come out, even though these new kids meant less attention came his way, Zach was a loving presence in their lives. It was no longer the two of us against the world, but his tenth birthday had to be special. He was long past Chuck E. Cheese and Lazer Tag. There was only one place we could celebrate this great decade: Vince Young's house. We had circled the Texas Tech game back during the summer and I told him he could take two friends. Little did I know that Tech would fire out undefeated in their best start in eighteen years and be ranked in the top ten when they got to Austin on October 22. This wouldn't have presented a problem at all had Erin and I not given up our season tickets in favor of having two children. What the hell were we thinking? Talk about a lousy decision. Now I was face-to-face with a seller's market for the biggest Longhorn home game of the year, which I had already made a birthday promise to deliver. After a series of machinations and wheedling left me two tickets short on Friday afternoon, I sought the last refuge of the desperate fan. I pulled out a credit card and dialed a ticket broker.

"I need four in the end zone."

I was astonished at the answer and asked for the broker to repeat the quoted price.

"How much?"

He kindly repeated his terms again.

"Holy shit! Umm, I mean . . . No, no, yes, I understand. We all need to make a living."

I paused briefly and then came to my decision.

"Yes. MasterCard 5395..."

Erin came home from running an errand. Why is it that all wives since the dawn of commerce have an innate sense that cash is leaving a bank account?

"What did you do?"

I looked at her, eyes blinking like a stressed rat trapped in a lab experiment.

"How much?"

There was only one thing for a man to do in such a circumstance. This required guts and honesty. There was only one response to this challenge to my masculinity.

"I'm not telling you." I said this quietly and then returned to silent prayer.

She smiled and headed up the stairs shaking her head as if our two-year-old had misbehaved and had gotten away with it simply by being so darn cute that anger was impossible. Of all the blessings God had given me, of all the things in my life that I had taken for granted, one super-seded all others. I was married to exactly the right woman. I said a short prayer of thanksgiving as I raced out the door to pick up my tickets.

Austin in October is about as hot as a pie right out of the oven, except with a much less pleasant odor if you happen to be crammed into a space with 84,000 college football fans. Keeping up with three ten-year-old boys would be the easy part; avoiding a call to their parents explaining why they were hospitalized for dehydration and heat stroke was a much larger concern. As we took our seats, I had another uncomfortable thought. It struck me that I had just paid major coin to sit in the same end zone where I was sitting when Texas Tech's Tony Manyweather had scored the winning touchdown against Texas in 1989. I hoped that some-where Juan Shepperd had taken a six of Lone Star to whoever had invited him over for the day. The Tech players obviously knew where I was sit-ting and made a game of it, forcing Vince into two picks and hanging in there for a 10–10 tie in the early going. But my superstitions were no match for the Longhorns, who turned the game on a blocked punt and coasted to a 31–10 halftime lead. Vince Young came out for the second half and treated us to a 75-yard bomb to Billy Pittman, who now only went by his initials: B.P. Big Play. He ran this one straight down the middle of the field. How could he be so open? The game, for all practical purposes was over. Time to make the most of it.

The problem for a boy growing up at DKR was that he couldn't ex-plore, not like at Kimbrough Stadium, where I was always released on my own recognizance as a child. You could not responsibly release three ten-year-olds into the wilds of this massive place. Of course, this didn't stop you from going with them if you were so inclined.

"Come on." I jumped out of my seat and headed down the aisle. The boys followed. We went right down to field's edge and hung out for a while with the Tech fans, shoehorned, as always, into the northwest corner of the end zone. When enemy territory no longer held any thrill—the depressed Tech fans were being slow-roasted into submission by the unforgiving sun—we headed over to the west side of the stadium. This was the home of the ancient and wealthy Longhorn season ticket holders, many of whom believed it was their divine right to watch college football without having their view obscured by anyone with the gall to stand up and scream on a crucial third down and almost all of whom believed that they should not have to endure a traveling band of ten-year-olds and their thirty-eight-year-old chaperone flirting with his lost youth. We played a spirited game of "avoid the usher" and crouched down at one of the tunnels to watch Vince Young set up under center directly in front of us, so close we felt like we could reach out and touch him. I looked at Zach.

"This is where we would sit if we were rich."

"Cool."

We watched our hero until the usher politely made eye contact. Time to move on, I led the boys up the stairs to the top of the section. A sign there simply said: NO STOPPING OR STANDING. Reading the fine print, this was apparently by order of the university fire marshal. Faced with this declaration, we did what any group of ten-year-olds would do. We stopped. We stood. We dissolved into laughter. An old man in an aisle seat caught my eye and smiled, no doubt remembering a day just like this one when he had brought his own son to this same sacred ground.

The clowning ceased as we settled into four abandoned seats that must have cost a small fortune when the week began. With one last sack of the beleaguered Tech quarterback, Texas put the finishing touch on a 52–17 dismantling of the best Texas Tech team in two decades. We sang "The Eyes of Texas" and raced down the ramps, impolitely cutting and sliding through the thousands like Jamaal Charles avoiding tacklers. We arrived at the car out of breath from bounding up the parking garage stairs. I drove home having captured and bottled all of the pleasures of my boyhood. The best thing was, I had two more boys at home and they would also be ten someday. And I could be ten with them for a while.

During those seasons of Longhorn disappointment, was God simply waiting for them to come of age?

"We didn't win in 2002 because Ben and Charlie weren't here, right? I am beginning to understand you."

God would never answer such a question. But somewhere in the air of a perfect Saturday, I knew my mother needed no explanation. Her smile, no doubt, illuminated the heavens.

17

THE MOMENT

*The University of Texas vs. the
University of Southern California*

THE ROSE BOWL,
PASADENA, CALIFORNIA, JANUARY 4, 2006

Texas had been unstoppable after the Texas Tech game, although
they did have one hiccup against Oklahoma State (why was it always Oklahoma State?). The Cowboys tried to derail Texas by flying out
to a 28–12 lead at Laymon Lowery Lewis Field (which by this time had
been renamed for the famous OSU alum, oil tycoon Boone Pickens; Dr.
Lewis may have been beloved, but he never did lay a multimillion-dollar
donation on the athletic department), but Vince crushed their spirit by
opening the second half with a remarkable—even by Vince Young
standards—80-yard touchdown run that led to a 47–28 runaway victory.
My nephew Chris was a freshman in the Cowboy student section that
night. I made a mental note to taunt him about the second half when I
saw him over the Christmas holidays.

Meanwhile, the USC Trojans, behind an unstoppable offense, were calmly destroying everything in their path. After escaping ninth-ranked Notre Dame on the road in one of the nation's great rivalries, the Trojans were on cruise control: 51–24, 51–21, 35–10 . . . The Trojans seemed to name the score against the Pac Ten. Other than a close call against the feisty giant-killer Fresno State (think a West Coast version of Oklahoma State), 'SC barely got their uniforms dirty.

As for the Longhorns, after returning from the near disaster at Stillwater, Mack's guys ran roughshod over Baylor and Kansas, but came out flat against Texas A&M. Vince was off his game, but Texas still put away the Aggies 40–29. The only thing left to do was win the Big 12 Championship Game against Colorado. Again, I had been here before. At the end of 2001, all Texas had to do was beat Colorado, a team that we had easily beaten during the regular season, and a trip to the title game awaited. Such a victory wouldn't have cured my mother of cancer, but it would, for a day anyway, have made me believe the world was still a friendly place. That was the night of the great Chris Simms meltdown; the Longhorns were upset, and I was convinced the world held no redeeming value. Now Texas was in exactly the same circumstance, the 2005 Longhorns had destroyed Colorado earlier in the season 42–17, but the Buffaloes had worked their way back to winning the North Division of the Big 12 and would travel to Houston for this year's conference championship. Had God granted me one of life's great do-overs? There was no question that he had; it was impossible for me to believe otherwise.

Vince Young was coming home, but instead of playing in the gloomy half-full Astrodome, this game would be in the immaculate temple of Reliant Stadium on a perfect 80-degree day with 71,000 watching him perform a few miles from the practice field at Madison High School. The little boy from Hiram Clark had come full circle. His friend Michael Huff helped him out by forcing a fumble on Colorado's first possession. The Longhorns then proceeded to play an almost perfect football game. The final score was 70–3.

USC, not to be outdone, clobbered crosstown rival UCLA 66–19. The

Trojan players must have been inspired by watching Texas in the locker room before their own game began, for they, too, played to perfection. Only one game remained in the college football season. The Trojans and Horns would meet in Pasadena.

Reality tends to trump romanticism. Only when the two intersect does life truly seem transcendent. On January 4, my life was extraordinary, for on this night the Texas Longhorns would play in the national championship game in front of 94,000 spectators, God, country, and the Lone Star Drinking Club. This game played by twenty-year-olds mattered in my life. Not only had I waited for it for thirty-five years, I had largely acted out all of the possible scenarios. I hadn't just watched Earl Campbell as a child, I *had been* Earl Campbell, crashing through spectral tacklers on Olsen Park's field. There wasn't a single Longhorn star of the last thirty years whose spirit I had not aspired to embody at some point or another, and the great moments of my adult days consisted of *being* Vince Young, throwing passes to my ten-year-old Billy Pittman. Even when Zach wasn't at my house I would take a football with me on walks around the neighborhood, tossing it ahead of me and catching it at a leisurely pace. The curbs were out-of-bounds and my inner Limas Sweed always managed to have the awareness to get one foot down, puzzling the neighbors I'm sure, but no one called the mental health deputies. Even had they arrived, they would have understood the fundamentals: on venturing out of the house in any season, no man should ever leave behind a ball under any circumstance where a game might break out and score would be kept.

When my parents held any kind of grown-up party, my siblings and I were consigned to the downstairs bedrooms. This was cool with me; as the youngest I was guaranteed the undivided attention of the older kids. Of course, during the fall I didn't require much of their attention—it would detract from whatever college football game I was watching. I can still remember 1974 when USC's diminutive tailback Anthony Davis spurred a comeback against Notre Dame. The Irish had gone up 24–0 before Davis went to work, returning the second-half kickoff for a touchdown and leading Southern Cal to an astonishing 55–24 win. There's not much I don't remember about that day. The smell of my mother's tenderloin wafting through the house meant the holidays were just getting under way. My mind can recall all of the awful 1970s golden harvest colors and looking at the pictures in *Sports Illustrated* when it came in the mail every week. The picture of a Notre Dame cheerleader crying on the sidelines after Anthony Davis ruined her day still haunts me and informs my thoughts on why so many people care so much about what happens on those fields. I knew then that the University of Southern California was a very big deal. They had Heisman Trophy winners—O.J. Simpson and Marcus Allen had played there—and every time Bob Hope introduced the college football All-American team on his Christmas special, which I never missed, a Trojan or two were always in the picture, just like there was always a Texas Longhorn. If Bob Hope introduced your team to the world, then you were part of the big time.

Maybe Zach had similar nascent memories somewhere within him. The University of Texas was a real place to him, a childhood playground. He didn't have to conjure it in his imagination like I did. When he was two, my parents were in town, and we walked the campus. Mom held Zach's hand and let him explore the turtle ponds behind the biology building in the shadow of the tower, just off of the West Mall. I made the mistake of hustling them along. My mom stopped me short.

"The problem with dads is that they are always in a hurry. Where do you have to be?"

I knew better than to cross her. I pulled up a rock and enjoyed my son's fascination with the turtles. A few months later I bundled him up and took him inside the stadium believing with all my heart that he would remember seeing the great Ricky Williams with his father. When he was three, we watched Ricky Williams win the Heisman Trophy. Later that year his mom and I got divorced. I hoped that he would remember the good times: the Posse and pool tables and being cozily stuffed into a tiny condo down the street from the Texas Longhorns with his dad and Truman, the burnt orange and white Brittany.

Regardless of how much our past he remembered, Zachary Peace Jones was certainly going to remember the night the Texas Longhorns played Southern Cal for the national title. Austin was in a state of complete euphoria that day. When Erin came home from running an errand, she informed me that even the homeless guys had scrawled HOOK 'EM HORNS across their signs as they solicited passersby on the Mopac access road. Our lifetime house on Highland Hills was prepared. Erin and our three sons were ready to welcome our guests, and the world seemed full of possibility. The second meeting of the Lone Star Drinking Club was called to order. Vince Young was in the house.

As Keith Jackson welcomed us to the greatest venue in college football, with the San Gabriels glistening behind him in the early evening light, Vince didn't look like he had a care in the world. Young was well known for joking and clowning, dancing, singing, cutting loose, and bringing an attitude to Texas football that it desperately needed: fun. For the past few years, Texas players under Mack Brown looked like they weren't having any fun, that the burdens of simply being Texas were too much to bear. Vince changed all of that, famously even convincing Mack to listen to the rapper 50 Cent on his iPod in an effort to relate better to his players.

What Young's brilliant smile and dance moves from the Rose Bowl sideline kept hidden from view was a searing emotion that would be extremely dangerous for the USC Trojans: Vince Young was pissed. During the long break between the Big 12 title game in Houston and the New Year, Vince had traveled to New York for the Heisman Trophy presentation. He sat on the aisle of the front row with USC stars Reggie Bush and Matt Leinart to his left. When Bush was announced as the winner, Young looked down in disappointment and politely clapped. Then he craned his neck up and glanced around the room as if he would rather be somewhere else. There was no smile, no grand gesture toward Bush other than a casual acknowledgement, which wasn't like Young, usually an enthusiastic hugger.

How could he not have known that Bush was going to win the award? The Heisman is one of the most famous awards in sports, but it is also one of the worst-kept secrets. Many of the voters reveal publicly who they have chosen long before the ballots are counted, and in this case the voting wasn't close. Bush, the speedy Trojan tailback, had won easily. In fact, Bush had won over 90 percent of the possible points, the biggest landslide in Heisman history. The result, or at least the margin of victory, was bullshit, but then, so often is the Heisman, sometimes degenerating into a popularity contest honoring the skill position player with the best career résumé playing for a top-ranked team. It was simply Bush's turn.

Vince didn't care that it was Bush's turn. He was disappointed that he had "let down"—his words—the University of Texas, his teammates, his family, the city of Houston. A nervous press corps looked on at this bizarre sideshow wondering if Vince Young was a spoiled child who had completely taken leave of his senses. The weeks got worse. USC, which had won the previous national championship by routing Big 12 standard-bearer Oklahoma, 55–19, was considered unbeatable. Leinart, the unflappable Trojan quarterback, had won the 2004 Heisman, so Bush's win meant Texas would face two Heisman winners in the same backfield. In addition, wide receiver Dwayne Jarrett was arguably the best in the country, and his companion on the other side of the field, Steve Smith, was also exceptional. Bush traded carries with another USC tailback, the bruiser LenDale White, who, like Jarrett, was among the nation's best at his position, even though his light didn't glow with the intensity of Bush's. All of these stars operated behind a deep and talented offensive line that had pancaked Trojan opponents for an amazing thirty-four games in a row. ESPN profiled the Trojans from every angle possible, even going so far as to create a fantasy tournament in which the Trojans were matched against the greatest squads in college football history. The result was the proclamation that these Trojans were the best college football team of all time. They simply had too much for Texas: too much speed, too much heart, too much talent.

By January 4, the Texas players were sick of this. Why play the game at all? They were seething at kickoff, but it was all masked by Vince Young's bright smile and happy feet. He didn't have a care in the world. The last shot of the great quarterback before the game commenced showed him in prayer in the end zone. I would have given anything to know how that conversation went, but I was only privy to my own prayers.

"Do the players sometimes ask you to help them win?"

"Of course. People ask for all kinds of things, usually when they are scared."

"But you don't determine outcomes."

"I don't keep score. You can determine your own outcomes; your life is on you, no one else."

"Yeah, most people just need grace and peace, I guess. Sometimes courage."

"Maybe you have been paying attention all of these years. Usually when you look for peace, it finds you."

"I think that's right. That's what my mom would say."

"Yes, it is."

My house was full of the people I loved. Juan arrived last, with Ann. They had married since we last saw them for the Ohio State game. Shortly after the wedding, Erin and I had asked Ann to join Holly Jacques as Charlie's godmother; we figured he needed another Catholic in his life, which made me wonder if we were secretly worried about his eventual salvation. Ann the Nebraska Cornhusker brought a gift for my youngest son. Juan brought a six-pack of Lone Star. We put it in the fridge hoping we would not have to bring it out.

Texas kicker Greg Johnson started the 2006 Rose Bowl with a high kick past the USC goal line. Reggie Bush collected it three yards deep and headed upfield. Longhorn linebacker Robert Killebrew and corner-back Tarell Brown buried him at the twelve-yard line. Game on.

On the first play from scrimmage, Michael Huff stuffed the Unstop-pable Heisman Trophy Winner for a loss of two. Texas forced a three and out on the first Trojan possession, and I felt the peace of victory be-ginning to flow over me. As I have mentioned before, my stupidity still knew no bounds. Disaster struck when Texas fumbled the ensuing punt, giving the ball back to USC. Leinart deftly led his guys down the field, hitting David Kirtman on a long pass out of the backfield. Cedric Griffin hit Kirtman like a pissed-off longshoreman wielding a two-by-four at a union riot, causing the Trojan fullback's helmet to fly off, but Kirtman held onto the ball. These guys were good. Before I knew it, LenDale White was coasting into the Texas end zone and it was 7–0. Texas got the ball and Vince made a few good plays, including a great pass to Da-vid Thomas off of play action. The drive stalled, and with a fourth and one at midfield, Mack took a page from the Bob Stoops playback and decided to go for it. Selvin Young ran wide but had nowhere to go. USC had the ball again and I had apocalyptic visions of 14–0 dancing in my head. Could the Trojans throw a knockout punch this early?

USC headed the other way, and when the drive stalled at the Texas 17, it was the Trojans who went for it on fourth and one. As Leinart took the snap, the Texas defensive front made the stronger surge, the USC quar-terback was hemmed in by linebacker Drew Kelson and couldn't gain any traction.

I leapt from my brick perch and screamed. "You didn't make it, Matt, you didn't make it, *Matt*," as if the attempt was some personal affront to my pride as a Longhorn fan. Which, in fact, it was. College football is nothing if not personal. This was my school, these were my guys, and Pete Carroll, the USC coach, might as well have said some-thing insulting about my mother as to go for it on fourth down and one at the Texas 17. The Texas defense had risen to the first big challenge of the night. More importantly, Vince Young got the ball back. The game was still in the first quarter and I was already exhausted. Every play was emotional turmoil. A wafer-thin margin separated failure from success on every Texas drive. Vince didn't appear to be stoppable, but mistakes by his teammates kept derailing him. He needed to raise their level of play somehow. The first quarter ended with USC ahead 7–0; this was the first time all season Texas hadn't scored in the opening frame.

Two plays into the second quarter, time stopped. In my past history as a football fan, these moments when I sensed divine intervention always meant bad things for the Horns. I remembered this all-encompassing dreadful feeling when Craig Curry muffed the punt on the Cotton Bowl floor, when Chris Simms threw his second pick in the 2001 Big 12 Championship, when Brodney Pool took away Vince's touchdown in his Oklahoma debut. The unavoidable dread stalked me like death and taxes. Tonight it caught up to me when Leinart perfectly read the Texas blitz and lofted a soft middle screen over the top of it to Bush. The sight of Reggie Bush flying unimpeded through your team's secondary is ghastly. Bush runs low to the ground, and his hips rotate like a spinning gyroscope, causing him to bounce off tacklers and change directions like a human pinball. Like Vince Young, he never seemed to take a direct hit; he was making cuts like a man on water skis. I wondered how his ankles could withstand the force. To watch defenders pursue him at his best Heisman-winning form was to watch a group of children trying to catch a greased pig at the county fair. Had I been an objective observer, I would have given him his full due as the amazing college football player he was. At the moment, I was instead dread-filled and speechless as Bush burst inside the Texas twenty. Then time stopped. With Drew Kelson wrapped around him, Bush turned to his left and *lateraled the ball* to a trailing teammate. This was not in the playbook. His shocked comrade ran straight past the ball, which fell to the turf. Michael Huff, the only person in the entire stadium who seemed unfazed by this turn of events, pounced on it. Texas ball.

"What the heck was he thinking?"

Zach's analysis was dead on. The "heck" came out with the rising

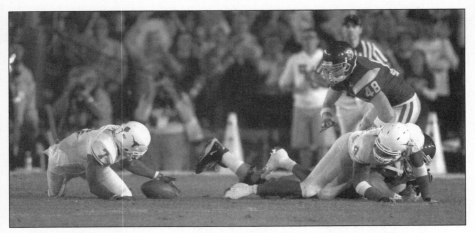

Michael Huff pounced on Reggie Bush's first-half fumble, one of dozens of huge plays made by the Longhorns' defensive MVP. *(University of Texas Athletics)*

inflection of a cute sitcom kid questioning his father's buffoonery. All that was missing was the laugh track. I didn't know, or much care, what Bush was thinking—young athletes believe in their invincibility in ways I cannot comprehend—all I knew was that USC had just made the kind of mistake thirty-five years of conditioning had led me to expect from the Longhorns. Texas took over and drove the field. Vince was still unstoppable—8 for 8 passing, four rushes for forty-two yards—but a Ramonce Taylor fumble, which Vince himself had to recover for a ten-yard loss, forced Texas to settle for three. At least they were on the scoreboard.

Time stopped again on the next USC drive. This time Leinart went deep to an open Steve Smith down the left sideline. Texas safety Michael Griffin, demonstrating for all to see that Texas did not suffer from any speed deficit, regardless of what the geniuses in the national media believed, raced across the goal line, timed his leap perfectly and cleanly picked the ball, just as Smith was planning his end zone celebration. Griffin got one foot inbounds in the end zone and Texas took possession at the twenty. The Longhorns surprised the Trojans by running a no-huddle offense, forcing the Trojans to react quickly and preventing any strategic substitutions. Vince Young used every weapon available. David Thomas was seemingly open on every play. Limas Sweed got into the act. Jamaal Charles went for fifteen, frustrating USC defenders at every turn. From the USC 22, Vince took off on an option play to the left. Finding a crease, he bolted to the 12 before he was wrapped up and forced down, but on his way down, he decided to taunt Reggie Bush. Young pitched the ball to his best friend Selvin Young, who plucked it and took it into the end zone. Vince may have already had a knee down when he pitched it, but the referees granted him artistic license. Texas now led 9–7, missing the extra point in a rush to keep the replay officials from reviewing the play.

USC faltered with a series of ill-timed penalties on their next possession, and Texas set up shop again, this time at midfield. Working the ball to the 30, Vince set up in the shotgun formation and made an inside handoff to Ramonce Taylor. Taylor slipped a tackle and decided himself to put the lie to the USC speed myth by exploding into the open field straight into the Trojan end zone, his path having been cleared by Limas Sweed, who mauled the last remaining Trojan defender and threw him into one of his own pursuing teammates for good measure. Texas now led the national championship game 16–7. A USC field goal at the end of the half cut it to 16–10, but a lead was a lead. Thirty minutes of game time remained as I went to the backyard with Zach and tried to make sense of it all.

This was actually happening. It was real. What happens when your dreams begin to seep into your reality? This was like the moment when the nurse informs a nervous mother and father that the time has come and the obstetrician heroically sweeps into the room to deliver your new son. Life forces you to live in the moment. You have no other choice. I went back inside to put Ben and Charlie to bed before the second half began. Charlie drifted off and I watched him content in the knowledge that the world would be a better place when he awoke.

The problem with all of this thinking is that somewhere in the world a father just like me was convinced that, as he put his own son to bed, his beloved Trojans would pull out the victory, because this is what his guys did. While I didn't have any desire to dwell upon these complicated moral ambiguities, I was very aware that USC had not won thirty-four games in a row by being a bunch of pikers. "Pikers" was a term my father always used. It occurred to me that I really had no idea where the term came from; Dad would just throw it out there when he meant someone shouldn't be taken lightly. It always made me laugh and I thought of my father home in Amarillo.

We had talked earlier in the day. True to his risk-averse nature, he noted that USC was one "whale of a ballclub" and would be very difficult to beat. Seventy-four-years old and the guy is still protecting me from disappointment. I am sorry he wasn't here; the night reminded me of all the *Monday Night Football* games when I was in grade school. The deal was that I could stay up until halftime. The informal deal, however, was that when I came back downstairs with teeth brushed and pajamas on, Dad was pretty lax about noticing I was still up. He would pretend not to see me, and often I would make it through the third quarter before his parental instincts would get the best of him and I would be sent to bed. As the second half of the Rose Bowl started, I pretended not to see Zach.

When we had last left Matt Leinart, he had been shaking free the cob-webs brought on by a vicious hit from Longhorn cornerback Aaron Ross at the end of a first-half scramble. But when he returned to the field for the second half, he was a different man. Somebody in the locker room must have reminded him that he was the best passer in college football. Whoever it was, I wished that he had left well enough alone. A confident Leinart was trouble.

On USC's first drive of the second half, Leinart hit Dwayne Jarrett with a perfect 24-yard strike. A few plays later, LenDale White was in the end zone yet again and the Trojans led 17–16. So much for the first-half lead. Texas responded by going no huddle and the Trojan defense was back on its heels. Vince executed a beautiful keeper off the zone read for fourteen yards, ending it by shoving a Trojan cornerback to the turf with his left hand and stretching the ball out over the right pylon. Bang. Bang. Texas 23, USC 17.

But Leinart was feeling it. He drilled six straight completions—all of which were to well-covered receivers—before LenDale White scored again, this time from twelve yards out to make it 24–23. Texas was in a shoot-out and Matt Leinart was Wyatt Earp. I nervously looked at Juan, who made no move to the garage to get the Lone Star. Perhaps we were still OK.

But some sort of cosmic payback continued to swirl. For almost two full seasons I had delighted in watching Vince Young beat teams and knowing that there wasn't a damn thing the opposition could do about it. Tonight, for the first time, a hot opposing quarterback was Young's equal. Matt Leinart was now giving me a belated dose of Christian empathy for the Oklahoma States of the world. Leinart gave me the cold chill of knowing that my team's margin for error had been taken away. The Texas defense was up against it; they couldn't play any better than they were already playing, yet Leinart continued to beat them.

Vince Young snapped my mental cold front. On a second and nine from his own 35, Vince was flushed from the pocket and took off, his jet trail leaving a wake behind him on a 45-yard scamper down to the USC 20. The third quarter ended with Texas primed to go back in front. But just when I thought my life was charmed, Texas stalled, and then missed an easy field goal. Uh-oh.

Leinart took the field like a lion on the hunt. He continued to throw to well-covered receivers, and he hit them all just to spite me. LenDale White battered the Texas defense and then, just to remind us he was still in the game, Reggie Bush took the ball inside and then bounced to the right. He slipped a tackle and outraced every single member of the Texas secondary. Michael Huff was the last guy with an angle. As our All-American strong safety closed in, the extraordinary Bush went airborne. Huff took the 'SC tailback's legs out from under him but Mr. Heisman used the inertia to spectacular effect by doing a front flip into the end zone.

Down by eight, Texas then executed the most deflating field goal drive in the 113-year history of the Longhorn program. The USC lead was cut to 31–26, but the Texas defense had yet to stop Leinart. I could feel the game slipping away. A few plays later, Wyatt Earp emptied his chamber, throwing a rope to Jarrett right between two Texas defenders. Michael Griffin and Tarell Brown collided with Jarrett, who slid between them and stretched the ball over the goal line. Neither Griffin nor Brown got up. Brown had been a warrior all night from the very first play when he brought down Reggie Bush on the opening kickoff, but now his night was over. His arm was broken. With the score now 38–26 with only 6:42 to go, the Longhorn defense sat dejected on the sideline.

Ten-year-old children all over Austin were being sent to bed, a parenting decision that never occurred to me. Zach and I had been through too much for me to put him to bed now. He was one of us, a proud member of the Lone Star Drinking Club. My favorite football fan looked as dejected as the Texas defense. In the kitchen, Ann Erickson, the Cornhusker fan who ostensibly had no rooting interest, was slowly and deliberately pounding her head against the sheetrock. With her comforting cranial rhythm in the background, I got up from the hearth and went to the garage. I brought back three Lone Stars and distributed them. Juan looked at me as if I were grasping for straws. I was not going to go down without a fight, and I did not believe that Vince Young would either.

He trotted out to the UT 30 to start what may well have been the last drive of his career. After fifty-four minutes of football, the boy from Hiram Clark still looked like he didn't have a care in the world. My only regret in life over the next six minutes and forty-two seconds of this college football game was that my mother wasn't alive to see it—not that I didn't think she was watching, of course. Texas had to score quickly and hope for the best. Their margin for error was now nonexistent.

Young went to the air, to Sweed, to Cosby, to the ever-dependable

Thomas. Vince ran the ball himself one play and then went back to Sweed, to Thomas again, and Texas was on the USC 17.

"Sam Baugh would roll out and look for Jimmy Lawrence out of the backfield here," Bulldog noted.

"I don't know about that, but Vince won't be looking for anybody. He's keeping this one himself." Mom never assumed my grandfather held the final word, even concerning football strategy.

Young took the snap and drifted left with the Texas offensive line an impenetrable wall moving with him. He pivoted quickly, went back to his right, slipping momentarily, but then regained balance, picking up one last block from his great center, Lyle Sendlein, and coasted into the end zone. Now we were down to four minutes, trailing 38–33. The Texas defense had to come through. We all stood and took a hopeful swig of Lone Star. Leaving nothing to chance, I muted Keith Jackson and turned up the great Craig Way on the Longhorn radio call.

The Trojans started with a LenDale White run for three yards, then Leinart looked to Jarrett for a first down. Now only three minutes remained. Leinart had gone an astonishing 14 out of 15 for 182 yards in the second half. 'SC had the ball four times in the second half, and Leinart had led them to a touchdown on all four drives. Lone Star beer had its work cut out for it. Leinart and his mates continued to drain the clock as White ran for three more yards. Leinart finally missed on a pass, and on third and seven the ball went to White again. He blasted through the right side of the Texas line and stretched out for another first down that would have just about ended the game. But as White fought for the last yard, Aaron Ross knocked the ball from his grasp. The leather ovoid hung there for not even a second before USC wide receiver Steve Smith snatched it out of the air. But the miscue cost the Trojans a vital two yards. Leinart now faced a fourth and two with 2:13 remaining. Make it and they repeated as national champs. Fail and Vince Young would take the Madison Marlin trot out to midfield one last time.

Mack Brown knew what that meant. He gave his defense very simple instructions: Stop them and you will be national champions.

Texas hadn't stopped LenDale White all day. Once again, he got the call. Time completely slowed as Matt Leinart seemed to take forever to call the signals. The ball was snapped, the battle joined. In the ugly ballet of the trenches, Texas defensive tackle Rodrique Wright fired out and fought his man to a draw. Bodies stacked up all around the middle of the line. Next to Wright, defensive end Brian Robison knifed low into the middle of the scrum and, flat on his back, reached his arms up and was the first Longhorn to grab White. Middle linebacker Aaron Harris walloped the 235-pound Trojan tailback head up and eye-to-eye. Drew Kelson beat his block and wrapped up White from the side, pushing him sideways to the right. White's forward progress was halted, and the pile collapsed around him. The whistle blew and the side judge charged in. On the very bottom of the pile, hanging on for dear life, and finally uncovered as the play stopped and the refs tried to make sense of it all, was Michael Huff. The officials brought out the chains, but it wasn't close. The Texas side of the Rose Bowl erupted over the radio a second out of synch with the television picture and the Lone Star Drinking Club knew what had happened before the chain was stretched taut. The Trojans were a yard short.

Vince Young took the field. For the first time all evening, Pete Carroll began to gamble, sending a cornerback blitz on first down. Young read the defense perfectly and slipped a screen pass to Ramonce Taylor. If USC defensive end Frostee Rucker hadn't made a remarkable play to bring Taylor down by his shoestrings, the speedster would have been off to the races. On second down, Trojan defensive back Brandon Ting came free on a blitz and Vince threw the ball away. Texas had lost two yards on two plays and the clock was now down to 1:35. On third down, Vince's best friend, Selvin Young, picked up the blitz, giving Vince just enough time to deliver the ball to Quan Cosby, who was wrestled down by his face mask. The penalty gave Texas a fresh start, first and ten from the USC 46.

USC blitzed again and Vince calmly hit Brian Carter on a hot route for nine. When a USC player stripped the ball after Carter was down, the guys in the replay booth for some reason decided to review the play. Terry Lynch and I traded expletives. Zach was going to have to hear them at some point in his life. The referees rightly awarded the ball to Texas. Vince took the snap on second and one, taking the ball himself for six yards and an easy first down. Another effortless pass to Carter and the ball was at the USC 14. Vince threw incomplete on first down trying to hit Sweed at the back of the end zone. On second down, he ran a draw to just inside the nine. Thirty seconds remained, and seven adults and a ten-year-old were huddled around a twenty-seven-inch television set shoulder to shoulder. We might as well have been posing for a family picture in front of my father, who never could quite squeeze everyone into the frame. Vince took the shotgun snap and threw again, incomplete to Sweed. Fourth down and an entire lifetime of my dedication to the Texas Longhorns to go.

From nine yards away, Vince Young lined up in the shotgun with his best friend to his right. He took the snap and the men of the Texas offensive line engaged. Jonathan Scott fanned out to the left, drifting back and cutting off the initial Trojan rush. Kasey Studdard was to his right and moved with him in perfect harmony. The other linemen, center Lyle Sendlein, guard Will Allen, and tackle Justin Blaylock, acted as the fulcrum, moving the entire pocket left and back as Vince eyed his options. Number 10 looked quickly left, then checked down to the middle for an open man, then another, scanning the field in three directions before he slid to the right, away from his protection. Going through his receiver options, he found no good choices. Vince chose himself. He was out of the pocket and all alone as Trojan cornerback Josh Pinkard, coming on a delayed blitz, had Vince in his crosshairs. Coming from Vince's right, Blaylock flashed over and dropped Pinkard like a sack of bricks as Vince darted off Blaylock's right hip and committed himself to run. He crossed the line of scrimmage . . .

A lump formed in my throat. Tears streamed down my face and I could barely breathe, but my lungs managed to force out a faint "He's gone" as I clung to Zach's shoulders.

Vince Young into the end zone and into college football history, disbanding forever the Cult of 1969. *(University of Texas Athletics)*

The Red Sea of Trojans had parted and the child of God raised up by the people of Hiram Clark and anointed by Mount Horeb Missionary Baptist Church exploded into the light. His right foot touched down on the end-zone stripe and his left foot glided past the pylon.

Lifting his head, he bounded over the barrier at the edge of the end zone and launched himself into history. This man who transcended Longhorn football might as well have taken flight. It was as if he would float over the stadium's side, for he could not be contained. Gliding into the ether, he left the broken pieces of the Cult of 1969 trailing behind him like the loose particles of a comet's tail.

I looked up to see him surrounded by photographers and embraced by a college student in a mascot costume with a giant foam longhorn head. This was the memory I would carry from the greatest moment in my life as a sports fan.

The Moment

As the clock ticked off on a last Leinart incompletion, the champagne came out. The Lone Star Drinking Club celebrated an end to thirty-five years of frustration. I never wanted this moment to end. We stayed up late into the night to listen to every second of the postgame. I drifted off to sleep on the floor of the living room, sharing a pillow with Zach. Truman slept in the corner. The postgame show ended and KVET went back to country music, playing first all the great songs about Texas, which provided our lullaby for the night. I awoke when they finally went to a station break. I heard the familiar voice of country singer Ray Benson:

The Lone Star Drinking Club in joyful celebration. *(Jones Family)*

You're listening to K-V-E-T FM, the flagship station of the national champions.

The words "national champions" hung there in the air as I remembered where I was.

Mack Brown told his players in the locker room after the game to make sure not to make this the greatest moment of their lives. He said that they needed to move on and become great husbands and fathers and role models. That was all well and good for a bunch of twenty-something college kids, but where did that leave me as the thirty-eight-year-old father of three? I could not possibly ever feel this way again, for no other emotional need in my life had stretched so far back into the plains of my memories without being fulfilled. Christians sometimes pray to be freed for "joyful obedience." Perhaps now I was free. God had paid in full. The question was: What did I owe him? Where would all of this emotional energy now be spent? I looked over at the boy to my left and wondered when he had grown too big to be carried upstairs. Before waking him, I sat silently and wondered what kind of person he would become.

Somewhere up in heaven, Bulldog looked over at Mom.

"That Vince Young is remarkable."

Mom smiled. "Yes, he is." My mother and I were connected that night, and as she looked down upon this house, she knew that her son was living in the moment.

My heart was full.

EPILOGUE

*"Don't ya'll think that's beautiful right there?
. . . and it's coming home to Texas. It's coming home
all the way to Austin, Texas, bay-bee!"*

*—Vince Young,
on receiving the National Championship Trophy,
Pasadena, California,
January 4, 2006*

A Lone Star six-pack caddy sat on top of my television set. I pondered it, trying to comprehend the previous night's event. I went to the kitchen and dug out the ibuprofen. Returning to the triumphant cardboard trophy, I set it aside (eventually I would deem it suitable for

Suitable for framing. *(Chris Carson)*

framing). There was much to do. I called in Zach sick to school—it turned out seven other classmates were sick that day, and to my knowledge there has been no analysis of the state funding thereby lost by the Austin Independent School District on January 5, 2006. I then headed up the street where my neighborhood grocer had a full set of major Texas dailies. I bought one of each. PERFECT FINISH said the *Austin American-Statesman*. If the paper reported it, then it must be true.

Vincent Young had nothing left to prove. He had rushed for 200 yards in the Rose Bowl and passed for 267 more. It was simply one of the most amazing performances ever seen on the college gridiron. Shortly after his greatest moment as a collegian, he announced for the NFL draft. His hometown Houston Texans owned the first pick, but passed on him in favor of Mario Williams, a defensive end from North Carolina State. The people of Houston may never forgive the Texans for this. Vince instead went third overall to Tennessee. All he did after that was become the NFL's Offensive Rookie of the Year, beating out his friend Reggie Bush, now a New Orleans Saint.

Perhaps somewhere close to where you live, on some fall Sunday, the Tennessee Titans will emerge from the locker room. And Vincent Young will do amazing things on the football field. Count on it.

The 2006 Texas Longhorns lost their September rematch with Ohio State. The Buckeyes spent the entire season at No. 1, but eventually lost in the national title game to Florida. Texas, for their part, played great football at times, but collapsed down the stretch to finish 10–3. Included in the loss column was the first defeat in seven years to Texas A&M. All good things must come to an end. The new Texas hero at quarterback was the cherubic Colt McCoy, from tiny Tuscola-Jim Ned High School. He drinks nothing stronger than milk and in the summer of 2006 swam across a lake to save the life of a neighbor in the midst of an epileptic seizure. Reality continues its three touchdown lead over mythology in the world of Texas football. You simply can't make up better stories than this.

Lots of characters in this book are now big-time professional football players. Chris Simms started the 2006 season at quarterback for the Tampa Bay Buccaneers, but in week three of the NFL season, he ruptured his spleen in a game against the Carolina Panthers. Remarkably, Simms returned to the game and led Tampa Bay to a lead that they eventually lost on a field goal with two seconds to play. Simms was rushed to the hospital for an emergency splenectomy and to this day his NFL career is very much in doubt. Of course, he could have died. Anyone who ever questioned his courage or commitment may send him a note of apology care of the Buccaneers.

Roy Williams is a Pro Bowl receiver for the Detroit Lions, and Nathan Vasher is a budding star for the Chicago Bears. Michael Huff,

Cedric Griffin, David Thomas, Bo Scaife, Jonathan Scott, Derrick Johnson, Cedric Benson, Cory Redding, Michael Griffin, Aaron Ross, Lyle Sendlein, Justin Blaylock, Brian Robison, Kasey Studdard, Selvin Young, and many other Longhorn heroes hear Sunday cheers, and the list gets longer with each passing year of the Mack Brown administration.

Major Applewhite, for his part, became the youngest offensive coordinator in the NCAA for the Rice Owls in 2006. The next season, he moved on to become the quarterbacks coach and offensive coordinator for the Alabama Crimson Tide. The big time called and Applewhite answered. For those of us who lead a rich fantasy life, he is already the Longhorn head coach of the future.

Not every story ends well. The brilliant Ramonce Taylor got into trouble with the law and never played another down for the Texas Longhorns.

In the wee hours of January 18, 2007, Bert's Barbecue burned to the ground. The great shrine to the 1969 National Champions is no more.

The Rose Bowl warrior, Tarell Brown, recovered from his broken arm and had an up-and-down season for the 2006 Horns. He was suspended for the Ohio State game for disciplinary reasons and fought injuries all year. After the season, while preparing for the NFL draft, he was arrested. The charges were dropped; Brown may have been guilty of nothing more than riding with his cousin "driving while black"—still an offense in some Texas counties. It was another tough day for Brown, whose father had died in February. In his dad's casket, Tarell had placed the number 5 Longhorn jersey that he had worn that magical night in Pasadena. Sports heroes will come and go over the years of my life, but I am certain that I will never stop pulling for Tarell Brown, who is now a San Francisco 49er.

My father, at seventy-six, still goes to work every day with a passion for medicine. We can all hope to be so lucky as to find our lifelong passion. After Mom died, he sought out Reggie Spencer at a West Texas alumni function. Dad was unsurprised to find that Mr. Spencer was a successful businessman in Atlanta. Number 7 and my dad had a long talk about the loud woman in the red chairback section. I would like to think that maybe Reggie, competing on the playing field at Kimbrough, had somehow felt the unconditional love of that great woman so many years ago.

The Buffaloes, now the West Texas A&M University Buffaloes, can't seem to lose. The Buffs have racked up the last three Lone Star Conference Championships, going 33–5 under Coach Don Carthel and becoming a major power in Division II. They also lead the division in attendance, averaging just under 14,000 per game. If you are ever in the Texas Panhandle, check them out.

Erin and I continue to try and keep our sons out of trouble. Ben has an uncanny knack for making the world just a little bit happier for anyone who encounters him. Reba Jones apparently lives on in this one. And in Charlie, too, who only has one speed—his life moves fast and with unparalleled enthusiasm.

The good life moves ever forward . . . *(Chris Carson)*

Zach went off to fifth grade in the fall of 2006. His flag football team won the West Austin Youth Association championship with back-to-back cliffhanger finishes. These games were more exciting to me than anything I had ever seen Vince Young do. Never again will my spiritual life be immersed in the kind of wild race that he finally brought to the finish line. The Longhorns are the 2005 national champs and that can never be taken from their fans. Do I want them to do it again? Damn straight, but now I will find joy in whatever they accomplish. Knowing what is possible and seeing it done has lifted my blasphemic neurosis about college football. The best gift Vince Young gave me was the freedom to live in the moment. Mom must have had something to do with this. She was right, I do just fine in the moment.

God and I don't talk about college football much anymore. Yet the good life continues to move ever forward.